MANAGEMENT

Strategic Management in the Fashion Companies

STEFANIA SAVIOLO
SALVO TESTA

ETAS

Titolo originale: *Le imprese del sistema moda. Il management al servizio della creatività*

Traduzione dall'italiano di J.T.F. Butler
Redazione di Christopher Howell
Copertina di Maria Teresa Pozzi
Fotocomposizione: Nuova MCS, Firenze

ISBN 88-453-0994-0

CONTENTS

Foreword

*Domenico De Sole**

There are two types of competitor in the current international panorama of the fashion system: firms that build their market strength on the basis of a *power brand*, and those that can draw on an *exclusive brand*. The first kind of firms, mainly Anglo-Saxon, base their competitive success on the strength and reputation of the brand within a lot of product categories. Accessibility is the leading concept of their offer. The second kind of firm, mainly European, belongs by nature to the luxury world. They have been able to build up exclusivity and prestige through the levers of product quality and style recognition that guarantee both a *premium price* and greater profitability.

Gucci was able to become an *exclusive brand* through its brilliant process of repositioning that brings together product and communication creativity and management discipline. This synthesis seems a vital condition for all firms competing in the international fashion system. Intuition and stylistic inspiration are still at the heart of the system, but they have to be connected within an organised complex of resources and skills.

---

* CEO GUCCI GROUP

Gucci started from a correct brand repositioning strategy, taking into account the new rules imposed by the fashion market. These new rules concern the obsessive control of "consistency", through direct actions on the international retail network and control over product quality and supply system productivity. The production network is rigorously localised in Italy, and can guarantee the workmanship that is expected from the 'made in Italy' label. Formulating a strategy is only the starting point. It is strategy implementation that requires competent and committed management and this is frequently the most difficult process. At Gucci the creative process is entrusted to a designer who has demonstrated over time the qualities of a creative director. These qualities do not include just inspiration but also market vision and the ability to co-ordinate all the levers that have an effect on brand identity – style, communication and visual merchandising – in harmony with the firm's strategic positioning, in order to create value for shareholders and customers.

Creativity, quality and discipline are the lessons we have learned from our experience in these years, and I feel they are the key words for leaders in the international fashion system in the future. While creativity, taste and manufacturing quality are usually the gift of talented individuals or the historical skills of some national systems, such as Italy and France, managerial discipline, on the other hand, can be built up and maintained through the establishment of a new managerial class for fashion firms. The importance of managerial discipline will be increasingly decisive, the more that fashion firms become *multibrand companies* without the presence of the entrepreneur/designer who created the brand.

This book moves towards a first, fundamental presentation of a specific managerial model for fashion firms. The hope is that other, similar works will follow, contributing to the debate about the importance of management for the lasting success of these important industries.

Foreword

*Renzo Rosso**

Fashion is inspiration, creativity and intuition. But it is also organisation, strategy and management. These two apparently contrasting sets of elements have to come together to ensure the success of a business idea.

The current scene presents new challenges such as the increasing sophistication of consumers, the constant need to innovate, the importance of attaining specific critical masses in order to meet growing investment requirements in retailing and comunication, the micro-segmentation of the market, hypercompetition, and brand management, just to mention a few.

It is increasingly difficult to find professionals in the fashion industry that are capable of 'managing creativity', that means leading creativity without impeding or deforming it. Firms and managers have to know how to innovate, breaking free from competitive rules while still remaining loyal to the core values of their brand. The fashion market is in a constant state of excitement, the consumer constantly wants new stimuli, and it is up to the actors in the industry to create and maintain a relationship with their own target.

* President of Diesel

A fashion firm always works in a circle. Any decision, any action undertaken, has decisive consequences on brand and corporate image. Let us take the example of retail directly managed by the firm. This affects only one functional department of the firm, retailing, but how can one forget the overall effects in terms of brand image, let alone business organisation? Production, logistics, information-gathering, reporting, and communication at the retail level all have to operate effectively and efficiently in order to maintain overall consistency.

There is another key point that should not be forgotten, the enlarged concept of communication. In the past one hardly talked about advertising, and the product was the focus of all the company's efforts. In the 1980s, and above all in the 1990s, communication became a key success factor in the fashion world. Today, communication does not just mean advertising or public relations. An advertisement (whether on press or on television) no longer has a rational motivation ('to inform and persuade') as much as an emotional content ('to seduce'). Communication means working with the new technologies (from the Internet to Videogames), and above all expressing the corporate philosophy in every way, not only through business communication but also through shop windows, direct marketing, customer service.

The brand has to be created, managed, sustained and protected. A brand is much more than a simple logo for a fashion firm. It evokes values, atmospheres, benefits that can never be ignored. This list of tangible and intangible factors attracts the consumer and ensures his loyalty. It ensures an economic advantage and represents a genuine weapon in the fight against competitors. It is also vital for the firm's growth (if not for survival as well).

The clients of fashion products often do not have national limits or national taste. Thinking internationally, but at the same time respecting diversity among markets is another key success factor within an industry that is becoming global. A book like this helps to analyse and understand the complexity and potential of the fashion system. But it is only a start. I strongly believe in learning by doing. Making mistakes does not matter to me; it is reaction time that makes the difference. This is why I let my managers make mistakes. This way they will develop the necessary antibodies for what is increasingly a daily fight.

Introduction

We have been involved with the fashion system for the last ten years as management researchers, lecturers and consultants. At first our reason for approaching the fashion world was more curiosity than a genuine belief that we would have found fertile terrain for our business activity. In the beginning we had to face some jokes from our academic colleagues from business administration and economics who could not understand the reason for all this interest. The fashion world was totally ignored by business schools, at least in Italy. Economic, management and organisational issues were dominated by frequently sterile debates about image, creative people and models, which still attract a lot of media attention. Despite this, we took the risk of entering the world of the firms and institutions, of going 'backstage' in this phenomenon that the public finds so fascinating. We gradually discovered the enormous cultural, knowledge and innovative endowment of this industry. Considerable changes took place in competitive systems in the last ten years of the 20th century, and these changes were a watershed for the fashion system as well. The growing internationalisation of the industry, both in terms of trade and in terms of factors of production, the entry of new competitors, the distribution revolution, and the ever-increasing amounts of money invested in brand and image, have all contributed to the definitive overthrow of the craftsman approach and orientation towards products that traditionally characterised the industries that we group under the word fashion. The fashion system is currently witnessing processes of productive delocalisation, distributive concentration and the industrial and financial aggregation of brands and firms into the celebrated luxury and fashion conglomerates. All these factors are breaking up the traditional logic of the industry, and making it front-page news in newspapers as well as in economics and finance journals and magazines.

This increasing complexity requires a new managerial approach enabling firms to cope with the new competitive threats. Therefore, our leading question was "What model of management do fashion companies need in order to survive and grow in the new century"?

We argue that traditional managerial science and discipline, which developed and established itself in very different industries, must be enriched with new perspectives in order to be really helpful within fashion companies. Fashion industries are based on assets that are symbol-intensive, more than capital or knowledge intensive: the culture of creativity, the striving for continuous product and process innovation, the sociological interpretation of the market, and the importance of communication. Managers, the 'rational spirit' of fashion firms, will be increasingly important, but they will have to interact with the creative people who represent the 'emotional spirit' of these firms (designers, architects, visual merchandisers, advertising agencies,...). We believe that this marriage, this necessary integration of management and creativity, requires a unique corporate culture and a new model of manager. Managers with strong business backgrounds but also an interdisciplinary culture, sensitivity, dynamism, and high communication skills are strongly required. They must also be able to interpret market 'weak signals' rapidly; to act quickly, and to direct and value stimuli from creative people. The current literature on fashion management is not very large at an international level and it mainly focuses on sociology, product design and fashion marketing/merchandising from an American perspective. This book is intended to be the first European and Italian contribution to students, researchers and companies in the field of management for fashion companies. The objective is to deal with all the management issues and business processes that are most significant for these companies. We also adopt a European perspective by considering the reality of small and medium sized firms, generally managed by an entrepreneur or a family, willing to upgrade their managerial approach. We believe that the Italian way of managing creativity in fashion can nowadays be interesting for other countries and also other industries, given the durable leadership that Italian companies maintain in fashion. We have included a lot of examples and case studies from the industry to facilitate the reading and provide empirical evidence to the conceptual arguments. The book begins with two chapters that provide an interdisciplinary approach to fashion: the phenomenology of fashion and the management of creativity. Then *chapters 3* and *4* present the competitive environment of fashion describing the logic of the fashion pipeline and comparing the competitiveness of nations in fashion manufacturing and distribution. From *chapter 5* onwards we present in detail each business process that is peculiar to fashion companies: starting from business definition and demand segmentation we go through product and seasonal collections development, operation and logistics, sales and retail management, communication management. The book is the result of the common project and effort of the two authors, who have both written the introduction and conclusion. Stefania Saviolo wrote *chapters 2, 3, 5, 6,* and *sections 4.1, 4.2,* and *4.3.* Salvo Testa wrote Chapters *1, 7, 8, 9,* and *section 4.4.* We had also a guest contributor, Erica Corbellini, an expert in fashion communication who wrote chapter *10.*

We acknowledge the comments provided by Claudio Dematté, Franco Amigoni and Severino Salvemini. Thanks are also due to all our colleagues of the Gruppo Interdisciplinare Sistema

Moda at SDA Bocconi: Andrea Antognazza, Giovanni Comboni, Erica Corbellini, Cesare Ferrero, Giorgio Lazzaro, Emanuela Prandelli, Davide Ravasi, Edoardo Sabbadin, Flavio Sciuccati, Giovanni Tomasi, and Paola Varacca Capello.

Although the origins and intellectual stimulus of the present work are related to our research and teaching activities at Bocconi University in Milan, the inspiration and most interesting advice came from business people, professionals, and many others in the fashion industry whom we had the good luck and pleasure to work with over the last few years. It is obviously impossible to mention everyone without running the risk of leaving someone out, but particular thanks go to those who gave up some of their precious time and those that we spent most time with: Silvio Albini, Giorgio Armani, Alberto Aspesi, Andrea Balestri, Stefano Barbini, Valerio Astolfi, Luca Bastagli Ferrari, Susanne Basini, Gianluigi Berrini, Gianni Bertasso, Ornella Bignami, Arnaldo Cartotto, Renzo Crotti, Brunello Cucinelli, Giovanni DallaColletta, Elio Fiorucci, Barbara Gianelli, Aurelio Giorgini, Vittorio Giulini, Daniele Kazem-Bek, Andrea Maccaferri, Maurizio Marchiori, Marina Mira, Umberto Monte, Francesco Morace, Carlo Pambianco, Giuseppe Pavan, Agostino Poletto, Maurizio Romiti, Renzo Rosso, Gilberto Rossi, Giovanni Scialpi, Daniele Selleri, Gildo Urbano, Valentina Ventrelli, Franco Veroni, Santo Versace and Anna Zegna.

Finally, affectionate thanks are due to Marco and Valeria, to whom we dedicate this book as a symbolic compensation for the time we took away from them to make the book possible.

Stefania Saviolo
Salvo Testa

PART ONE

The phenomenological context of the fashion system

1 The phenomenology of fashion

1.1 What is fashion?

A lot has been said and written about fashion. Great historians, starting from Herodotus, used to explain in details the customs and ways of dressing in their societies. Men of letters, poets, sociologists, psychologists and economists have all discussed it. Consumers, journalists, retailers, creative people, managers and entrepreneurs talk about it. And yet, like every issue that is hard to define but that affects the sensitivity and taste of everybody, it seems that everything is the opposite of what could still be said. It is claimed that fashion is a pointless subject, but also a very serious one, that it is shows and magazines, but also institutional conferences. It is said that fashion only exists in the minds of those who create it, but that everyone can create his own fashion. Fashion has been celebrated but also considered as something useless and even "atrocious". In his essay on fashion Georg Simmel[1] writes:

---

1. G. Simmel, "Fashion", *The American Journal of Sociology*, 1957, p. 544.

"...fashion is merely a product of social demands... This is clearly proved by the fact that very frequently not the slightest reason can be found for the creation of fashion from the standpoint of an objective, aesthetic or other expediency. While in general our wearing apparel is really adapted to our needs there is not a trace of expediency in the method by which fashion dictates...Judging from the ugly and repugnant things that are sometimes in vogue, it would seem as though fashion were desirous of exibiting its power by getting us to adopt the most atrocious things for its sake alone".

What everyone seems to agree about is the fact that fashion allows certain so-called 'mature' industries to achieve a satisfying dynamism and profitability thanks to the continuous stimulus that fashion gives to the enlargement and renewal of demand.

According to common sense a product or a service, or even a social behaviour, is considered 'fashionable' if it is widely approved by a specific public, in a specific time and social context. If the consumption of a fashionable item is removed from its specific social context then changes in fashion do not entail any improvement in product quality. This specific public may be intended according to a geographical perspective, New York rather than the Italian city Parma, or it may be socio-demographic, the provincial middle-class, urban women working in the service industry, shop-assistants, or teenage snowboarders.

In the past the concept of fashion was only associated with clothing, and in particular with the most specialised women's clothing segment: *haute couture* and, more recently, ready-to-wear. In the last ten years, however, fashion has increasingly spread to further segments – fur and hosiery, perfumes and cosmetics, glasses, accessories (watches, jewels, pens, mobile telephones), furniture and household goods, and even travel destinations and domestic pets. It has been said that nowadays one can talk about fashion in industries that are a long way from the dimension of aesthetics and taste, such as computers, scientific research and law.

Up to now, however, there has been no other field of human activity where the systematic change of the product has been institutionalised in the way that it has in clothing and the consumer goods closely related to clothing (accessories, perfumes, glasses), where change has really become an obsession.

This is due to the fact that clothing is, or ought to be, the expression of a development in custom, social context, culture and lifestyle, in a phenomenological context that is much wider and more complex than clothing itself.

Knowledge of the meaning of fashion, of the why and how of its creation, spread and consumption, is central to understanding the fashion business and its management. The traditional management studies, from marketing to communications, from strategy to operations, however, have not focused much on fashion. This can be related to the difficulty, from a theoretical and empirical perspective, of understanding, explaining, forecasting and then managing the typical features of fashion. Besides, there is no awareness of these features even among those professionals working within the business. This is why it seems appropriate, before entering the economic and managerial dimensions of fashion businesses, to illustrate briefly the so called phenomenology of fashion, and present those aspects that make its competitive logic unique.

1.1.1 The etymology of fashion

It is hard to provide an unambiguous definition of the concept of fashion, as there is no objective and unanimous interpretation of it, above all at an international level. We start from the Italian language as fashion, as we know it nowadays, has been mainly an Italian phenomenon. The Italian dictionary *Garzanti* defines fashion as 'the more or less changeable usage that, deriving from the prevailing taste, is imposed on habits, ways of living, and forms of dress'.[2] Another Italian author confirms that clothes represent only one aspect of fashion. He argues that 'fashion is a universal principle, one of the elements of civilisation and social custom. It involves not only the body but all the means of expression available to people'.[3]

---

2. *Il grande dizionario della lingua italiana*, Garzanti, 1993.
3. G. Devoto, *Il dizionario della lingua italiana*, Le Monnier, 1995.

Going back to the etymological roots of the word, the Italian word for fashion *moda*, introduced into Italian language around 1650, derives from the Latin word *mos*, and has the different but related meanings of: a) usage, custom, habit, tradition, b) law, rule, kind, c) regulation, good manners, morality. However the fashion phenomenon had existed for a long time before the introduction of the word *moda* into the Italian language. Right from the start it was considered as a strange and crazy phenomenon: Leonardo da Vinci in his Codex Urbinate described with humor the changes in the way of dressing of Florentine people.

This list of meanings makes it clear that although it is the expression of an individual orientation, taste has to face a system of social rule that defines what can be considered 'fashionable' at any time or place. A presumed etymological overlap between fashion (moda) and 'modern' is not thus the result of pure chance. It emphasises the developing and institutional aspect of taste. The French, English and German words *mode* confirm this matrix. This word derives from the Celtic words *mod* and *modd*, which have the same meaning as the Latin word *mod*, usage, custom or manner.

The commonest word in the international setting, *fashion*, seems less interesting and explanatory. It derives from the French word *façon*, through the Latin *facere*: do, build, make.

1.1.2 Clothing and fashion

Before the word 'fashion' entered common language, presumably in the late medieval period, the phenomenon of fashion itself already had a social meaning, with particular reference to clothing. The history of clothing is closely related to the history of mankind.

One constant feature of the social role of clothing, that is still evident today in even semi-primitive societies, is man's willingness to use fashion as a bodily adornment, as if there were something unsatisfying about natural attributes.[4] At different times

---

4. J. Anderson Black, M. Garland, *A History of Fashion*, Orbis Publishing Limited, 1990.

and in different places there has been a desire to make the head seem larger or the neck longer, the chest broader or the hips narrower, the feet smaller or the hands more tapered.

Myths, legends, and taboos, and also events such as war, political alliances, scientific discoveries, inventions, and the development of international trade, have always influenced the history of clothing. Marco Polo brought the silk-roll from China to Europe, and this resulted in the gradual development of the finest processing industry that is still active in France and Italy. Adventurous merchants set up the Indies Company, discovering cotton and the art of weaving. England obtained strong influence in the industry by introducing a new textile, muslin, and this became a valuable alternative to the historical predominance of French and Italian silks. Indian cottonseeds found an ideal terrain in the green land of the United States of America where, thanks to the work of the Southern slaves, a large cotton clothing industry came into being. This industry is still the productive basis for the present American market.

Clearly the aesthetic dimension has always had a certain importance as well, but only when fashion became really popular did the awareness come that it could be used as an instrument for communicating people's identities through their bodies.

According to historians[5], clothing developed for very basic reasons such as the need for protection against the elements, modesty, sexual exhibitionism, and social identification.

The first reason, protection against the external elements, is related to the technical function of clothing. This has always had a limited role in the development of fashion, given that people have always preferred decoration to usefulness. The proof of this is that many populations living in the coldest climates, such as the Inuis, Tibetans, and Peruvians, dress more for the sake of adornment than for protection.

The sense of modesty was undoubtedly the second fundamental reasons for clothing. It varies enormously, however, over time and in different places. Images of women with exposed

---

5. J. Anderson Black, M. Garland, *op. cit.*

breasts have survived from ancient Crete, for example, and later, from the Paris of the French revolution. In our own times there is a clear difference between Islamic women who wear the bourka and the *nude look* of the catwalk in Paris or Milan.

Many people think the main reason for the development of clothing can be attributed to sexual dimorphism, and thus indirectly to man's reproductive urge, by analogy with the sexual dimorphism that is common among animals. Women's desire to look more attractive and men's desire to look stronger would appear to be the third significant reason for the development of clothing among primordial humans. This has not prevented some historians[6] from emphasizing the importance of emulation between the sexes in western history, that is the desire, sometimes evident, sometimes repressed, to imitate the other sex's look.

The desire to affirm social identitities in modern societies has been more important recently than the three motivations of ancient times in diffusing fashion. It is from the beginning of social upgrading that the phenomenon of changing the way of clothing starts, or accelerates, thus giving rise to the modern concept of fashion. Some historians[7] underline a contrast between oriental and western societies. Oriental societies are seen as stable, where conservatism is also carried over into clothing, behavior and manners. In such societies large political upheavals are the cause of change. Western societies are seen as mobile, dynamic and fascinated by fashion. There is also a difference in western societies between the rural and urban environments. Although they are subject to change, the inhabitants of the countryside and poor people do not change their dresses so much. There is more change within the urban population, among those belonging to well-off social classes, and the so called "nouveaux riches". Fashion is a phenomenon that presupposes an intense social life, free and frequent human contacts, and a certain social class mobility, because of its propagatory characteristic.

---

6. F. Davis, *Fashion, Culture and Identity*, Chicago University Press. Chicago, 1992.
7. F. Braudel, *La dinamica del capitalismo*, Il Mulino, 1984.

As we have already emphasized, fashion is thus a phenomenon with a relatively consistent duration and extent that makes up a *gestalt*, a defined and structured set that is clearly distinguishable and observable. Furthermore, it has an identifiable character and spirit, even when it is not dominant. The Mary Quant mini-skirt, for example, or the Chanel tweed suit or the Marlon Brando 'leather jacket' in *The Wild One* all belong to the collective imaginary and to a specific historical moment, whether they are fashionable at a particular time or not. Fashion is thus rooted in a specific context that fulfils the needs, tastes and culture of a dominant group, or rather a contextual or simply new group. Fashion is the creation of great designers whose points of reference are the catwalks and fashion magazines and opinion leaders; but fashion is also that of young people who have the street as the source of inspiration. The socio-cultural framework for adoption in both cases is very different, but both phenomenons have recognition and solidity within their environment.

1.2 The fashion cycle and the fashion process

1.2.1 Fashion variability

The fleeting nature of fashion is closely related to its variability over time. The process of change is partly driven by the cycle of the seasons, and partly to the fashion cycle itself. Seasonal change is mainly related to functional attributes, such as climate and occasion for use, with their implications about products, styles, materials and colors. Change that is related to the fashion cycle can be explained by two perspectives:

- It can be regarded as a phenomenon brought about by the industrial, retail and communication system of the fashion business. This is tied to the need to encourage and control a certain product turnover. 'Forced' obsolescence encourages season after season a new demand for products that could last longer considering only their functional and technical features

- Variety and variability are part of a system designed to guarantee the consumer a wide range of choice and the greatest satisfaction in terms of the product's match with personal needs, whether these are expressed or tacit, tangible or intangible.

1.2.2 The fashion cycle

We can define the fashion cycle as the period of time between the introduction of a certain fashion (a new product, a new look) and its replacement by a new one. The degree of innovation of the replacement may concern basic features (concept, style, basic materials, accessories), or variants (colors).

Every fashion has its own life cycle, usually made up of three stages - introduction, peak, and decline. Opinion leaders adopt the new fashion during the first stage, when it is emerging. Opinion leaders are small groups of consumers and distributors who want to look different from the mainstream for several reasons (class differentiation, identification with a particular system of values, and so on). There is a process of diffusion and adoption by much wider segments of the market during the second stage, but not all fashions are lucky or good enough to reach this stage. There is often an aspirational element supporting the diffusion, the desire to be trendy among those who follow an imitative model of behaviour, the so called followers. The final stage is decline. All short-term fashions go through this. For fashions that last more than a few seasons decline is often related to structural changes in people's habits and lifestyles (for instance, the use of a hat or suspenders or overcoats in menswear. While scholars agree that fashion follows a cycle, there are different points of view about the nature and content of the cycles. There is no agreement, for example, about a direct relationship between fashion and degree of social development. Some experts see fashion as a universal phenomenon that can also be found in primitive societies.

In the Lobi society of the Upper Volta the only women's clothing consists of a cord around the waist. Women hang twigs with leaves on them around this, both in front and behind. It might seem to a superficial observer that there is no fashion here. An ethnologist who spent three years in the community, however, was able to see that certain women in the apparently highest sections of the hierarchy, or who were the most beautiful, varied the kind of leaves they used. These changes were then imitated for months on end by the rest of the population. These variations might include the number of twigs or leaves, sometimes very uniform, that made up the fashion of the prominent branch. Certain types of leaf could be sought out, and this meant that women had to go a long way into the forest to collect them. Finally, fashions might concern the colour of the leaves, from light green to a dark green that was almost black.[8]

Despite disagreements about the beginnings of fashion in the history, scholars agree that, despite a certain variability in the duration of cycles, the flow of change underwent a first acceleration in the 13th and 14th centuries. The institutional origin of the concept of fashion, in the sense of a systematic process of socially accepted variations in a particular custom and clothing style, took place early in the Renaissance in the protocapitalist Italian cities[9]. It later spread to the whole of Europe, in particular to the Boulogne courts, an early sign of the crucial role of Paris as the place for the creation of new fashions in later centuries. There was a second acceleration of the phenomenon that seems related to the emergence of the merchant social class, alongside the established social groups such as the nobility, the army, the clergy and farmers. The diffusion of rich merchants around Europe encouraged the creation of a new dressing code no longer conditioned by ostentation (the nobility and clergy), poverty (farmers), or usefulness (the army), but by the search for social legitimacy. Thus the association between clothing and cyclical change was strengthened.

The rhythm of the fashion cycle underwent a further considerable intensification in the 19th century, and especially since the end of the Second World War. At first it was the role of the designers that was fundamental, and then the role of the industry and distribution, in supporting or anticipating the development of the end consumer.

---

8. F. Galli, *Moda e management. Il connubio*, degree dissertation, Pavia University, 1993.
9. V. Steele, *Paris Fashion, a Cultural History*, Oxford University Press, 1988.

The first independent *couturier* was Charles Frederick Worth, an Englishman who established himself in Paris in the 1850s. Before Worth, tailors had been unknown by the general public, and worked on commissions from individual customers, principally ladies of the aristocracy. Paris became the global centre of new trends during the 20th century, with its Haute Couture, thanks to great *couturiers* such as Poiret, Chanel, Dior and Saint Laurent.

The last acceleration in fashion cycles took place in the late 70s, with the relative democratisation of fashion as a result of the emergence of ready-to-wear that bore the name of the designer on the label of the industrial product, and the move from Paris to Milan for the exhibition of new collections. Ready-to-wear also helped to create a much more complex relation between the designer and an increasingly demanding market, less willing to accept a standardized industrial product.

1.2.3 The fashion process

The fashion cycle takes place within the structure of seasonal collections that are connected to trade fairs and fashion shows. These events were once the exclusive domain of women's couture and ready-to-wear clothing, but have now been penetrated by the whole clothing system and pipeline, including fibers, textiles, leather goods and hosiery (menswear, children's wear, sportswear, leather goods and hosiery, cloths, yarns and finishing, and so on). The trend is towards the continuous increase in the number of annual collections shown and delivered to the point of sale, so that the concept of the season has almost become redundant.

> Some retail brands like Gap, Zara and Promod are structured so that they can design, produce and deliver new collections throughout the year following a model of flow delivery. These are destined to have very short sales, purchase and consumption periods.

The fashion system has been speeding up this cycle for some time, making use of all the possible synergies such as the mass media and the star system to nurture it.

Nowadays, the democratisation of fashion means that there is even more reason for speeding up the system, and the diffusion of brand and product is encouraged by the use of all the media tools available. Those involved in this complex process include fashion designers (independents, or those operating within a fashion-house or industry, or retailers), producers (of semi-finished or finished products), distributors, retailers, mass media, research and trend institutes (including fairs), consumers (opinion and market leaders), product category associations, banks and government.

1.2.4 Fashion and style

If, as has already been stressed, the dominance of the fashion system has prevailed over the last thirty years, this nowadays has to come to terms with consumers' greater awareness and independence. Consumers are increasingly creating their own fashion, combining brands and products so as to express their personality or style. The consumer is attracted by fashion offers, but does not simply accept them passively. This is the crucial point for understanding how the collapse of *total look* happened. The *total look* intended as a women, man or child completely dressed by a single designer down to the accessories, was a real feature of the 1980s, and the best expression of the dependence of the consumer on the designer.

Now there is a move from the concept of fashion to the concept of style. Personal style is the manifestation of an individual identity (of values, lifestyles, taste) that can be transversal to fashion – that is, it can cross freely over different fashion offers, taking from each of them that which serves to define a completely personal result. This view of style thus reflects the emotional and cultural need not to accept fashion passively, but not to reject the opportunities offered by it either.

1.3 Theories about fashion

The complexity and appeal of fashion have allowed it to be studied from several perspectives. There is first the sociological approach. Veblen[10] and Simmel[11] both point out the importance of social differentiation processes (distinction, affirmation-imitation, differentiation): the *trickle down* theory or 'class differentiation'. According to this approach, higher social classes adopt three strategies for contrasting themselves with lower ones – conspicuous consumption, ostentation and change. Fashion is launched at the highest social levels and then moves downward to penetrate the lowest ones. During this process what has been aesthetically innovative to the initiates is progressively trickled down until it is mass-produced to meet the needs of a wider market, and becomes ordinary. Whenever a certain fashion reaches the lower classes, the higher classes begin a new cycle, renewing themselves and again being imitated by those beneath them, and the cycle starts from scratch once more. Ostentatious wealth predominates in historical and geographical contexts where there is a rigid socio-economic hierarchy. Elegance does not just have an aesthetic function in such societies, it also represents a status symbol. As socio-economic mobility between classes increases (for example with the advent of the middle class), the strategy of trend-setting in order to distinguish from emerging classes dominates. The emerging classes tend to imitate the élites. Simmel[12] defines fashion as the convergence of a need for individual differentiation and social equality, and that implies mobility between classes.

Psychological studies were an early effort to explain the content of fashion. These studies usually focus on competition among sexes. Flugel[13] in particular investigates the conflict between adornment and modesty. Clothing is charged with the cultural equivalents of sex, and these perpetuate sexual competitiveness

---

10. T. Veblen, *Theory of the Leisure Class*, Penguin Classics, 1994.
11. G. Simmel, *op. cit.*
12. G. Simmel, *op. cit.*
13. J.C. Flugel, *The Psychology of Clothes*, Hogarth Press, 1930.

in the social arena as much as power, wealth or authority. The marked sexual dimorphism of western societies is interpreted in terms of a more widespread and localised sexuality in women that results in the development of adornment difference, and to some extent decorative variability. We have already explained how others, more recently[14], have seen sexual emulation as the key to understanding fashion trends.

> Giorgio Armani[15] said, 'I wanted my jacket to create a clothing concept for working women that was similar to what the suit has always meant for men, but I wanted to adapt it to the aesthetic and physical needs of women.'

> The main sources of inspiration for Ungaro's couture and ready-to-wear collections are military uniforms and the clothing of the 18th century dandy. These styles are so transformed, however, by frills and combinations of precious fabrics that they become symbols of ultra-feminine clothing.[16]

More interdisciplinary approaches have predominated recently. Konig[17] distinguishes an early, anthropological, dimension of the fashion phenomenon. He shows the importance of curiosity and the search for novelties. He admits the significance of distinction-imitation theories for explaining fashion change and diffusion from a sociological perspective. The *trickle-down* view loses its validity with the advent of mass production and an increase in lower-class incomes. These events contributed both to a horizontal diffusion of fashion among different social groups not determined by income and class (trickle across) and a bottom-up effect where trend originated from the street and "bubble up" to the designers' catwalks. This is the result, among other things, of the pluralism and poly-centralism that characterises the contemporary western way of dressing. The bottom up effect seems better able to explain fashion for the youth market.

---

14. F. Davis, *op. cit.*
15. S. Testa, G. Scialpi, *Caso Armani*, DIR-SDA Bocconi, 1995.
16. B. Morris, 'In Paris, the past inspires couture', *The New York Times*, 24 February 1987.
17. R. Konig, *A la Mode; on the Social Psycology of Fashion*, Seabury, 1974.

Here, the consumer is seeking to communicate his or her own desire to belong to a particular lifestyle and value system. The fashion designer has to provide a stylistic response to a style that already exists in the mind of the consumer. The *trickle across* theory[18] shows the limits of earlier reductionist assumptions in which the concept of the status symbol was central (imitation, versus differentiation). It provides a first explanation of why, beyond the dynamic fact, a fashion trend is created, diffused and destroyed. Further, the *trickle-down* theory pays little attention to the set of institutional, organisational and market structures that direct the fashion process of today, as these features did not exist when the theory was formulated. It cannot be denied that the social construction of seasons, shows, the fashion circuit, buyer choices and promotional strategies, are all closely related to the form that fashion takes.

Blumer[19], who talks about 'collective selection', also denies that hierarchical class relationships are the motive behind today's fashion. He speaks of a generic process that involves many areas of social life. This process is closely allied to modernity and can introduce order into the continuously changing and potentially anarchic present. According to Blumer, tastes are the product of experience. They generally develop from an initial, unclear state and reach a state of definition and stability. Once they are formed, however, they may decline and disintegrate. They are formed in the context of social interactions as a response to definitions and suggestions from others. People with a shared area of interaction who have similar experiences develop similar tastes. The fashion process implies both the formation and the expression of collective taste. Collective taste is initially a confused set of inclinations. It is amorphous, undeveloped, vaguely balanced, and lacks specific direction. Fashion innovators use models and suggestions as possible lines along which the incipient taste can pursue objective expression and take on definite form. By set-

18. C.W. King, 'Fashion Adoption: A Rebuttal to the Trickle-down Theory', in *Perspectives of Fashion*, Burgess, 1981.
19. H. Blumer, 'Fashion: from class differentiation to collective selection', in *Sociological Quarterly*, 1969.

ting limits and offering directions, collective taste is thus an active force in the resulting process of selection. It undergoes a process of increasingly precise refinement and structuring during the long fashion cycle. 'The origin, formation and direction of collective taste constitute the enormous problematic area of fashion.'[20]

Blumer, then, attributes a kind of social function to fashion. This social function is tied to the effort of rationalize the direction of taste, to the concept of modernity in the sense of 'adaptation to the social and cultural context'. Without it, taste evolutions would be out of control.

In recent times fashion has been studied also in semiotics. Semiotics studies the meaning and social processes that link fashion to consumers, producers, retailers and publishing. The communicative aspect of fashion, as well as its apparent negations, has always been evident although semiotic studies are a comparatively recent approach that is not yet able to offer full interpretations. Barthes[21], with his study on the language of fashion and the relationship between the signifier and significance of clothes was the pioneer of this line of research. Eco[22] introduces the fundamental concept of the communicative code with reference to clothing. This is a very different code to written and spoken language, with different rules and above all, it is continuously changing.

According to Sapir, 'The main difficulty in understanding fashion and its apparent extravagances is the lack of exact knowledge of the unconscious symbolism of forms, colours, materials, postures and other elements that express a given culture. This difficulty is considerably increased by the fact that some expressive elements tend to have different symbolic references in different areas.'[23]

The same dress, the same style, on one occasion or in one season rather than the next, can communicate something completely

20. *Ibid.*
21. R. Barthes, *The Fashion System*, University of California Press, 1990.
22. U. Eco, *Theory of Semiotics*, Indiana University Press, 1979.
23. E. Sapir, "Fashion", in *Encyclopedia of the Social Sciences*, 1931.

different with regard to the trends that are current at a given moment in time. Further, the dependence on context has to be taken into account, and this means reassessing the work of Veblen and Simmel about the importance of social class differentiation, at least to show that the same item does not have the same meaning for all social classes at the same time.

> One thinks of the process of the acceptance of jeans during the 1970s. Their controversial and revolutionary component as part of the youth movement had nothing to do with the social class of the miners and builders who had always worn them. What is more, the controversial element has almost disappeared now. This is shown by the adoption of jeans by conforming adults and their 'labelling' by fashion names.

Apart from the disagreement among scholars about the origins and diffusion of fashion, the fundamental concept is the existence of a relatively distinct centre whose innovations and changes radiate outwards towards the edge (hierarchically or horizontally). The image of a centre of innovation lingers on (Paris for couture, Milan for ready-to-wear, Florence for male fashion, London for streetwear, and New York for sports and casual wear). Going beyond this model can be explained in the *bubble-up* and *bottom-up* theory. This theory has always been more useful for explaining phenomena in youth fashion (jeans, leather jackets, anoraks, windsurfers, snowboards). It assumes that it is the bottom of the market, the street, which elaborates behaviours that are later institutionalised and transferred to the top of the market. The relationship between the consumer and the fashion system (the designer, the producer, the distributor) is inverted in the sense that it is the individual or the group that reject the trend and thereby actually dictate fashion. The reasons for rejecting the trend can, at the end of the process, be nullified by the institutionalisation and mass diffusion of the new fashion.

> Jeans, as observed, have all but lost the original connotation that made them the symbol of youth revolution. They have become clothes just like others. The fashion system has transformed them into an elegant, fashionable and exclusive product. Further, we can nowadays identify different interpretations on the market – those that look back to their origins (faded, 'fake poor' jeans, Levi's 501), those that take jeans into ready-to-

wear (Gucci, Fendi, Cavalli), those that make a male sex symbol of them (Calvin Klein), and those that emphasise their feel good and innovative component (Diesel).

This is why it is now possible to talk about the pluralism of fashion in different senses. It means, in the first place, that a single fashion can no longer dominate as in the past - crinoline, knee-length skirts, the new look, or the trouser suit. Fashions today are no longer able to impose conformity on the whole society for all social classes and every occasion. Further, styles and fashions have recently become much more specific for each occasion. There is daily wear and evening wear, work wear, leisure wear, clothes for the cruise, for travelling, for the countryside, for the seaside, and for the mountains. What dominates in one context cannot necessarily be spread to other contexts.

It is for this reason that the relationship between creative people and management, whose function is to select the firm's target, is more crucial than it used to be in establishing a brand or product.

The designer's creativity increasingly needs to be directed towards satisfying the specific needs of the market. This implies a greater complexity than in the past, and makes the management of creativity a more critical subject. The definition of management for creativity is the subject of the next chapter.

The relationship between creativity and management is a central issue for understanding the management model for fashion firms. The historical success of firms in this industry, particularly French and Italian ones, is deeply rooted in creativity: the creativity of designers, manufacturers, artistic directors, photographers, visual merchandisers. These people's range of activities and the importance of their role has no comparison with other industries. This is aside from their place on the organisational chart, given that they are often freelancers who work outside the firm. They have been able to give the whole pipeline a capacity for continuous innovation, and have created a strong appeal for the product among increasingly different segments of consumers. This is so true that, at least as far as the press and public opinion are concerned, the name of the creative people is more well known and acclaimed than the name of managers and entrepreneurs. Creativity has also national roots and it grows more strongly in some countries.

Italian creativity has solid roots in history and culture from the Renaissance onwards. From 1450 to 1500 Italy gave birth to artists that changed the world of art from then on: Leonardo da Vinci, Raphael, Michelangelo Buonarroti. Leonardo da Vinci, in particular, has been a symbol of the Italian capability of designing and managing creative projects. He was indeed a man of "both" worlds. He found a plane of thought that encompassed both the world of art along with the world of the sciences. Leonardo was a painter, sculptor, architect, musician, engineer, inventor, and scientist. He is surely the epitome of the renaissance man.

Italy is still nurtured by a pronounced and widespread taste and aesthetic sensitivity, and this is true not only of people working in fashion, but of large parts of the population generally. This historical and cultural asset has developed a fertile terrain in recent decades for the creation of the productive systems in the textile, leather and design furniture pipelines. These pipelines have been able to interpret the stimuli for product innovation coming from Italian designers.

After years in which the fashion industry's success was inextricably linked to the ability of creatives, the expression of the 'emotional spirit' of fashion firms, there has recently been a greater awareness of the importance of the managerial dimension, the expression of fashion firms' 'rational spirit'.[1]

The fashion system has organisational structures and professional management just like other industries. But the importance of creative people and the way that they condition how the rest of the firm works, are a peculiar feature that is worthy of further examination. Before going into detail about the relationship between creativity and management in the fashion system, it may be useful to offer some general remarks about creativity.

2.1 Artistic and commercial creativity

In the past traditional industrial systems used to have relative stability in terms of markets, technologies and competition, and the task of the manager was mainly to maintain the routines.

---

1. D. Goleman, *Emotional Intelligence*, Bantam Books, 1997.

Firms nowadays live in a complex environment in which breaking the rules has become the new competitive rule. Knowledge,
imagination, intuition and talent, in a word creativity, are what
the international business community of today values above all
else. The importance of creativity is linked to the evolution of the
competitive arena. Firms are increasingly valued on the basis of
their knowledge and intangible assets rather than their tangible
assets. The interconnection that is encouraged by information
technologies enormously increases the acquisition of stimuli
from different cultures, and this increases the creative potential
at global level. As creativity is nurtured by ambiguity, improvisation and complexity, new managerial techniques are necessary.
No industry or business activity can afford to underestimate the
need for greater creativity. But creativity does not have to be the
sole prerogative of so-called creative firms (fashion, design, publishing, and so on). All firms nowadays should know how to anticipate change with original and sustainable positions. The demand for creativity has increased a great deal and industries have
responded quickly. We buy a lot of products that incorporate creative work, such as fashion, publishing and entertainment (television, radio, music, and cinema).

Creativity is not the same as art, although the boundaries between artistic creativity and commercial creativity are increasingly blurred. The main difference between them is that artistic
creativity has a value in itself. The purpose of artistic creativity
is not to satisfy the needs of a mass market. Artistic creativity is
above all the means through which artists express themselves.
Commercial creativity, on the other hand, does not have this freedom of expression. This is because its purpose is to achieve another subject's objective, the firm. The firm's reason for existence lies in its ability to satisfy market needs.

In this book we define creativity as the process through which
new ideas are generated, developed and transformed into economic value. The point of view is always that of the firm and
'since the firm is an institution for making things, creativity without any operational result is a mere attitude[2]. It is useful to clar-

2. V. Bertone, *Creatività aziendale*, Franco Angeli, 1993, p. 36.

ify the differences between creativity and innovation. From the economic viewpoint, innovation can be defined as the development and diffusion of new products, services or processes that offer what customers perceive as better benefits.

Every innovation can be classified as a function of its *newness*. The idea of newness allows a distinction to be made between radical and incremental innovations. Innovation can also be defined as a function of the *object of innovation*, and this may be a product or process, or both (systemic innovation). The innovative process is usually conceived as a sequential series of events that is set in motion by creativity, on an input-output basis. In practice, creativity should be regarded as not just the source of innovation, but more widely as the fertile terrain where the process of innovation takes place. Creative ideas are thus the condition for innovation. They have an important role not only in the initial stage of the process, but throughout the whole innovation process.[3] The creative process has been effectively compared[4] to a *jam session* in which musicians begin with a theme that is then replaced by improvisation. The ensuing music then takes the initiative, following its own grammar and a series of conventions, towards a completely new and unexpected result. Like jazz, creativity also has its own rules and vocabulary. It is both art and discipline, an exploratory process rather than an end in itself.

2.2 The origins of individual creativity

Creativity is a fascinating subject, and has been the object of considerable psycho-sociological study, focused above all on the personalities of creative people. The romantic stereotype would have creative people be insecure, individualistic, perfectionist, and indifferent to time and the search for fame.[5] This may be true in certain environments, but not all creative actions inside firms can be attributed to people with these characteristics.

---

3. For more on this topic, see S. Vicari, *La creatività dell'impresa*, Etas, 1998.
4. J. Kao, *The Art and Discipline of Business Creativity*, Harper Business, 1996.
5. See T. Fisher, 'The designer's self-identity. Myths of creativity and the management of teams', in *Creativity and Innovation Management*, vol. 6, n. 1, March 1997.

Studies on creativity start from the human mind. The mind is a modelling system. It creates models that are based on environmental information which are then recognised, stored and used according to necessity.[6] As the order in which information arrives conditions the way in which it is processed into a model, the models are always less than the best possible elaboration of the information. Updating the models requires an intuitive restructuring mechanism. This cannot be logic, which works for relating concepts among them but not for restructuring them. One example is lateral thinking, through which the mind combines information in new ways in order to produce new ideas. While vertical thinking is concerned with proving or developing conceptual models, lateral thinking concerns the restructuring of old models (intuition) and the stimulation of new thoughts (creativity). Lateral thinking can therefore be defined as creative thinking. Research has endeavoured to examine the links between creative thought and personality features such as intelligence, age, competence and risk avoidance. The relationship between intelligence and creativity is not, as one might think, directly correlated. Research[7] has shown that, above a certain level of intelligence required to carry out a particular task, creativity level is not correlated with rational intelligence level.[8] The relationship between age and creativity seems, however, to have an inverse correlation, although it is greater in some fields than in others. Experience gained with age seems more important for the purposes of creativity in the arts than in science, for example. Experience gained through the generation of ideas seems to support creativity in all cases. If experience helps, however, the technical knowledge related to a specific problem seems to place a limit on creativity, as Simon argues.[9] Finally, there seems to be no doubt about a positive link between risk propensity and cre-

---

6. For a complete investigation of the subject of the mental handling of information, see D. Goleman, *op. cit.*, 1995.

7. S.G. Isaksen, *Frontiers of Creativity Research*, Bearly Press, 1987.

8. H. Gardner, *Frames of Mind. The theory of Multiple Intelligence*, Basic Books, 1983.

9. H.A. Simon, 'Understanding creativity and creative management', in R.L. Kuhn (ed.), *Handbook for Creative and Innovative Managers*, McGraw-Hill, 1988.

ativity[10], even if this can lead to simplistic and misleading conclusions about creative people as whimsical, heroic and solitary inventors to whom firms allocate disproportionate resources and patience.[11]

In brief, definitive results have not emerged from the conclusions that have been shown. Age, experience, competence and risk propensity may or may not support the creativity of individuals in a work environment if they have attained the level of intelligence that is required by their tasks. If something is known about creativity at the level of the individual, however, there has been no substantial study of creativity within firms. Quantitative studies have never taken account of the environment in which individuals work, or the way that structure and operating mechanisms influence creativity. This, however, is a fundamental issue as it is not unusual for environmental factors to have greater influence than personal characteristics in the development of creativity. The analysis of the creative process within organisations requires a definition of the creative act, and then an examination of the reasons that push individuals to perform creative acts, the means that they use, and the occasions that stimulate its occurrence. There is no theory explaining how creativity emerges, how it is managed, and how it can be increased. Single aspects of the working environment have, however, been examined, for example the issue of the motivation for creativity. The usual methods for stimulating work productivity are rewards and incentives, but these mechanisms support *extrinsic* motivation. In other words, they motivate the individual to produce for some external reason, the reward.[12] Psychologists seem to agree that creativity depends more on *intrinsic* motivation, that is working for a personal stimulus that consists in the creative process itself, in exploration, discovery, and the challenge that is implicit

---

10. R. Schank, *The Creative Attitude*, MacMillan, 1988.
11. P.F. Drucker, *Innovation and Entrepreneurship: Practice and Principles*, Harper Collins, 1985.
12. Rewards as incentives are a central theme in the behavioural school. The limits of this approach have been demonstrated recently. In particular, see A. Kohn, *Punished by Rewards*, Houghton Mifflin, 1993.

in the process. Several different studies[13] have recently come out, usually based on case studies, of the origins of business creativity. Creativity is defined as the possibility that employees make something new or potentially new for the business without having been explicitly told to do so.

The general conclusion of these studies is that a firm's creativity is limited by prejudices about who should be creative, the activities that are creative, and when and how the creative process should be produced. For the purposes of business creativity the establishment of a supportive environment for creativity is more important than individual *pre-established* elements. According to research and to our experience in the field, the following elements make up this environment:[14]

- Alignment, in the sense of the degree to which employees' interests and actions support the objectives of the business, is commonly regarded as the most important factor. Creativity always has to be related to the firm's objectives if it is to generate value.

  Renzo Rosso, Founder and president of Diesel, the leading Italian jeanswear company, succeeded in putting his own mark on the whole business in a way that is consistent with his own spirit of modernity and non-conformism, and with the target of young people looking for something different and original. Diesel employees, whose average age is less than thirty, all identify with their entrepreneur-leader, and are perfectly aligned with the business's target. They are proud to wear Diesel products. It is amusing to meet the Diesel employee tribe on the streets of Marostica, a medieval small city located in Veneto, Northern Italy, very near the firm's headquarters. The tribe stands out among the local inhabitants and employees of 'traditional' firms in the area, because of its hairstyles and colours, make-up and accessories.

---

13. See studies by Amabile: T. Amabile, 'A model of creativity and innovation in organisations', in *Research in Organisational Behaviour*, vol. 10, 1988: T. Amabile, B.A. Hennesse, 'The condition of creativity', in R.J. Sternberg (ed.), *The Nature of Creativity*, Cambridge University Press, 1988: T. Amabile, 'How to kill creativity', in *Harvard Business Review*, September-October, 1998.

14. See A.G. Robinson, S. Stern, *Corporate Creativity*, Berrett-Koehler Publisher Inc., 1997.

- Most creative actions in firms take place spontaneously. They are unplanned and are undirected by management. The unofficial activity is performed without the support of the firm, and it produces the most unexpected and creative results. This evidence would seem to be confirmed by the fact that creative abilities are related to a series of personal characteristics such as the lack of conformist thinking, independence from others' opinions and perseverance. These characteristics find their best expression in environments that are free of routine, borders, deadlines and appraisals.[15]

3M's culture has fostered creativity and given employees the freedom to take risks and try new ideas. The company allows technicians 15% of their time pursuing their visions on their own. In fact the policy is loosely applied with some 3Mers spending 50 percent of their time doing their own thing. This culture has led to a steady stream of products. With no boundaries to imagination and no barriers to cooperation, one good idea swiftly leads to another. At the Body Shop founder Anita Roddic characterizes her organization's culture as "benevolent anarchism," meaning that everyone has been encouraged "to question what they were doing and how they were doing it in the hope of finding better working methods."

- Creativity is supported by heterogeneous stimuli, but not all of these have the same effects on individuals. Further, the best quality stimuli come into existence 'in the field', that is from the work itself.

- Communication is a strong creativity supporter, but if it is to allow for interaction between people and roles that would normally not have contact with each other, it has to take place in unconventional channels. This is because creativity often seems linked to combinations of things that are not usually related to each other. An effective and conti-

---

15. These factors were studied in the area of creative training programmes such as brainstorming by Osborn and Gordon. For a critical review of the best known methods for developing creativity see S. Parnes, *The Magic of Your Mind*, Bearly Press, 1981; R.W. Weisberg, *Creativity: Beyond the Myth of Genius*, Freeman, 1993.

nuous interface between the creative function, marketing and production increases the probability of success in creative projects.

At Motorola teams drawn from marketing, research, engineering and sales are often brought together and assigned a project. Members of these teams are first trained in creative tactics, such as associative thinking, and to work on a cross functional team with training in the areas of conflict resolution. Ford Motor Company has also taken the cross functional team approach towards process improvement and creation. Ford believes that getting people from all parts of the process together allows them to see the forest rather than just their individual trees and is the key for creativity and innovation to occur[16].

2.3 What kind of management for creativity?

The importance of creativity does not imply that management has to acquire artistic qualities or scientific research skills. Nor does it imply that firms have to support a chaotic environment. Leonardo Da Vinci used to say that *"art lives from constraints and dies from freedom"*.

The task of managers in developing creativity is quite clear. They have to create environments supporting and nourishing the creative process. Managers in creative firms work as integrators who connect values to objectives, culture to strategy, and results to rewards. The role of management is to operate in the paradox, or in the central tension between art – the free play of intuition, imagination and inspiration - and discipline. This implies making a series of decisions. The first of these is who to involve in the creative process, and what abilities and responsibilities. Secondly, the agenda. Thirdly, the rhythm and what roles, and lastly, what the final product of the creative process will be.

The management of creativity has been considered like the orchestration of a conversation, an interaction among people, cultures, and points of view. The conversation has to be centred on individuals, and it has to use

---

16. For these examples in managing creativity *www.thebesemer.com*.

their language whenever possible. A creative culture that can stimulate vision and generate enthusiasm can never derive from an autocratic environment. It has to come from a boundary-less organisation, where communication flows freely. Some limits to creativity are also needed or creative people lose a sense of direction.

The manager of creativity also needs to understand the interdisciplinary nature of the skills that are required, in addition to the strictly management skills. The heart of the strategy for all firms is interfunctional integration, and this does not mean so much the ability to improve the individual process or activity as the ability to integrate activities along and outside the business value chain, so making the activities complementary.

The responsibilities of the management of creativity do not end with maintaining existing skills. They also have to include the continuous nourishment and enrichment of the creative skill base within the firm. The following alternatives can be pursued, with regard to building new creative skills.

- Acquisitions of new companies, in the hope that the personnel from the acquired businesses will continue to be creative witin the new corporate culture. Nowadays this represents the challenge for most fashion and luxury conglomerates after several acquisitions of brands and designers
- Structured inter-firm agreements, in order to share the benefits of a joint creativity. Large pharmaceutical companies have this kind of arrangement with small biotechnical laboratories
- *Scouting* for personnel and independent creative structures that can be used in short to medium term partnership in order to contribute to the creativity of the whole organisation.

The last of these three is the most common route in creative industries, but it is also the most difficult. It establishes a temporary project culture that sometimes does not create alignment in visions between the external creative structures and the corporate interest.

One interesting example of creativity management is the film industry. Historically, the great Hollywood studios were vertically integrated empires. They controlled actors, studios and writers through long-term contracts that imposed strict planning of activities. Some major studios also controlled cinema sales chains that showed their productions exclusively. This system entered a crisis due to anti-trust legislation, and actors in particular understood that they had box office power. Nowadays, the studios are essentially capitalist ventures. They manage distribution channels and some technical skills, but the true creativity lies in the world of independents who are not tied to a single organisation. They join individual projects from time to time through their agents.

A further example is related to the pharmaceutical industry in the biotechnology segment. Biotechnology research is not currently flourishing in universities because of the shortage of funds, nor in the large pharmaceutical companies that are slow acting and bureaucratic. Instead, it flourishes in small firms that are supported by venture capital. Such firms came into being from the research of a single creative group. Scientists can pursue their vision without cultural or financial conditioning in these free and flexible environments, and then enter into agreements with the large companies for the very costly development of the clinical tests.

2.4 The management of creativity in fashion firms

Creativity is a necessity for all firms, although it exists in different quantities and qualities for different firms. Firms that are based on artistic-creative ability, such as fashion ones, are different from other firms because they produce and sell a *creative* product. This product is conceived in a context that brings together art, craftsmanship and management. The fashion product blends together the artistic vision, the action and physical skills of the craftsmanship, and the strategic thought of management. Every product, or product line, is to some extent at least always original and different from the previous one, as it is the result of a creative activity that continuously renews itself. Change is the essence of these firms, as they serve needs that are constantly changing. Constant innovation, along with a process of planned obsolescence, is their reason for existence. The market is only willing to buy if the creativity meets its own tastes, and change has therefore to be in harmony with customers and the development of the socio-cultural context. The problem lies in the fact that these tastes are difficult to predict. Although there are no scientific methods that can help predict the success of a creative product, there are still some more or less established methods for motivating and leading creative people to come up with ideas that consumers will want, whether they are aware of it or not. For this reason, fashion firms will continue to depend on creative people, but also and above all on the ability to manage the innovation process on which they are engaged. Defining creativity as synonymous with personal inspiration and invention for its own sake, with no limiting conditions or reference to socio-cultural or market conditions, is one thing. It is quite another to see creativity as a tool for innovation within a clear market and product strategy, and as something aware and durable. The former case certainly has fascinating elements, and it can sometimes be possible to obtain extremely good results from this route, thanks to its strong innovative content. The other side of the coin, however, is the risk of not focusing innovation, of triggering schizophrenic behaviour within the firm, and of disorientating the market and internal and external partners. This way of defining creativity is difficult to manage because it excludes any limit and above all, any setting of objectives from the outset.

Conversely, creative people who agree to serve a firm and a market without giving up their independence, can only benefit from managerial support.

This is a crucial point. Fashion firms and creative people in fashion, and more generally all those in industries of symbolic intensity and a high rate of change, need 'special' managers who can understand the culture and language of creative people. Such managers have to be capable of great flexibility. Above all, they have to accept one of the basic rules of the industry – it is not enough in fashion to offer the market what it wants today, as this would already be an old product! Instead, it is necessary to understand what will happen in the next few seasons, but without looking too far ahead.

This aspect is subtle and complex, but also important in the fashion system, and it requires interaction between the 'emotional-creative spirit' and the 'rational-managerial spirit'.

In this respect it may be useful to consider that the most successful fashion people in the past were often couples where it was nearly always possible to define one member of the couple as the pure creative and the other as the rationaliser, the manager.

> Some of the most significant cases where a perfect mix between creative and managerial spirits was reached are these: Yves Saint Laurent and Pierre Bergé, Giorgio Armani and Sergio Galeotti, Valentino Garavani and Giancarlo Giammetti, Ottavio and Rosita Missoni, Mariuccia Mandelli (Krizia) and Sergio Pinto, Alberta and Massimo Ferretti, Gianfranco Ferrè and Franco Dei Mattioli, Gianni and Santo Versace, Tom Ford and Domenico De Sole, Calvin Klein and Barry Schwartz.

The most interesting aspect is the specificity of the situations in which this harmony is achieved. The two roles are often played by a couple who are linked together in a long-lasting friendship, or have a personal affinity. It is as if this were a necessary condition for overcoming the cultural and structural barriers that obstruct the positive interaction of the two people. It often happens in fashion firms that the management seems to consider the creative people as 'crazy', and the creative people in turn think of managers as 'sad and grey office workers oriented to the past'.

This situation of apparent conflict conceals enormous potential, but it is tied, in our view, to management's capacity to develop attitudes, methods and behaviours that fully appreciate the indispensable creative potential of the firm's artistic part. If one cannot ask creative people to be more managerial because this would immediately be translated into a limit on their innovative potential, it is legitimate to expect managers to adapt their professionalism to this context, and to enter into harmony with the creative dimension of the business. Thus the fashion manager has to have innate creative attitudes, or to agree to take on some of the creative people's culture. This does not mean that the manager has to abdicate the managerial role, which is to support, rationalise, and give objectives to the creative process.

One result of this is the need to accept that fashion firms have a dual culture that has implications on organisational structures and professional roles. The problem is above all to avoid this duality becoming a struggle for dominance between the two parts, as this would reduce the complementarity that is needed. This challenge is also the ultimate purpose of this book. The authors want to offer a contribution to the development of a managerial culture aimed at satisfying the particular characteristics of the fashion industries.

PART TWO

The structural and competitive context of the fashion system

3 The fashion pipeline

3.1 The structure and competitive context of the fashion system

3.1.1 The structure of the fashion pipeline

The fashion system is so large and complex that it can be considered as a cluster[1] of closely interconnected industries. Often attention is focused only on the finished products (apparel, knitwear, hosiery, accessories...), but these are the result of a long and developed chain of stages and activities whose interaction is largely responsible for the product's final success on the market. A fashionable suit is much more than the creative effort of the designer. It is the result of innovative fibres that have been woven by specialised machines into fabrics of the colours and shapes that the fashion system has presented through its trade fairs and specialised operators, such as the *Bureau du Style*. Nor

---

1. A cluster can be defined as a group of economic operators and organisations whose competitive advantage is increased as a result of the interactions and links they develop among themselves. For more on the concept of industry clusters and the effects on competitiveness, see M. Porter, *The competitive advantage of nations*, The MacMillan Press Ltd., 1990.

is this enough. The role of distribution in selecting the offers is fundamental in affirming a fashion trend, as is the critical opinion of fashion editors. A fundamental concept for analysing the fashion system, intended as an interrelated system made up of different stages, is the concept of the fashion *pipeline*. Sometimes defined as the supply chain, the pipeline identifies the vertical system that starts from the production stages of raw materials (fibres from the agricultural or chemical industries) down to the manufacturing and distributive stages of the textile and clothing industries. The fashion pipeline is thus made up of different sectors (fibre, textile, clothing, accessories, ...) that can be further segmented according to categories of merchandise and price range. Therefore the fashion pipeline is characterised by an unusual length – fibre to yarn, yarn to fabric, fabric to garments and retailing with an enormous variety of end-products. Industries that do not form part of the vertical productive cycle, but which support the whole system, are also part of the fashion pipeline. These include the textile machinery industry and various sections of the service industry (fashion publishing, fashion trade fairs, advertising and communication agencies, design studios, and so on).

A country's development of a competitive advantage within several stages of the fashion pipeline is important to achieving international leadership through its finished products. The success of 'made in Italy' in fashion has always been linked to the control of the entire textile and leather pipelines, from yarn to distribution, and at a very high level of innovation and technology. No other industrialised country has developed a leadership in cashmere, linen, cotton and wool weaving and knitting, in manufacturing technologies, in the most advanced finishing technologies and in fashion design. A great part of the creativity and flexibility supporting the competitiveness of the Italian fashion system relies on the relationships between textile firms, clothing firms and specialised distributors. These firms, at different stages, work together like a large workshop in the creation and manufacture of a wide and innovative range of products. "Physical proximity" is not the only factor supporting innovation and the ease of interaction of Italian yarn and textile producers with knitwear and manufacturing firms. Also the average firm dimension counts: Italian textile firms' average size is lower than that of European producers as a whole. This results in advantages in flexibility, an increase in the variety of semi-finished products, and a shorter product life cycle. Even in the industrial environment, where the size of firms is greater, textile suppliers and producers of finished goods have developed strong relationships with their clients based on exclusive supply, small batches, delivery timed in relation to the clothing cycle, and so on. The greater flexibility of Italian textile and clothing firms is also related to the development of sub-contracting. This is encouraged by the presence of industrial districts made up of small firms that specialise in a single stage of the manufacturing processes rather than in product technology or in a particular raw material.

Two pipelines are usually identified within the fashion system: textile-clothing and leather-hosiery-accessories. The focus here is on the former. This is the more important from the perspective of market dimension, demand and supply segmentation and advances in technology. It was also the first to develop that fashion cycle that later has been transferred, thanks to product and business diversification, to other pipelines and industries.

Figure 3.1 shows the different stages of the fashion textile-clothing pipeline, from raw materials to the fibres, yarns, fabrics, end uses and distribution of the final product. The textile machinery industry and supporting services work transversally to the entire pipeline. In terms of total employment and output, the three largest segments are fibres, fabrics, and clothing. However, the extensive linkages within the entire textile pipeline underscore the importance of analysing it as a whole and not just its individual segments. The largest of the three final production stages in the textile pipeline is clothing.

The structure of the fashion pipeline as presented originates from a classification traditionally used by the Italian Textile Associations.[2] This gives the following order:

- Fibre industry
- Textile industry:
  – wool

---

2 . The fashion system in Italy is organised for the textile industry by Federtessile, a federation that heads all the textile associations: Associazioni cotoniera (cotton), liniera (linen), laniera (wool), serica (silk), dyeing and finishing. The downstream industries are represented by Moda Industria that includes clothing, knitwear, accessories and other finished products.

FIGURE 3.1

THE TEXTILE PIPELINE

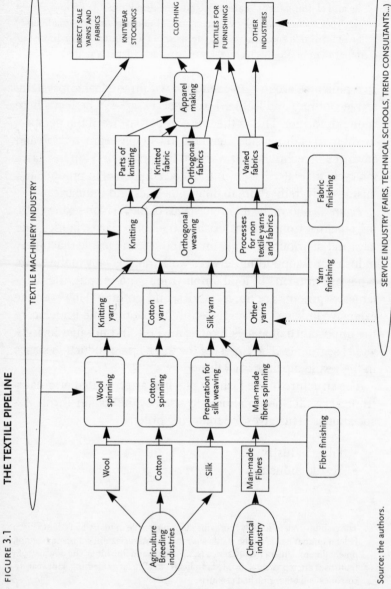

Source: the authors.

- cotton and linen
- silk
- finishing and textile ennobling
- other textiles and product techniques
- Clothing industry:
  - Textile clothing
  - Knitwear and hosiery.

A brief description of the clothing distribution industry (which is the subject of *Chapter 9*) and the mechanised textile industry, a typical supporting industry, completes the background.

Firms' success in fashion, above all on the Italian market, is strongly connected to the competitiveness of all the stages of the textile pipeline. Partnership, co-operation, co-marketing and co-design are the key words for understanding the nature of the collaborative and competitive relationship among fashion companies. Michel Porter[3] explains the important phenomenon of "clustering" in which related groups of successful firms and industries emerge in one nation to gain leading positions in the world market. The management of creativity in the fashion industries is above all a *management of boundaries*. It is designed to promote innovation in all those parts of the system of actors, competencies and resources that converge on the needs of the end consumer. In the following, each industry will be analysed from the viewpoint of the type of product offered and the structure of the competitive environment. Particular attention will be given to the contribution that each industry provides to the innovation process within the whole pipeline.

3.1.2 The fibre industry

The first link in the textile pipeline is the fibre industry. Fibre is the smallest component in a fabric. It is also the one that gives

---

3.   M. Porter, 1990, *op.cit.*

the fabric its colour, weight, solidity and 'hand'.[4] Fibres can be natural or man-made, depending on the type of product being offered. Natural fibres come from the animal world (wool and silk) or the vegetable world (cotton and linen). Man-made are produced from natural substances such as cellulose or petrol derivatives. There are two broad categories of man-made fibre: artificial and synthetic. Artificial fibres are natural raw materials that have been chemically treated, like cellulose from wood, and linters from cotton. They generally have similar properties to natural fibres. Synthetic fibres have their origins in different polymers that have been obtained through chemical treatment. Man-made fibres also include some inorganic fibres such as glass-fibre and ceramic-fibre. The real advantage of man-made fibres over natural ones is that they can be 'made to measure' to meet particular applications. Thus it is possible to have brilliant or opaque fibres, elastic or rigid ones, very soft or hard fibres, delicate or super-resistant fibres, or coloured or transparent ones, according to need. As they are made in the laboratory, there are many more man-made fibres than natural ones. There are about twenty types, and these are classified under a generic name, with producers making their own variations of each type. The principal and best known artificial fibres are: rayon-viscose (this is the oldest artificial fibre and was already in use in 1889) cellulose, acetate. The synthetic fibres include: polyamide, polyester, acrylic, polypropolyn, and elastometric fibre. *Table 3.1* lists some of the best known trade names on the man-made fibre market.

One important innovation in the area of chemical fibres was the introduction of microfibres. This began in the 1970s and was developed with particular reference to polyester and polyamide. Microfibre is about ten times thinner than human hair and much thinner than wool and cotton or even silk. It has a soft feel but is resistant to folding and washing.

---

4. The 'hand' of a textile refers to the feelings that are produced when it is touched by hands. These include softness, elasticity, weight, thermal properties, touch or roughness. A textile is said, more or less properly, to have a *rigid, smooth,* or more or less *fine* hand.

TABLE 3.1 **GENERIC AND TRADE NAMES OF SOME CHEMICAL FIBRES**

GENERIC NAME	TRADE NAME
Polyester	Terital (Montefibre), Dacron (DuPont)
Acrylic	Acrilan (Solutia), Leacril (Montefibre)
Aramid	Kevlar (DuPont)
Lyocell	Tencel (Courtaulds fibers)
Nylon	Cordura (DuPont), Tactel (Dupont), Zeftron (BASF), Meryl (Nylstar)
Rayon	Enka (Akzo Nobel Faser)
Spandex	Lycra (DuPont)

Source: the authors.

Du Pont introduced another enormously successful fibre, which is known by its trade name, Lycra. It is an elastometric synthetic fibre known in the USA under the generic name Spandex, and in Europe as elastane. It has elastic properties that allow it to stretch to six times its own length and then recover its original shape. It is never used by itself, but is combined with either natural or chemical fibres to give the finished product elasticity and comfort.

Man-made fibre is sold to the spinning-mill in the form of continuous yarn or staple. Natural fibres are bought unbleached by the spinning-mill (in balls or skeins) directly on the global markets for natural raw materials. The quality and price of a fibre are determined by its fineness (its suitability for spinning depends on this) and length (the longer a fibre is, the stronger will be the resulting yarn).

The fibre industry, and particularly the man-made fibre industry, is the part of the textile pipeline where the most important innovations in terms of new functions and materials take place. It is thus capital intensive, given the need for high investment in research, technology and machines.

Further, the environmental issue has become increasingly important in the last ten years, and this has led to increased costs for firms in the industry. These costs derive from respecting the stringent rules about the discharge and recovery of the auxiliary chemicals that are used.

The chance for technical innovations to reach the market for finished products depends on the interaction of stages at the bottom of the pipeline (spinning-mill, textile and manufacturing industry) with the innovative process.

The industry is concentrated, from the competitive point of view. Competition is in the form of an oligopoly, where a relatively small number of producers – chemical groups in the case of chemical fibres and commodity markets in the case of natural fibres - control the global market. The fibre producers further increased this market dominance thanks to the power of their brand names. The final consumer often knows these names, which act as a guarantee of the fibre's quality.

For the apparel manufacturer the possibility to use fibre brands that are known by final customers usually implies the concession of licensing agreements that contain some restrictions on the use of the fibre. These agreements also increasingly provide for sharing the costs of communication and promotion of the brand between the fibre producer, the textile producer and the clothing firm.

> Du Pont, for example, defined a new relational marketing approach for the Lycra brand with the different actors in the pipeline: from the textile firm to the manufacturing firm, up to the sales point where joint promotions of Lycra products were made.

> In order to stimulate the global demand for wool in the face of the growth of cotton and chemical fibres, the International Wool Secretariat (IWS) defined the 'pure virgin wool' brand. It implemented a marketing strategy that provided for collaboration on all the stages of the textile pipeline. The strategy is designed to make wool more modern, to reduce its weight, to bring out products and styles, and to make machine-washable woollen clothes.

In the 1990s there was a global change in both the mix of fibres that were bought and in the geographical map of the industry. Man-made fibres have overtaken natural fibres in the industrialised countries in the last ten years. The increase in man-made fibre consumption is also linked to the growing use of innovative fibres, or fibres that are mixtures of natural and man-made types.

Global production of manufactured fibre was 34.2 million metric tonnes in 2000, an increase of 130% from the 15.0 million tonnes produced in 1980. Over the past twenty years synthetic types, e.g. polyester, have shown strong long-term growth, while cellulosics have declined. Synthetics now account for 94% of worldwide production. Over the past twenty years, polyester has maintained a substantial lead in volume. Olefin fibres have shown strong growth from a low base and now surpass nylon and acrylic fibres in production volume. Growth in synthetic fibre production has resulted in a major shift in production from North America and Europe to Asia. In 2000 Asian production was 19.1 million metric tonnes compared with 5.5 in North America, 3.9 in Europe. The Asian share of synthetic fibre production was 61% in 2000. This compares with a North American and Western Europe combined share of 57% in 1980, down to 30% in 2000. The other significant shift in the twenty-year period was Eastern Europe – moving from 12% to 3%. From 1980 through 2000 trend growth for all manufactured fibres was 4.3%. Synthetics grew at 5.2% per year, while cellulosics declined at a rate of 1.9% per year. Within the synthetic group, olefin grew at 9.1%, polyester at 6.7%, both nylon and acrylic at 1.3%. The twenty year average annual growth trend by region reflects 8.6% growth in Asia, 1.3% growth in North America and Western Europe, and 8.4% for all other regions. Eastern Europe declined at 4.2% per year with the decline starting in the mid-1980s.

3.1.3 The textile industry

The textile industry includes the activities that transform fibres into yarns and then fabrics. This macro-industry can be broken up into segments according to the technology or stage covered in the productive cycle. One method of segmentation is based on the type of fibre used. This distinguishes between the wool and cotton cycles,[5] the silk cycle, and the non-textile and mixed textile cycles. The four cycles make up well-differentiated supply chains, even if they share some common industrial stages: the fibre preparation and spinning, the fabric-making (knitting and weawing), and the finishing process. Technological variables dominate in the spinning stage. These are related to the type of fibre employed. In the fabric-making stage there is a greater fo-

---

5. Linen is regarded as part of the cotton section.

cus on the final market destination (for example fabrics for shirts, technical fabrics, fabrics for clothing, for furniture, knitwear, and so on).[6]

The fibre spinning stage

The different types of raw material are prepared before entering that process whose purpose is to create the yarn. In the case of natural fibres, for example, unbleached skeins are turned into semi-finished products for spinning so as to obtain cotton, wool or silk reels. According to the nature of the raw materials, productive cycles differ even at this preliminary stage. Therefore, textile firms usually specialise in one technology only. Plants that work to produce cotton reels are different from plants producing wool[7]; furthermore wool yarn can be carded or combed.[8]

The weaving stage

This stage prepares and works on the yarns in order to produce fabrics. A first criterion of differentiation among woven products is technological, and refers to the distinction between orthogonal and knitted fabrics. Orthogonal fabric, or simply cloth, is obtained by laying the warp on the loom - the warp is the longitudinal spread of fibres, and the weft is the transversal spread of fibres. The different ways of laying out the warp and weft are known as the framework. Once orthogonal cloth has been cut into pieces and sewn, it is used for making apparel (shirts, jackets, trousers, and so on).

The preparation of material for knitted fabrics takes two forms:

- *Woof*: the techniques are based on horizontal knitting, and the industrial process is similar to the elementary opera-

---

6. For more on this, see M. Bona, F.A. Isnardi, S.R. Straneo, *Manuale di tecnologia tessile*, Zanichelli-Esac, 1981.
7. Fibres have different lengths. Cotton is about 2 cms., and wool about 5 cms. Silk is a continuous thread and chemical fibres are usually obtained as a continuous thread that can be cut to the same length as cotton or wool.
8. Carded yarn is made up of fibres that go through a process that makes them warm and coarse, while a combed yarn is smoother and softer. The main combed yarns on the Italian market are found in the industrial district of Biella, and carded yarns at Prato.

tions of the knitting needle. The result is not a fabric, but a weave that is ready for use after finishing (we will deal with these stages later on)
- *Chain*: here the yarn (or chain) is fed to the loom to obtain the weave.

At the end of the pipeline, manufacturing processes differ technologically according to the type of fabric, knitted or orthogonal. Both types are cut and sewn. It is the market positioning that characterises the manufacturing firms as clothing or knitwear firms.

There are then other innovative processes that allow for the making of non-textile fabrics (these are made without the use of looms). This avoids the process of spinning and textile making. These products currently hold the record for growth throughout the whole textile industry. Research on new fabric types has led textile production to great creativity and versatility favoring the development of new fabrics using weaves combining natural with synthetic and artificial fibres. This has led, for example, to the stretch materials which are fundamental expecially for easy-care garments. Classic fabrics have also evolved thanks to research on finishing.

The concept of quality for textile products is essentially related to fibre quality. Cashmere weavers, for example, are regarded as quality producers while cotton producers are regarded as in the average-to-low segment of the market, even where the cotton itself is of high quality. There is monopolistic competition for both orthogonal and knitted textiles. Although the technology is more important lower down the pipeline, the differential advantage is based on firm's skills and capabilities within all the stages of the chain from purchasing to production and sales, with a strong orientation on market needs.

Firm structure has changed over the years. In the past textile firms tended to integrate vertically in the different stages of the pipeline; starting from the 1990s there was a tendency to specialise. Even medium size firms tended to concentrate on single manufacturing stages, and to outsource low value activities. Further, the importance of firms focused on commercial activities and pipeline co-ordination is growing.

Regarding the non-textile section, the few firms that have the technology, knowledge and capital to invest in research and development operate in a competitive system that is largely oligopolistic. Italian firms dominate the medium-to-high market segment of orthogonal and knitted textiles, particularly in natural fibres that are produced in specialist areas.

Italy is in the lead in wool textiles. Almost 95% of the natural raw materials come from foreign markets (Australia, CSI, New Zealand and China). The spinning, weaving and manufacturing stages are carried out in Italy. The sector is made up of many small and medium sized firms as well as a few large ones such as the Marzotto group. Most companies are located in the two industrial districts of Biella (located in Piemonte) and Prato (located in Tuscany). There are different types of firm within the district:
- importing firm
- services firm (for example research on fibre combing in the Biella area)
- spinning firm (combed wool at Biella, carded wool at Prato)
- wool mill (orthogonal textile activities)
- integrated firm (from the purchase of raw wool or worsted to the weaving stage).

Prato's textile production is coordinated by the wool mills whose role is to define and market the sample collections. Wool has always been a fundamental raw material for Prato since the year 1000 when Prato's craftsmen developed increasingly refined weaving techniques and began selling their products. Between the XIII and XIV centuries a new figure appeared on the scene, the merchant, who took orders, placed them and delivered the finished goods, thus laying the basis for the existing system of intermediaries. Nowadays the Prato wool mills invest a great deal of resources in research into new blends, in trend studies, and in the creation of innovative textiles.

As regards the market viewpoint, the textile industry can be segmented on the basis of the final destination (clothing or knitwear, furniture, industrial uses), on the basis of the price range (high, medium-high and low) or on the basis of the characteristics of the supply system (firms specialised in a particular product/technology, firms oriented to serving the market with a wide range of products often sub-contracted). With regard to the fibre and textile industries business communication addressed to the final consumer is very rare at the international level.

English Harris Tweed is one of the best known carded wool trademarks, as is the Italian Ing. Loro Piana in the field of cashmere and lambswool fabric, the well known Tasmania.

The textile treatment stage

This stage that includes a series of treatments (dyeing, printing and finishing). These can involve the fibre, the yarn, or more frequently the fabric, or in some cases the finished item of clothing. For this reason it is correct to consider the sector as transversal to the entire textile pipeline. There are highly specialist firms that use treatments which give a specific feature or touch to materials without changing their nature. These treatments can be divided into colouring (dyeing and printing) and finishing. The latter consist of chemical processes designed to wash, dry, soften, shine, or stabilise yarns, cloths and finished items of clothing. They are often performed within the same firms, whereas printing and dyeing require very specialist skills. Finishing is nowadays the most important phase in textile manufacturing. The finishing techniques are extremely innovative and can give to any product a particular look and "hand". The financial commitments required of the companies in this field are enormous: research, upgrading machinery, experiments on increasingly innovative treatments in some cases absorb up to 10% of their turnover. The finishing sector is made up of medium to large size firms, often located near their clients.

3.1.4 The clothing industry

It is usual, with regard to the stages lower down the pipeline, to use the generic term of clothing, without making any distinction between the two types of production process - apparel making and knitwear (*Figure 3.2*). There are, however, profound technological, productive and market differences between the two processes. Apparel making includes cutting and sewing both from orthogonal fabrics and knitwear, while knitwear includes making garments directly from yarn (wool, cotton or blends). The expression 'fragmented system' well describes the com-

FIGURE 3.2 **THE PRODUCTIVE CYCLES OF TEXTILE APPAREL AND KNITWEAR IN THE CLOTHING INDUSTRY**

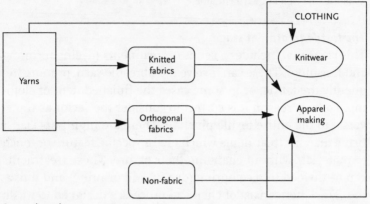

Source: the authors.

plex structure of the clothing industry. These are made up of a lot of competitive sectors, each of which has its own competitive model. The competitive sectors are defined by the technology that is used, the clients that are served, and the product end-uses. The nature of productive cycle causes further fragmentation. Both clothing and knitwear technologies present low economies of scale with regard to plant dimensions. This is because of the low degree of standardisation of production driven by the need for seasonal flexibility in the use of the materials and processes. Unlike the industries higher up the pipeline (fibres and yarns), the productive cycles lower down the vertical chain can be highly decentralised. It is thus possible in both apparel making and in knitting to organise the production in just one stage. A low level of concentration and vertical integration in Italy has been a marked feature of the two sectors from the beginning. The fragmentation of the system is made clear from the frequent references in journals and specialised literature to productive areas/districts rather than individual firms.

The main stages of the productive cycle that are common to both apparel making and knitwear are cutting, manufacturing, ironing, and the quality controls and packaging of the final product. The manufacturing stage is then divided into several sub-stages such as sewing, glueing, embroidery and quilting (*Figure 3.3*).

FIGURE 3.3 **THE PRODUCTIVE CYCLE OF APPAREL MAKING**

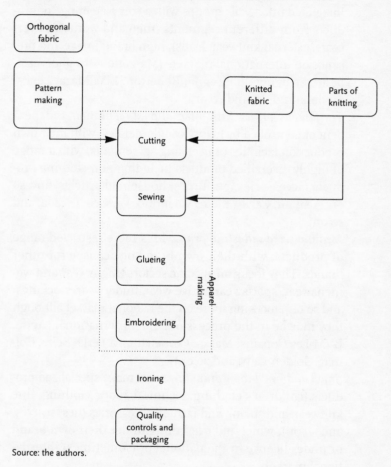

Source: the authors.

Although the various stages of the cycle have been involved in automation (particularly for cutting) in recent years, the sewing stage has always been labour intensive. The technology here (sewing machine) dates back one hundred years and can hardly be replaced. This means that manufacturing in the most industrialised countries is not competitive compared to low costs countries. Regarding the structure of firms competing in the industry, clothing firms can be classified as follows:

1. *Large industrial firms.* These are sometimes industrial groups integrated into textile groups with a complete range of products from different segments (men and women's overcoats, external knitwear, jeans), high brand image and presence on international markets (Marzotto, Miroglio-Vestebene, Ermenegildo Zegna, Benetton, Max Mara, Levi's, Steilmann, Fila, and so on)

2. *The famous 'griffes' with international reputation,* independent or controlled by luxury conglomerates, with their own production facilities or licensing agreements, with a range of highly diversified products including non-clothing products (accessories, perfumes, household articles, and so on: Armani, Calvin Klein, Valentino, Versace, Escada, and so on)

3. *Medium sized industrial firms* with a more restricted range of products, with their own brand or licensee for other brands. They focus on specific sectors (menswear and womenswear, sportswear, active wear, underwear, stockings, and so on), focusing more on the national market although they may be in the process of going international (Aeffe, BVM-Les Copains, Maska, Corneliani, La Perla, Belfe, Colmar, Golden Lady, and so on)

4. *Small and small-to-medium firms* that make specialised products (children's clothing, technical sports clothing, fine knitwear, and so on), and fashion accessories (ties, scarves, and so on), which put everything under their own brand or under licence in the national or (sometimes) international markets

5. *The suppliers* of the above firms. These can be divided into 'sub-contractors' (medium and medium-to-small), that can make the finished article or do most of the work related to it, and the so called 'façonists' (smaller and often craft-based firms), that exclusively carry out some manufacturing and finishing on semi-worked products of the commissioning company.

Chapter 5 deals in depth with the competitive dynamics of the clothing industry, the definition of the competitive environment, and market segmentation.

3.1.5 The distribution industry

Distribution is the final stage in the pipeline. It consists of selling the final product, the item of clothing or accessories, to the end user or consumer. Modern distribution in the fashion system can be defined as general (addressing several categories of merchandise or several targets of consumer) or specialized (one category of merchandise or one target of consumer). There are then several different distribution formats within each category, and these differ according to geographical area, location, price positioning and service level. They include department stores, specialist stores, chain stores, discount stores, to name a few.

A further criterion of distribution segmentation is the proprietary formula. There is a distinction between independent distribution, groups of shops that are centrally owned (chains), and franchise shops. Although it is the final link in the pipeline, distribution is in many ways the heart of the textile-clothing pipeline and the fashion system itself. The sales point is no longer just a distribution channel. It is the place where the commercial strategy of the whole fashion pipeline is given shape. The sales point communicates, offers products, provides a service and, above all, builds and reinforces the loyalty relationship with customers. Further, the sales point in the fashion industry is unlike sales points in any other industry, because it provides the most reliable and well-timed inputs about the development of customer tastes and needs. It is through the sales point inputs that clothing producers and their suppliers can redesign their strategic choices: product strategy and innovation, image, range policy, pricing and service.

In recent years a fundamental issue in the clothing industry has been the evolution of distribution and industry relationships. There has been a transfer of power from manufacturers to distributors all over Europe, and the clearest signs of this are:

- The increase in the market shares of the large distributors (department stores, specialist department stores, factory outlets, and so on)
- The development of retail chains (of both producers and distributors)
- The development, within multi-brand specialist retail, of retailing strategies like trade marketing and visual merchandising (corner, shop in shop) with an accurate selection of industrial suppliers.

Further evolutions in the fashion market are the increasing internationalisation of distribution and the development of the private label. Many apparel firms in all specialities are commissioned to manufacture clothes for large department and chain stores that wish to sell garments under their own brand name or private label. A store may use a single brand name to identify all merchandise produced for it, such as "Made expressly for X's". Or it may vary the label with the clothing line (ABC brand for sportswear and XYZ brand for lingerie and night-wear).

This shift of power had a structural effect on producers in the fashion industry, modifying their contractual power with respect to retailers. Some industrial firms reacted to this by investing in directly owned stores and by establishing very strong relationships with distribution partners. Conversely, those firms that have left market relations to other actors (agents, intermediaries and importers) now find themselves in a position of great weakness.

In this chapter we have analysed the pipeline according to its technological features and starting from the fibre stage. A strategic interpretation, however, should start directly from distribution, because the retail outlet is the place where the end consumer and the offer system really meet. The success (or failure) of the entire pipeline depends upon the final consumer reaction to retail environment (merchandising mix, location, service, experiences, comparison between competing brands...) where the physical product is only one variable. *Chapter 8* contains more on the relationship between the clothing industry and distribution.

3.1.6 Related and supporting industries: the textile machinery industry

No analysis of the textile-clothing pipeline would be complete without some mention of the textile machinery industry. This is one of the most important sections of the largest industry of instrumental mechanics. It includes the machinery and plants used for transforming raw materials and semi-worked products from other firms. It is a typical supporting industry in the textile pipeline, and was identified by Porter[9] as the source of Italy's competitive advantage in clothing. Concerning the types of product offered, *Table 3.2* shows the different types of specialist textile machinery for each stage of the pipeline.

The machinery and equipment industries play an important role in each of the major segments of the textile pipeline. Many of the manufacturing breakthroughs in the textile pipeline have occurred from the utilization of new equipment developed by equipment firms. Most of the new equipment has been more labour-saving and efficient than its predecessors and, as a result, has increased the international competitiveness of higher labour cost countries as they substituted equipment for labour.

The activities of a machinery producing firm are sub-divided into four macro areas: machinery design, the supply of raw materials (electrical and mechanical parts), the productive and logistic process (the assembly of electronic and mechanical systems, testing, packaging and transport), customer service (assembling, testing, training and after-sale service). The most valuable activities for firms are design and customer service. The former can be divided into a preliminary stage and a performance stage. The preliminary stage is fundamental, and concerns the design of the machinery, and thus its personalisation for all the firms which provide made to measure solutions rather than selling standard products from a catalogue. The next step is the preparation of 'design' laboratories at clients' firms, where the new machinery and productive methods are tested. The service stage can

9. M. Porter, *op. cit.*

TABLE 3.2   **STAGES IN THE TEXTILE PIPELINE AND TYPES OF MACHINERY**

STAGE	TYPOLOGY OF MACHINERY
Fibres	Machines for the production and treatment of chemical fibres and continuous yarns
Spinning	Machines for preparing spinning Machines for yarn treatment
Weaving	Machines for preparing weaving Weaving machines
Knitwear stockings	Knitting and stockings machines
Ennobling finishing	Machines for bleaching, dyeing, printing, finishing
Apparel making	Machines for unrolling fabric before cutting: sewing machines, embroidering machines; labelling, folding machines

Source: ACIMIT.

also require a lot of interaction with the clients, and this is naturally made easier if the two firms are sited close together.

The industry's most important fair, ITMA, is held every four years in a rotating list of countries, and it is here that the most important textile machinery innovations are presented.

A mechanical industry that is internationally competitive leads to considerable advantages for the whole pipeline. The most significant advantage is the continuous innovation that is the result of the close relationship between suppliers and customers. This innovation is spread through the whole pipeline. Different industries in Italy provide examples of this process, such as textiles, jewellery, hosiery and pottery.

Textile machinery is highly fragmented in Italy, with relatively small firms compared to the main international competitors (Germany, Japan, and Switzerland). The underlying reason for this structure is to be found in the client market – the fashion system.

Given the dynamism and fragmentation of lower sections in the pipeline, machinery suppliers are required to provide a specialised and flexible system that favours small size.

Further, firm investment in basic research is not high[10] in the Italian textile machinery industry. The innovation, which is incremental more than radical, is the result of partnerships that have been set up between machinery suppliers and their customers.

The industry's role in maintaining the competitiveness of the Italian pipeline seems more and more important, given the competition from emerging countries: technology has to be constantly renewed in order to reduce production times and labour costs.

3.1.7 Timing in the textile pipeline

Timing the presentation of the offer within the textile pipeline varies among the different sectors (*Table 3.3*). The fibres and the textile industry have to operate months earlier than the clothing industry, and have to inform it of fashion directions and trends.

The firms offering yarns are the first to start, usually two years before the final item appears in the shops. They study new materials and colours and present their collections to textile producers. This way of operating is deeply rooted in the industry, and also conditions the events that regulate the timing of the pipeline, such as fairs. Yarns and textiles collections are shown at the fairs, the main ones being in Italy (Pitti filati, Moda In) and France (Premiere Vision).

Table 3.4 indicates the length of the entire process of designing, manufacturing, presentation and sales of yarns, fabrics and finished products in the fashion pipeline.

The complexity of the fashion pipeline cannot be fully understood if production times are not taken into account. *Table 3.4* gives an idea of the length of the pipeline as it existed for most woven fabric apparel until very recently[11]. According to Hunter, an expert in textile pipeline management: "For apparel made

---

10. G. Dossena, S. Frova, A. Nova, A. Ordanini, *L'industria meccanotessile in Italia. Comportamenti strategici, commerciali, finanziari*, Growing, 1996, p. 15.
11. This example is taken from Hunter A. "*Quick response in apparel manufacturing. A survey of the American scene*", The Textile Institute, 1990 p. 20-21 and represents a traditional vision of the textile pipeline for mass market products.

TABLE 3.3 **THE DESIGNING PROCESS FROM YARNS TO APPAREL**
(collection A/I 2003-2004)

STEPS	TIMING	EVENTS
Research on fashion trends from yarn producers	October-November 2001	
Spinners and weavers' technical cycle and collection of information	March 2002	
Presentation and sale of intermediate products:		
fibres and yarns	June-July 2002	Pitti filati, Modaprima, Premier Vision (Paris), Expofil (Paris)
fabrics	September 2002	Moda In, Prato Export, Idea Biella
Presentation and sale of finished products (apparel):		
menswear	January 2003	Milano Collezioni uomo, Pitti Uomo
womenswear	March 2003	MOMI, Milano Collezioni Donna
Delivery to retail	July 2003 (abroad) September 2003	

from woven fabrics the pipeline represented in the table is 66 weeks, and of that only 11 weeks are taken up with processing: the balance on over one year is storage time. For knitted goods the pipeline length is shorter – 6 to 7 months, including time in the store – because processes are faster, simpler and more flexible than those for wovens. But even for knits the time in inventory accounts for over 2/3 the pipeline length.... The term 'work in progress' is itself misleading. A large proportion of WIP time is in fact that spent by the product between process steps".

Regarding production times in the textile pipeline, some clothing firms can operate with a very much reduced timing. These are the so called pronto-moda[12] firms. Traditionally fashion firms adopt the so called 'pro-

---

12. Pronto moda can be strictly translated into English as "ready to wear" taking into

TABLE 3.4   **APPAREL PIPELINE INVENTORIES AND WORK IN PROGRESS (WEEKS)**

	INVENTORY	WIP
FIBRE		
Raw material	1.6	
WIP		0.9
Finished Fibre	4.6	
Fibre to textile	1.0	
	8.1	0.9
FABRIC		
WIP – Greige*		3.
Greige goods*	1.2	
Greige goods* to finish	1.4	
Finishing		1.2
Finished fabric to textile	7.4	
Fabric to apparel	6.8	
	16.8	5.1
APPAREL		
WIP		5.0
Finished apparel	12.0	11.0
Ship to retail	2.7	
Apparel to retail distribution centre	6.3	
Apparel to store	10.0	
	31.0	5.0
TOTALS	55.0	11.0

* Greige goods = Unfinished fabrics bought by converters

grammed' model, scheduling their production on the basis of orders they receive from distribution (samples go out nine/ten months before the effective sales season). Pronto-moda firms, on the other hand, are able to present a high number of samples with an immediate or short-term delivery. The main innovation is the elimination of the research and design phase, as pronto-moda firms imitate trends at the fairs and catwalks, and can immediately reproduce the models thanks to a network of external sub-contractors. The pronto-moda model has both advantages and drawbacks. In the programmed model distribution takes more risks because it has to buy many months in advance and has more limited opportuni-

account that ready to wear also identifies the upper segment of the fashion market where designers compete.

ties for infra-seasonal replenishments; however, sales are supported by brand image, merchandising, and brand communication. This does not happen in the pronto-moda business where firms are very small and do not invest in brand management.

The timing of the textile pipeline has been deeply affected by recent evolutions in the fashion market. The uncertainty and volubility of the end consumer affect the entire pipeline up to the highest stage. Planning in advance is very hard and risky and no stage wants to take risks any more, including distribution. Orders increasingly arrive late, and this causes obvious problems in production and delivery. The search for partnership in the pipeline seems the most interesting direction for increasing the effectiveness of offers and the level of service.

3.1.8 Towards partnership in the fashion pipeline

The need for co-ordination and optimisation of the 'vertical and horizontal interrelationships' among firms' value chains within the textile pipeline used to be a relatively neglected area of action. Technological innovation and new management systems were more directed towards the improvement of individual stages of the pipeline and/or single activities within the firm value chain. This lack of attention by firms and management scholars can be explained by the fact that each sector in the fashion supply system has traditionally regarded itself as a separated business with its own strategies. This narrow view of the relationship between firms and the business system had several causes:

1. The complexity of the problem, due to the need to consider a wide number of technological and market variables which were often interrelated
2. The lack of information and knowledge, and thus control over activities in the whole pipeline of the firm
3. Conflictual relationships between the firm and its suppliers, clients and external actors. These were more often seen as competitors than as partners.

The development of managerial disciplines and technologies, particularly with regard to information systems and telecommunications, allowed some of the causes of this delay to be removed in recent years. Thus, the spread of Japanese management models (just in time, total quality and lean production), and the development of 'firm networks', have helped to change the former attitude towards relationships with external actors. Despite the relative success of this new orientation in many firms, interrelationships between the chain of firms within the pipeline are still a grey area where there is much to be done in terms of reducing inefficiencies.

The industry has gone through a profound change in recent years. The difficulties of large historical groups, the downsizing of several medium-sized firms, and the closing down of producers and distributors, are the clearest signs of a worrying state of health. The increase in competitive pressure, above all from developing countries, forces firms to look at themselves in order to make as many improvements as possible. The aim is to reinforce their strengths and act firmly on their weaknesses. The areas for improvement are not only within individual firms, but are outside them as well. These include external actors – suppliers, clients, intermediaries, consultants and financing firms – and above all interrelationships between them.

The hypothesis is that, given the particular nature and structure of the fashion system, inter-firm strategies in the pipeline represent a source of competitive advantage both for individual firms and for the whole productive and distributive system. The implementation of these strategies implies, however, considerable changes by firms in the establishment and management of relationships within the pipeline. In particular:

- The development of a co-operative attitude founded on the concepts of trust and transparency
- The sharing of a series of basic strategies between customer and suppliers including the area of competition, in a way that is consistent with the specific business segment in which they operate
- The development of contracts and operating mechanisms

designed to improve the management of relationships with suppliers, customers and external partners.

The final objective is to initiate a permanent process of shared knowledge creation that can nurture a continuous process of innovation. This, in turn, will produce sustainable competitive advantages for the whole pipeline.

3.2 International pipelines

The basic functioning and general features of each segment of the textile pipeline do not vary much between different countries. The man-made fibre industry is more capital intensive everywhere compared to the textile or clothing industry. A line of manufactured clothing in India goes through substantially the same processes as its equivalent in Germany or the USA. Within individual segments of the textile or clothing industry, however, there is a certain potential for the substitutability of capital and labour. It is for this reason that the textile firms of one country may be more capital intensive than those of another country. Further, there are differences between countries with regard to the complexity of goods produced, the skills of the work force, the level of concentration, vertical integration, internationalisation, and the degree of segmentation of the industry. This means that pipelines in different countries and regions are not the same. The evidence shows that the actors in the world's textile pipelines are not so much individual countries as regions. Regions can display a wide range of combinations among productive factors (labour, capital and others) that allow for the localisation of both capital and labour intensive activities within them. Regions are also enlarging their markets integrating other regions along different trajectories: North-South (between the USA and Mexico), South-South (between the countries of South-East Asia), East-West (between the European Union and Central Europe).

The shape of each pipeline, whether national or regional, can be understood in relation to two elements:

- The *state of development* of the pipeline in terms of the maturity and degree of completeness of the different stages
- The *model of co-ordination and internal integration* between the stages of the pipeline.

There is a continuum in terms of stage of development, ranging from embryonic to decline. The pipelines of developing countries that are predominantly oriented to hand-made clothing for domestic consumption, with the use of natural fibres, are at the embryonic level. There is no textile industry here, and the countries are generally net importers of fibres and cloths.

When the domestic production of textiles and finished products improves considerably in terms of quality, quantity and consumer satisfaction, the pipeline can be considered as *emerging*. The export of finished goods usually begins at this stage, as does the internal production of fibre, although the most innovative fibres are still imported. The textile industry grows, becoming more diversified and concentrated. It is usually stimulated and supported by direct investment from producers and distributors from the most developed countries. The most advanced countries of South-East Asia and Eastern Europe are in this position.

The next stage of the continuum can be defined as *development*. The sophistication of the textile and clothing industries increases. The pipeline is complete in all its stages, it has a diversified product mix and starts with internationalisation. Countries like Taiwan and Hong Kong are currently at this stage.

When the pipeline reaches *maturity* it loses employees because of productivity increases (in particular in the clothing industry). During this stage the process of industrial concentration and product sophistication continues, and the pipeline becomes more *capital intensive* in all of its stages (given the need to substitute labour with capital and to guarantee more satisfying products). Japan, the USA and Italy are all in this phase, although with great differences.

The last stage of the continuum is *decline*, when the number of employees and firms reduces substantially and there are commercial downturns in terms of payment balances, above all in clothing. The textile pipelines of the principal European countries (France, Germany and Britain) have already reached this stage. Their de-industrialisation has been to the advantage of the Asian pipelines which are currently in the phase of maximum development, thanks to a mixture of low labour costs, growing internal demand, and high transfers of capital and technology from European firms.

Throughout the whole process of development international flows of capital, technology and know-how are very important. The faster and more diffused these flows at the global level, the more rapid is the development and maturity of the pipelines of the different countries. This makes the competitive global environment highly dynamic. The actors in this development are the large fibre and clothing producers, as well as the producers of technology and the large distribution chains. The countries that hold leadership positions in more stages of the pipeline have a sustainable competitive advantage in finished products.

The second element that allows for the differentiation of textile pipelines at the international level concerns vertical integration.

Vertical integration means the control that individual firms have over the whole pipeline through internal hierarchy mechanisms – from the production of yarns and cloths to manufacture and distribution.

Where there is high integration, the outputs of the individual stages (fibres, yarns and fabrics) are internal operations in each firm. In the opposite case these inputs are exchanged through market or semi-market mechanisms. Three pipeline shapes can be distinguished as a result of vertical integration:

1. *Vertically integrated pipelines*: the main advantage of integration is the possibility to overcome complexity and fragmentation in the textile cycle. The disadvantage, however, is loss of flexibility due to the need to saturate productive capability. Vertical integration, particularly in developing countries, allows for cost reductions associated with imported materials (on which heavy import tariffs are applied). Where there is no efficient market system, vertical integration allows for better management of information flows

along the whole manufacturing cycle. The production of vertically integrated pipelines is limited to basic and mass market products as the lack of flexibility inhibits a quick response to the market's volatility for fashion products. There are large, vertically integrated textile firms in Japan, Indonesia and China.

Asian pipelines are usually more vertically integrated than European or American ones. One of the largest Japanese fibre producers, for example, is Toray Industries. It owns or directly controls many textile and clothing firms in Japan, Korea and other Southeast Asian countries. The same strategy was pursued by Toray's main Japanese competitor, Tejiin. These two giants dominate the local chemical fibre industries in Malaysia and the Philippines through holdings and trade agreements.

2. *Externally integrated pipeline*: this pipeline shape can be easily traced back to the model of Italian textile districts where stages and sub-stages are performed by independent actors all localised in the same geographical area who maintain relations oriented to partnership. Even where there are no hierarchical mechanisms, there is still a very high degree of co-ordination and control of the whole cycle by the district or by large firms (converters) lower down the productive cycle. The advantage of this type of pipeline, which generally manufactures products with a very high fashion content, is mainly related to flexibility. Flexibility allows a quick and customised response to market needs.

In an international scenario characterised by strong competitors that push towards productive relocation in low cost countries, Italy has strenuously defended its own spinning, textile, finishing and manufacturing activities. It has done this through local systems made of small and medium-sized family-owned firms. Apart from the size of individual firms, Italian industrial districts hold leadership positions at the international level with about 30% of the global share of international trade in wool and silk textiles. The best known districts are Biella (yarns and cloth, wool), Prato (yarns and cloth, wool), Como (textiles, manufacturing and silk accessories) and Carpi (knitwear); the Busto and Gallarate area, Northern Italy, for cotton yarns and cloth, Schio and Valdagno in Veneto for woollen yarns and cloth, Treviso for knitwear, and Alba in Piemonte for manufacturing. In central Italy Empoli (leather clothing), Pesaro (jeans), Ancona and Macerata and Ascoli Piceno (footwear).

3. *Virtual pipelines*: this is a model where the pipeline is shaped like a 'virtual' space where independent actors who are often a long way from each other work through market mechanisms. There is neither internal integration or geographical proximity, but a high degree of co-ordination from a pipeline leader who is generally placed low down in the productive cycle. This is the case, for example, of the American distribution chains that only control the distributive stage directly. They use market mechanisms to add an international network of independent suppliers in the different stages of the pipeline that change according to evolution of market conditions.

Nike, the global leader in sport shoes, is a virtual pipeline leader. One of the distinctive features of Nike's production system is that 100% of its products are made by external suppliers or, in the language of the company, production partners, based in East Asia. The productive partners are divided into two levels. The first group includes all partners involved in the final assembly of shoes. The second group includes the whole network of materials, components and sub-assembly suppliers. The first level partners are further divided into three categories:

- Developed partners: flexible medium-sized firms, responsible for the production of the most innovative and expensive articles (the so-called 'statement products'). They are based in Taiwan and in South Korea, and work exclusively for Nike
- Volume producers: large plants that are vertically integrated up to the dyeing and tanning of leather stages. They usually produce one article only (for example basketball shoes). They are mainly sited in South Korea, but do not work exclusively for Nike
- Developing sources: factories in Thailand, China and Indonesia. These are often replaced for reasons of economic cost, and they produce the most basic articles for Nike. They work exclusively for Nike.

Each pipeline configuration works better in some competitive context more than in others, as shown in *Figure 3.4*. The externally integrated pipeline is particularly efficient with fashionable and high end products with a short life cycle. In this case flexibility and creativity, more than low costs, are the key success factors for competing. The virtual pipeline is often found in cases of standard quality and short life cycle products as the market mechanism does not allow the establishment of a network based on mutual trust. The vertically integrated pipeline can work in both the previous cases but it lacks flexibility and it is best suited for products with a longer life cycle and with more predictable production trends that can profit from economies of scale.

FIGURE 3.4   **PIPELINE CONFIGURATION**

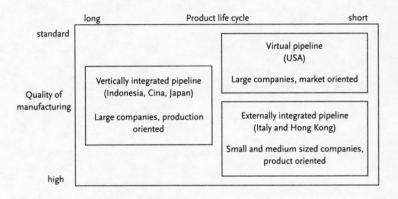

4   The competitiveness of national models

4.1 The French model: from haute couture to luxury goods

Haute couture[1], or *couture création*, the origin of ready-to-wear fashion, began in France. Until the 1950s Paris was the centre of the fashion world. This was where nearly all the fashion houses, the so called *Maisons*, had their headquarters. France's avantgarde position in fashion can be attributed to several factors. Firstly, the relationship between pure and applied art has always been a very close one, and Paris has always been a workshop for the arts and culture. The role of the institutions and actors within the fashion world was also fundamental. Even today, the co-operation of designers, institutions, the media and opinion leaders make Paris fashion shows a powerful communication event, centered on fashion, culture and national pride. The French attitude to fashion has always featured a luxurious, prestigious and exclusive character. This has made French fashion essentially an

---

1.   The French term *Haute couture* is frequently used at the international level to identify the highest segment of the fashion market in terms of price points. It can be translated as *high fashion* in English and as *alta moda* in Italian.

élite phenomenon. Even nowadays, *Haute couture* is an ambassador for the French tradition of quality and prestige. Fashion helps to reinforce the 'made in France' label.

Haute couture refers to the craftsmanship of the French fashion houses, whose designer-tailors create and present their own seasonal collections. These are either unique creations that are made to measure for individual customers, or very small numbers of the same article. The terms *haute couture* and *couture création* are legally protected descriptions. They can only be used by fashion houses that appear in an annual designer list approved by the minister of French industry. The Paris Chambre Syndacale de la Couture Parisienne was opened in 1968. It sets out the conditions that *Haute couture* houses have to meet, and thus manages the industry. Membership is still limited, and members are bound by rules about the exhibition of collections, the timing of these, possible copying of their work, and so on.

The English-born Parisian tailor Charles Frederick Worth (1825-1895) opened what is generally regarded as the first *Haute couture* house in Paris[2] in the 1860s. However, it was only in the 1900s that the development of *couture* really took off. The Universal Exhibition arrived in Paris in 1900, the fashion capital. Fashion was one of the Exhibition's most important sectors. The Worth brothers participated in it, as did the Callot sisters and Madame Cheruit. All the fashion houses showed their collections to foreign customers. Buyers from all over the world came to Paris to see the exhibition.

Paul Poiret was the first modern couturier. He wanted to liberate women from corsets and the heavy fashion of the new century. He opened a small studio where, for the first time, simpler gowns were shown that did away with the underskirts and busts of the past. He was also the first to use real women as models, and to tour Europe in order to 'exhibit' his work. His relatively comfortable lines were in ever increasing demand.

The most successful collections in the spring of 1924 were those of Coco Chanel. Chanel embodied the essence of the mod-

---

2. For the history of French *couture* see J. Anderson Black, M. Garland, *op cit.*

ern working woman, and her style is still current. By the mid-1920s, Coco had established her "Chanel look" consisting of a wool jersey suit with a straight, collarless jacket. Skirts were full-cut and short, and hair was often bobbed and covered with a sailor hat. Overall, Coco Chanel's clothing styles embodied much more than appearance in that it also contained a message about women. She celebrated women and their freedom, equality, and ability to express themselves through dress. At this time, fashion magazines were the primary source for news about the latest Paris couture, and Chanel was able to use this medium to relay not only her message about fashion, but her message about women in general. Chanel specialised in the use of jersey, which had been previously considered as basic fabric. Chanel jerseys were luxury items, and were rapidly copied so that the Chanel style became less exclusive. Chanel commented. 'I want my fashion to be out on the streets, even if I cannot accept that the streets inspire the style.' Thus Chanel anticipated the later coming together of *couture* and industrial production that was to give rise to ready-to-wear.

The fashion market came to a halt during the Second World War. Paris attempted to start up the activity again commercially, but it was only the first Christian Dior collection of 1947 that re-established French leadership in couture. Dior at first used a mix of natural and synthetic textiles for his creations. Although these were to become known as the 'new look', they harked back to the past, to pre-war elegance and femininity.

Up to 1940 the *haute couture* product was a luxury product, and it was only available to a small élite. Later, workshops and small firms began to reproduce high fashion items for a wider segment of the market. Dior made the first moves towards an international ready-to-wear industry in 1949, with the opening of a New York office for the sale of clothing to American department stores. This was also the era when American ready-to-wear clothing begun to spread. Designers such as Traina-Norell, Hattie Carnegie, Claire McCardle, Adrian and others showed clothes in very small but expensive series for their European customers. Their influence was felt in Europe, however. Here the new style was beginning to be appreciated. It was similar to *cou-*

ture, but did not require fitting and measuring. Ready-to-wear clothing manufacture was based on the development of standardised sizes. French fashion continued to offer *couture* and luxury ready-to-wear items during the 1950s. At the same time, from the United States leisurewear began to diffuse, supported by the image of the Hollywood movie star Lana Turner, the 'girl in the pullover'.

It was Italy, however, that led the way in knitwear. Italian jumpers were elegant and well made, and they ousted the dull products designed for informal occasions. The growing ready-to-wear market in Italy had its base in Florence, with Palazzo Pitti for the fashion shows and Palazzo Strozzi for commercial activities. Rome was the centre of Italian couture, with fashion houses like Simonetta Fabiani, Valentino, and Emilio Pucci. It was in accessories, however, that Italian fashion was particularly strong during this period – Salvatore Ferragamo's made-to-measure shoes were legendary for Hollywood actresses and European princesses.

New names appeared in French couture in the 1950s and 1960s, including Guy Laroche and Louis Feraud (1957), Pierre Cardin (1953), Yves Saint Laurent and Jean Louis Scherrer (1962). The new *couturiers* interpreted the new woman with inspiration and imagination – Courrèges through the style from space, Saint Laurent through the famous *smoking* or dinner jacket. Above all, these were the years when licensing of the great French names in perfumes and accessories began. Cardin and Saint Laurent promoted a phenomenon that was later to allow all the *couturiers* to leave the *couture* niche and create brands with strong market power. Cardin was barred from the Chambre Syndacale de la Couture for breaking the stringent rules regarding exclusivity that were imposed on *couturiers*. At the same time, the world of casual wear and youth clothing exploded outside France. England had Mary Quant's mini-skirt revolution and 'swinging' London, and the USA had James Dean and jeans. The English spirit was closer to young people, and it began to develop new market segments for young people's clothing in these years. The current English supremacy for streetwear and the American dominance in sportswear had their origins in this period.

Italian ready-to-wear won international leadership in the 1970s. Until that time Italian designers tended to be anonymous and it was the manufacturer's name that was on the label. Giorgio Armani, who was supported by a licensing agreement with the Gruppo Finanziario Tessile (GFT), appeared with his first collection in 1978. It was dedicated to the working woman, and it focused on refined and feminine jackets. Versace also appeared in the same year, with his more feminine and seductive lines.

The *International Herald Tribune* commented, in March 1980: 'the competition between Milan and Paris is in full force, and Milan is clearly winning. Paris provides the inspiration and the direction, and Milan interprets and manufactures ... France earns glory, but the Italians are much better at earning money.' In 1982 *Time* magazine gave Armani international status by putting him on the front cover.

The success of Italian ready-to-wear is closely related to a profound change in society, and the new, modern and accessible fashion was able to respond to this change. Further, although it was disadvantaged because it lacked the institutional protection and consensus that sustained the French industry, Italy showed that it could reach the same level of success thanks to high standards of workmanship and a superior textile industry. France went on offering inspiration and eccentricity in couture. Couture itself only had a market of aproximately 3,000 women worldwide, but it represented the launch platform for the wider and more profitable business of perfumes and accessories.

Italy definitively conquered the fashion world in the autumn of 1985, when Milano Collezioni became a seasonal appointment for international buyers.

Table 4.1 indicates the birth and development of the most popular fashion designers at an international level over the last 30 years.

Parisian couture was still at its height in the 1980s, but new designers were coming into the fashion houses – Angelo Tarlazzi to Laroche in 1980 and Gianfranco Ferrè to Dior in 1989. France was the first country to experience the problem of succession to the first generation of couturiers.

The relationship between couture and young talents was a dif-

TABLE 4.1   **THE MOST POPULAR FASHION DESIGNERS AT AN INTERNATIONAL LEVEL**

	1900/ 1920	1921/ 1940	1941/ 1960	1961/ 1970	1971/ 1980	1981 1990
France	Poiret Lanvin Callot	Vionnet Balenciaga Chanel Hermès (apparel)	Balmain Cardin Dior Givenchy Laroche	Lapidus Rabanne Rykiel Scherrer Y.S.L Ungaro	Castelbajac JPGaultier Montana Mugler	Alaia Lacroix Lagerfeld
Italy			Krizia Capucci Pucci	Valentino Albini Lancetti	Armani Coveri Ferrè Trussardi	Moschino Gucci (apparel) Dolce & Gabbana Prada (apparel)
United States			Adrian	De La Renta Ralph Lauren Calvin Klein Anne Klein	Blass Donna Karan	Steele Rohem Sui Abboud
Germany					Jill Sander	Ley (Escada)
United Kingdom			Westwood		Jasper Conrans Rhodes Zoran	Jackson Galliano McQueen

Source: the authors.

ficult one. New generations were rich in inspiration and extravagance but the *couturiers* of the past, Balenciaga, Dior, Schiappelli, Chanel and Valentino, were above all great tailors with a profound knowledge of proportions, materials and colors. It was their ability in technical skills that seemed rarer in the new generations. Therefore, couture ran the risk of becoming a mere communication event.

French couture currently has to face a series of problems:

- A smaller number of fashion houses
- The key problem of substituting *couturiers* with a second generation of designers who do not bear the name of the maison itself: Lagerfield for Chanel, Marc Bohan for Dior, and Galliano for Givenchy
- The smaller number of customers: it is reckoned that nowadays there are 2,000 customers, compared to 15,000 after the war and 3,000 in the 1980s. Further, today's affluent couture customers are no longer considered as international trend-setters. Ready-to-wear and the more recent blend of styles and life occasions have become the new style for consumers who create international trends.

Modern luxury conglomerates have nowadays taken the place of the historical *couturiers*. These are managed professionally, and are more oriented towards marketing and finance than towards style and creativity. Collecting new brands has become the core business for these companies as they search for multiple identities to keep growing. They have grown through a process of acquisitions, inheriting fashion houses that were no longer able to sustain the investment needed to preserve their brand identity. Perfumes and accessories produce most of the turnover from the French haute couture names. The role of clothing, which was the core activity of the *couturiers*, is today absolutely marginal. The current French model of luxury conglomerates seems biased towards wines, perfumes and cosmetics, and is losing turnover and credibility in the clothing business.

Further, the French textile pipeline seems less able to stimulate quality and innovation in clothing. The recent acquisitions of historic fashion brands by French multibrand groups can be seen as an attempt to restore balance in their portfolio, as well as an attempt to become involved in new market segments (such as youth clothes).

The French group Louis Vuitton Moet Hennessy (LVMH) is a global leader in the luxury industry of numerous categories of merchandise, including Wines and Spirits, Fashion and Leather Goods, Perfumes and Cosmetics, Watches and Jewellery, Selective Retailing.
The group regards itself as the ambassador of the 'art of living' and of

TABLE 4.2 **LVMH BUSINESS UNITS AND BRANDS (2001)**

WINES & SPIRITS	FASHION & LEATHER GOODS	PERFUMES & COSMETICS	SELECTIVE RETAILING	WATCHES AND JEWELLERY
Moët & Chandon	Louis Vuitton Malletier	Parfums Christian Dior	DFS	TAG Heuer
Veuve Clicquot	Loewe	Guerlain	Sephora	Ebel
Pommery	Celine	Parfums Givenchy	Speciality Retail Concepts	Zenith
Chandon Estates	Kenzo	Parfum Kenzo	Le Bon Marché	Benedom - CD Montres
Hennessy	Givenchy	Hard Candy	Miami Cruiseline	Fred
Château d'Yquem	Christian Lacroix	BeneFit	La Samaritaine	Chaumet
Dom Pérignon	Fred Joaillier	Bliss	Solstice	Omas
Krug	Berluti	BeneFit Cosmetics		LVMH/De Beers joint venture
Mercier	Marc Jacobs	Urban Decay		
Ruinart	Fendi	Fresh		
Canard duchêne	StefanoBi	Make Up For Ever		
Cloudy Bay	Emilio Pucci	Laflachère		
Cape Mentelle	Thomas Pink	Acqua di Parma		
Hine	Donna Karan			
Newton				
MountAdam				

Source: LVMH

French luxury. It came into existence in 1987 following the merger of Moet Hennessy and Louis Vuitton, a brand leader in leather goods. Responsible for the merger was the young Bernard Arnault, who already managed a holding company controlling Christian Dior Couture, and who had financed the rise of Christian Lacroix. The growth of the group in fashion continued with intensive acquisitions of historic brands – Givenchy (1988), Christian Lacroix and Kenzo (1993), Loewe and Celine (1996). In 1999 the group signed a joint venture with Prada for the acquisition of the Italian group Fendi and in 2001 it creates the De Beers/LVMH Jewellery Venture.

LVMH, with 11.6 billion euros of net sales, in 2000 employed 53,000 people, and the largest part of its turnover came from outside the French market. The group operates through five product divisions that control different historic brands, category leaders, and specialist distribution trademarks. The group's management philosophy of a wide portfolio of luxury brands can be summarised in three points:

1. rigorous control of industrial costs
2. large investment in communication
3. large investment in direct distribution

4.2 The American model: from workwear to vertical integrated chains

The American clothing industry came into existence at the start of the 1800s for menswear. This was a good half-century before fashion for women.[3] Up to that point, menswear had been based on tailoring for those who could afford it, or direct home production. Some small east-coast tailoring businesses (New York, Boston and Philadelphia) first had the idea of producing and selling low-price ready-to-wear clothing for the sailors who came ashore on leave and needed to replenish their wardrobe.[4] These first tailor-shops were both producers and distributors. The market grew from there. A mass-market within the middle class grew up during industrialisation in the first half of the 1850s. One of the greatest and most famous retailers of modern menswear, Brooks Brothers, was one of the first producers. Brooks Brothers was founded in 1818 as a tailor-shop, and in 1857 it already employed 75 tailors and 1,500 outside workers.

The 'gold rush' of 1848 had a significant effect on the development of the menswear industry. A man called Levi-Strauss, foreseeing that the prospectors would need tents, started in business in California. He had a certain quantity of a resistant textile from France – this was *de Nime*, which was later Americanised as *denim*. Levi-Strauss decided to use this material, not for

---

3. Cf. J. Jarnow, M. Guerreiro, *Inside the Fashion Business*, MacMillan Publishing Company, 1991.
4. This type of clothing was known as *slops*, that is careless and slovenly, and it was regarded as an indicator of poverty and lack of taste.

tents, but for work trousers with a large number of pockets that were strengthened by metal buttons. These trousers had a considerable success and, together with work clothes for the pioneers, contributed to the development of the manufacturing industry.

The main event that prepared the way for ready-to-wear clothing on the industrial scale was Elias Howe's invention of the first sewing machine in 1845. This was adapted by Isaac Singer for industrial use. This invention, together with the abundant immigrant labour force, sustained the growth of the industry. With the increase in mass production came mass distribution. Department stores and speciality stores began to devote a lot of space to the sale of clothing.

The origin of ready-to-wear clothing in the USA was thus very democratic, right from the start. The American industry came into existence because of the need for comfortable work clothing, which is known as workwear.

Although the industry would lose this feature over time, it allowed firms to develop native products, superior production methods and mass distribution channels. The firms developed with a strong market orientation and integrated production and distribution roles from the outset. This feature helps to explain the current American model based on the centrality of vertical chains, department stores, and a strong marketing orientation.

Up to the second half of the 19th century ready-to-wear clothing and women's fashion did not exist in America. Women made their own clothes. The few women who could afford to so, imported clothes from France.

Womenswear began to grow only at the end of the century. In the 1920s every large city already had its department stores and speciality stores, and ready-to-wear fashion was also available through catalogues. The industry and large department stores still looked to Paris for their inspiration. Buyers and owners attended the *haute couture* presentations twice a year, and then turned these into mass items. The expression 'Paris inspired' was the key to promoting fascinating apparel. It was only after the Second World War that the first American designers began to appear on the scene. It was Dorothy Shaver, the president of

Lord & Taylor, who promoted American designers for the first time in her shops – Elizabeth Hawes, Clare Potter, Vera Maxwell, and the woman considered by many to have been the first real sportswear designer, Claire McCardle. The development of the great American designers, who now battle against the Europeans for the world fashion market, took place in the 1960s.

Retailers played a particularly important role in the development of the American industry. It was they who, from the beginning, applied hints from Paris to their products. Nowadays, it is still the large department stores and vertical chains that make up the backbone of the American model. They are now in a position to teach their prestigious European 'suppliers' how to deal with service, deliveries and merchandising.

Finally, the invention of 'casualwear' and a superior marketing management, above all in the mass market, allowed the American model to enter the international markets by building competitive positions hard to be imitated by European competitors.

Levi Strauss

Levi Strauss started as a small shop run by its founder. In these early days, Levi Strauss was able to develop a patent for rivet-reinforced pants that would change the future of clothing. Thanks to this unique patent the company could charge premium prices and, thus, make management and organizational decisions based on other principles than strictly costs. The patent separated Levi's pants from the rest of the market, and therefore brand identification became possible. In addition to the rivets, a "V-shaped" stitch was sewn into the back pockets of all the pants in an orange thread that was meant to match the color of the rivets.

After the second World War the US were getting younger as a whole, largely because of the baby boomers. Levi's began to shift its advertising away from the "cowboy" and more towards the youth of American society. This also shifted the target sales area geographically. Most of America's youth lived in predominantly urban neighborhoods as opposed to the rural areas in which Levi's were most heavily marketed and sold. With the new urban market, the firm changed its distribution outlets. Levi's were now sold in large-scale department stores rather that in "mom and pop" stores. The fifties and sixties marked Levi's new image with American youth, its expansion into the European market, and the introduction of Sta-Prest jeans. Captivated by Dean and Brando's image, American teenagers clung to their uniform of T-shirts, boots, leather jackets, and most importantly, fitted, worn, blue jeans.

The strategy of Levi Strauss from the early 1980s was characterized by an alternation of periods of re-focus on core business and phases of diversification. Facing a major setback in its market at the beginning of the 1980s the first response of Levi Strauss was to change its business focus from manufacturing to marketing, more precisely to marketing of their core product, mainly the 501 jeans. This particular type of jeans (buttonfly, shrink-to-fit), being probably today the best known article of clothing in the world, is in fact Levi's great strength, the essence of its brand identity and reputation.

The Gap

Gap was born in 1969 in San Francisco, and was the result of work by Donald Fisher. Gap was a specialist jeans shop that sold all sizes. The business grew from one shop into a chain, at first in California and then throughout the US. From 1974 onwards, other merchandise was introduced with the Gap label. In 1976 Gap was listed on the stock exchange. Gap purchased Banana Republic, a chain store specialising in travel clothes, in 1983, when it already had 550 specialist shops over the whole country. In 1985 it decided to enter the children's market as well, and did this through the development of new lines and the opening of the first Gap Kids' Store the following year. In 1987 Gap began its international development with the opening of the first shop in London. In 1992 it created a new division for family clothing, Old Navy Clothing. This had a lower price positioning than earlier lines. Gap now employs 50,000 people and has a vertically integrated structure. It is directly involved in the entire supply chain, from the development of the product up to visual merchandising in the sales point. The network of shops is owned by the company. There are five divisions: The Gap, The Gap Kids, Banana Republic, Old Navy and The Gap International. The group is able to segment its casual clothing offer effectively. Banana Republic satisfies customers who are looking for items that are sophisticated from the point of view of quality and image, while Old navy offers lower-price items that are still fashionable. Within the USA Gap is seen as a 'social passport', in the sense that everyone, from child up to adult, possesses at least one of its items. The style has been defined as 'modern American classic with a twist', and the brand evokes informal values, style and fun.

4.3 The Asian model: from outsourcing to integrated production networks

For a long time East Asia[5] was exclusively an area for low-cost production by western firms. The countries of the region have shown themselves capable of astonishing growth levels in the last ten years, however. This has stimulated local consumption and promoted the development of new countries and actors in world textiles and clothing industries.

It is thus impossible to consider the analysis of national models complete without examining the case of East Asia: this region promises to be the largest growth engine of the new century.

Analysis of the industrial models

Before analysing industrial models in the Asian clothing industry it will be useful to make some general comments about the economic models and growth routes that have been taken in this area. The purpose is to clarify the industrial realities as part of a wider economic analysis. Recent empirical studies have shown[6] that the *economic proximity* of countries in the region has increased as a result of strong growth in the 1980s in trade and direct intra-regional investment flows.

The *flying geese* model has been used to examine trade and intra-regional investment flows in the case of textile and clothing. This theory concentrates on the relationship between changes in the stage of industrialisation and the comparative advantage of countries. According to the theory, the spread of technology is transferred through direct investment by leader country to follower country. Firms from the leader country move their production to the follower country, in an attempt to exploit their ownership advantages, and to take advantage of lower cost factors. The combination of direct investment and relatively cheaper

---

5. East Asia means the region to the east of the Indian peninsula and the west of Australia. It includes China, Hong Kong, Taiwan, Korea, the countries of Southeast Asia, and Japan.
6. GATT, *International Trade*, for different years.

factors of production helps to increase competitiveness on world markets and leads to an increase in the follower country's exports. The expected result of this process is the decline of the leader country's comparative advantage in a particular product, following the de-localisation of production, and an increase in the follower country's comparative advantage in the same product. There is some empirical evidence that countries in the Asian region have been pursuing the flying geese model since the 1950s with regard to international specialisation in textiles/clothing. The so-called 'first migration'[7] of production took place in the 1950s and 1960s. It moved the production of textiles and clothing from industrialised countries (mainly Japan, the US and Germany) to the 'three large' Asian producers: Hong Kong, Taiwan and South Korea. The large western firms, generally competing in the mass market, tended to transfer the most basic and labour intensive productions to Asia. Over time the transfer of the technology and controls for ensuring that qualitative standards were met produced a learning effect on the local producers. They became increasingly directed towards products and activities of greater added value, and also increased their share of production destined for export. The combined share of Hong Kong, Taiwan and South Korea was 10.3% of world textile and clothing exports in 1980, but this had jumped by 18.6% in 1990. Hong Kong is the leader of the three countries, and its exports over the same the ten-year period grew by 365%.[8]

The three countries progressively lost their attractiveness as production sites at the end of the 1970s, as a result of the increased cost of labour and the lack of export shares. They became logistic and service centres heading new productive networks and encouraging the growth of new producers in the area – China, Thailand, Malaysia, the Philippines and Vietnam. The strong development of textile trading companies[9] from Japan, Hong Kong

---

7. See S.R. Khanna, 'Structural changes in Asian textile and clothing industries: the second migration of production', *Textile Outlook International*, Economist Intelligence Unit, September, 1993.

8. GATT, *op. cit.*, 1992.

9. The trading company or *shosha* is one of the principal actors in the Asian clothing market. Its origins are in Japan, and it performs the functions of a central com-

FIGURE 4.1 **INTRA-REGIONAL INVESTMENT MODELS IN CLOTHING (ASIA FROM THE 1950s)**

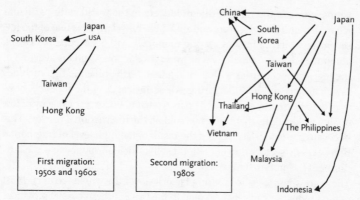

Source: the authors.

and Taiwan in the emerging areas suggests that they were forming regional networks organised on the flying geese model (*Figure 4.1*).

These changes have been called a 'second migration' of production in the textile-clothing industry, with migration being taken to mean the transfer of the production of the three large producers (Hong Kong, Korea and Taiwan) towards new areas within the region.

China seems to be the main beneficiary of this secondary migration of production. It will also be the largest beneficiary of the end of the Multifibre Agreement[10] and the liberalisation of exchanges in the industry at the global level. Since 1997, the return of Hong Kong to China has caused exports from both countries to increase rapidly. China is going to become the strongest

---

mercial office for the sale and purchase of various types of merchandise, both nationally and internationally. It offers the retailer and the producer a vast range of services including finance, technical assistance and the direct management of the sales network.

10. The Multifibre Agreement was first made in 1974. It provides a series of bilateral quotas that were negotiated between developed and developing countries for the international textile-clothing trade. The quota system should be wholly eliminated by 2005.

world producer in the new century, while Hong Kong is taking the role of a regional financial and services centre.

China is one of the main textile producers in the world, with particular regard to natural fibres (wool and silk). Silk, for example, is one of the few sectors in which China has a world monopoly, with its exports of raw silk accounting for more than 85% of world production. China is also one of the few Asian countries with an integrated textile pipeline that includes raw materials and manufacturing. All of the stages of the pipeline, however, are affected by a structural crisis related to the excess capacity of low quality productions that cannot be sold on the international market. This over-capacity is to a large extent the result of the high level of fragmentation of many sectors due to the local self-sufficiency policy that the government has pursued for years.

There are about 45,000 clothing factories over the whole territory. Most of the productive capacity is located in the two Southern coastal provinces of Guandong and Fujian. These areas have recently attracted strong foreign investment, and they are also the areas where most private Chinese firms are located. State-run firms are in Jiangsu, Zhejiang and Shangai. The clothes produced in the Shangai, Suzhou and Delian zones enjoy a very high reputation internationally.

The need to restructure the textile pipeline is very urgent. The problem concerns distribution. Raw materials do not go to the areas where they would be used most efficiently. The cotton producing regions, for example, supply all the inefficient local producers that make low quality products. Further, textile firms still depend too much on exports for achieving profitability. More than a third of Chinese textile and clothing production is destined for export, but the exports are of low quality and have low added value. They do not meet the standards of world markets, and so they continue the low profitability of the textile firms. Most of the state firms are unable to tune in to the needs of world demand by planning their own production. They have to bear the burden of an immense labour force that cannot be exposed to market effects. Obliged as they are to maintain inefficient workers, the firms find it impossible to invest in new technologies and productive processes. The main problem that the Chinese textile industry has to confront is this impossibility of reducing the labour force.

Analysis of the consumption models

Consumption models, like productive ones, have been subject to intense development in Asia. After a first stage (from 1980 to 1995) of high growth in purchasing power and consumption on the one hand (South Korea, Japan, Hong Kong and Singapore), and market transition or the end of the subsistence economy on the other (China and Indonesia), the Asian market is now converging towards a polarisation in clothing consumption.

- The success of imported labels (Italian and French) in the high end of the market
- The spread of local brands or international ones produced on licence in the low and medium price range for young people and value-driven adults.

This polarisation is more evident in some markets than others, but is still a general trend. The trend was reinforced by the rapid development of distribution towards modern formats (the shopping mall and the department store), and this has a strong influence on suppliers.

Compared with Europe, distribution is very concentrated. The Philippines, Indonesia and Thailand have adopted the American model of the shopping mall with shop in shop formats inside it. Japan, Korea and Hong Kong and China as well nowadays, have a more balanced use of the street shop, the department store and the speciality shop.

Japanese operators have the widest distributive base in Asia through trademarks like Sogo, Takashimaya, Yaohan and Isetan. The large Asian importers (Japanese, Taiwanese and Korean) in the high end choose the best *concepts* (a mixture of product, image, distributive layout, accessories and fair price) that can attract their customers. The historic French brands (Lanvin, Dior, Cardin, Yves Saint Laurent) were the first to import their own labels through production and/or distribution licences. This has now become the model for other countries as well. Italian labels have been on the Asian market for a long time, and Asia has been the first market for some Italian firms. The typical entry mode is the partnership with Japanese trading companies (MITSUI) or Hong Kong importers (Joice, BlueBell) through monobrand stores or corners within department stores in the Hong Kong market .

There is very strong local competition in the medium and low market bands. Hong Kong producers like Toppy (Episode, Toppy and Colour Eighteen brands) Theme, Bossini and Giordano are

"American inspired" vertical chains. They have an aggressive approach to the market, and offer a good fashion content in line with European trends, large advertising and brand investment, very careful visual merchandising, and information systems in the store.

4.4 The Italian model: from manufacturing industry to the industrialisation of creativity

The history of fashion in Italy started in the time of the ancient Romans, continued through the Renaissance Dukedoms, and reached the present through the success of the 'made in Italy' in the final decades of the 20th century. A single book would not be enough to outline its evolution. We will focus, therefore, on more recent history, and try to explain not only the success of Italian fashion, but also its potential weaknesses over the last ten years.

The hypothesis underlying the success, national and international, of the Italian fashion system, is that, from the 1970s anwards a series of conditions, regarding both supply and demand, and related to strictly national factors, have acted positively in the country. The development process was completed between the 1970s and 1980s. It created 'virtuous circles' that first produced and then strengthened the competitiveness of the whole industrial and distributive system.

4.4.1 The transformation of the Italian industrial system in the 1970s

The Italian textile-clothing industry, like other national industries, went through a profound restructuring in the 1970s. This resulted in considerable downsizing of the large textile firms that had come to prominence in the 1950s and 1960s (GFT, Monte, Lebole, Sanremo, Marzotto, Lubiam and Abital). It also resulted in the development of a strong and widespread network of small and very small firms and the reinforcement of textile-clothing local industrial areas.

These processes were all related to each other, and although it is difficult to establish which of them were responsible for the change, it is important to analyse their mutual interdependence.

The de-integration of the large firms

Strong trade unions and the related increase of labour costs dealt a deadly blow to the large Italian firm, as did the growing competition of products from low labour cost countries. Many entrepreneurs had to deal with a loss of competitiveness due to costs, and with internal conflict. They protected themselves from the general climate of hostility to business by dismantling their own structures and creating small productive units. During this process of de-integration the large firms were able to count on the strong spirit of independence and entrepreneurship of many Italian workers, and on the advantages that the move brought in terms of productivity. Once a specialised worker had become an entrepreneur, he could ensure levels of productivity and quality that were much higher than those that had been reached while he was an employee.

The difficulties of the large firms were also due to stagnation and an early change in demand. These encouraged the production of small series. Mass production and economies of scale were less important, and this restored competitiveness to small firms.

Many observers were worried by the industry's trend towards a reduction in concentration that could affect the internationalisation process of Italian firms. The increase in the number of productive units and the reduction in their average size not only increased entry barriers to foreign markets, it could also have resulted in the whole textile-clothing system's loss of productivity and competitiveness

As it turned out, however, the cost per unit of product was reduced by reduced labour costs. These were lowered even further by tax evasion and the greater mobility and productivity of labour. Smaller firms showed that they had strategic advantages in terms of flexibility and product innovation. The larger firms took account of these advantages, and this gave a further impulse towards sub-contracting.

The explosion of "pronto moda"[11] and outsourcing

The process of productive decentralisation from large to small firms was also encouraged by another, opposite trend: the

---

11. "Pronto moda" can be strictly translated into English as "ready to wear" (see page 59).

growth, all over Italy, of tailors' shops and small craftsmanship workshops that had survived the growth of the manufacturing industry. These workshops were able to develop more industrial structures, although remaining small and flexible. They took on new life towards the end of the 1960s because of the greater flexibility that was needed to satisfy a demanding consumer. The trade union claims, the explosion of the youth revolution, the new relationship between sexes, the attention to the 'social dimension', had all changed the values and lifestyles of the Italian people, and this also had an effect on the way of dressing. Specifically, informal clothing caught on with young people, following the jeanswear revolution. In the higher age group the "pronto moda" phenomenon took place. Both segments were populated by small firms whose flexibility allowed them to produce articles satisfying the new needs at low prices, and to guarantee better service to distribution. The central role of the small firm was also made possible by the low level of technology required by the new productions and by the small amount of investment in production compared with traditional formal wear.

After the first stage of development, the small firms had growing difficulties in accessing the final market and distribution. "Market orientation" required considerable communication investments and sales management techniques. Only a few of them managed to make the quality leap to become 'industrial fashion oriented firms', differentiating themselves from the mass production of the large traditional firms. The others, however, maintained their role as sub-contractors, and they thus supported the decentralisation of productivity that was being carried out by the large firms.

The development of subcontracting among large, medium and small firms was further supported by another specific feature of the Italian fashion system – the distribution and concentration of the productive units into specific industrial areas specialised in textiles (Biella, Vicenza, Prato, Bergamo, Milano, Torino, Carpi, Bologna, Ancona and Bari).

"Local systems" have always played an important role in Italian national development. Their contribution to the nation's economic activity is estimated as being 20/25%[12] of the gross national product and employment while their share of total Italian exports is over 25%. Local systems are characterised by a variety of sectors and organisational methods that differ widely from one another. Among these, the most easily distinguishable are the "industrial districts", due to their strong identity associated with a few strongly characteristic elements: specialisation in a manufacturing sector, the division of work between companies, high entrepreneurial levels and permeation between social and economic life. *Figure 4.2* presents a general overview of Italian industrial districts in fashion related industries.

FIGURE 4.2   **ITALIAN INDUSTRIAL DISTRICTS IN FASHION RELATED INDUSTRIES**

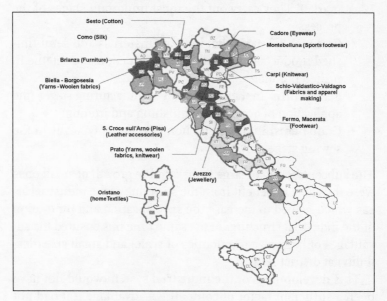

The development of the industrial districts

Each firm in the textile industrial districts specialises in a particular stage of production or a certain type of product or material. Physical proximity, cultural homogeneity, and social and

12. Data from the Italian Club dei Distretti, established in 1994 with the purpose of representing the specific interests of these industrial realities (www.clubdistretti.it).

What does this mean?

personal relationships encourage communication and the containment of logistics costs. Above all, they encourage the development of a very advanced know-how that acts as a lever on strong partnership and imitation processes. Thanks to the availability of labour and qualified personnel throughout a specific area, the districts make up a wide and continuous basin for the birth of new firms. These, in turn, contribute to reinforcing the stimuli for a further improvement in productivity and product throughout the whole system.

The districts are populated by different kinds of firms that interact together because of the nature of the productive process. These include:

- Vertically integrated firms that produce and sell on the market. They carry out the most important stages of the process
- Commercial firms that buy raw materials and semi-finished products. They outsource production and sell the finished product
- Service firms in the cutting and manufacturing stages (the application of accessories, finishing and ironing)
- Craftsmanship firms and home workers, typically in the sewing stage only.

The subcontracting of large firms and the growth of small ones were thus able to benefit from the stimulus of the industrial areas which helped to increase the specialisation and innovation of the industrial structure. At the same time this ensured the advantages of large size (economies of scale) and small size (flexibility) at district level.

This development of the industrial system would not have been a sufficient factor of competitive advantage if it had not been accompanied by two important and closely related factors for change. These were the birth and establishment of designers and the revitalisation of demand.

The fashion designers (stilisti) and the revitalisation of demand

The close relationship between designers and the industry is a further feature of the Italian model. This is the result of a comparatively recent process of development. Up to the 1960s some designers were unknown external contributors to the manufacturer's product office. Other designers were used to produce made to measure dresses for the élite (*haute couture*). They made unique pieces or, at most, produced a few dozen articles of the same kind. This was the case of Valentino Garavani, who opened his own maison in Rome in 1959. His dream was to diffuse a new style for elegant and feminine women. As one of the most famous French *couturiers* (Dior, Saint Laurent, and so on), Valentino achieved world success thanks to a concept of the suit as a work of art, as the expression of the designer's greatest creativity. This should be made to measure and was thus destined for a very restricted public – the aristocracy and movie stars. Starting from these assumptions it is evident that couture had long been regarded, and perceived itself, as quite separate from the clothing industry. This was particularly true in the moment when the clothing industry was offering mass production based on a strategy of low prices and high volumes.

The distance between the two worlds of couture and the industry finally disappeared thanks to some events that started in the 1960s and then was consolidated definitively in the second half of the 1970s.

The pioneering experience of Albini

In the spring of 1969 the designer Walter Albini showed his collection Misterfox at the Palazzo Pitti. This was an informal line that had been produced for an industrial firm, Papini. The line was a departure from couture. The Albini collection reflected the creation of an atmosphere, a certain style and a total look that was aimed at a specific target. The collection was very successful because of its innovative proposal. However the economic results were disappointing also because Palazzo Pitti was not yet considered as a commercial space where producers and national and international buyers could meet. The Misterfox line was shown in Milan the following year, where the industrial firms had already presented their own advance samples to Italian retailers and foreign buyers. Other collections with the same innovative features as Misterfox were shown alongside it in Milan

(Basile for overcoats, Callaghan for jerseys and Escargot for knitwear). The purpose of all these new collections was to emphasise the 'total look' concept. But the main innovation was that products carried both the name of the designer and the industrial firm for the first time, and this was the final celebration of the marriage between the two worlds. The designer identifies with a lifestyle and certain consumer and his image could be used as an integral part of the 'product system' offered by the industry. The partnership of Albini and Papini broke up some years later, but this was after it had signalled a fundamental stage in the development of the whole industry.

The crisis of haute couture

The youth revolution and the increasing emancipation of women had already thrust the values of femininity and affluent consumption into the background in the 1970s. This had caused a lot of difficulty for couture, as the acceptance of unisex and the crisis in elegant formal clothing in favour of the new "uniforms" (jeans, anoraks, tracksuits, folk, and so on) shows. The 1973 oil crisis and the recession of the following years were the deathblow to couture. Many of the great French tailoring studios, such as de Barensten and Schubert, were forced to close. The Italian designers Valentino, Rocco Barocco and Lancetti had worldwide reputations but they had to limit themselves to performing promotional activities. Couture thus lost its attractive and distinctive role, and Milan took the place of Paris in the high end ready-to-wear industry. It became the centre for international buyers. Industrial firms like Krizia, Mila Schon, Missoni, Genny and Basile grew up in the Milan area. They incorporated the designer's role without making it dominate over the entrepreneur's role. The move of European and world fashion to a new centre of gravity in Milan seems evidence of a widespread desire among the operators in the industry to have greater links with industry, efficiency and organisation. Although the preconditions for a profound change were already in place in the early years of the 1970s, the process itself could not move forward because of the recession of 1974-75.

The middle years of the 1970s saw a radical change in the economics and value system of the industry. This was due to the inversion of the economic cycle, growth in income, and greater social-political stability. There was a greater interest in the private dimension over the collective one, with a search for the daily pleasures of life.

Middle- to upper-class women were the first consumer segment to give in to the unprecedented scale of consumption. Advertising was now accepted willingly, and it became both a phenomenon of communication and the expression of the taste and culture of the time.

People's greater interest in themselves and the growing need for differentiation were behind the development of activities like body care and personal look: jogging, body-building, weekends, holidays and travel, quality restaurants, cosmetics and perfumes, accessories and so on.

This enthusiastic consumerism produced enormous opportunities for clothing as well, thanks to the increased willingness of the consumer to follow models and suggestions from the industry.

The main interpreters of the new trend were not, however, industrial firms but designers. The most developed firms, starting with Gruppo Finanziario Tessile (GFT) realised that it would be easier and faster to seize the new opportunities that were emerging from demand if they had a new relationship with the *couturiers*.

The development of high end ready-to-wear and diffusion segments

In 1978 the Gruppo Finanziario Tessile (the clothing manufacturing company located close to Turin, Nothern Italy, that had a fundamental role in the development of "made in Italy"), proposed to a young Giorgio Armani, who had just left Cerruti, a consulting agreement aiming at bringing to the GFT's industrial culture an innovative technical and stylistic know-how. Armani declined the simple consulting agreement and rather proposed a licensing agreement for the production of a line under his own name with a precise distinction of tasks between the two parts. The Armani case, with all its peculiarities, became the model from which in Italy the relation between industry and creativity was built. The experience of Gianni Versace in Genny and Giorgio Armani and Valentino in GFT during the second half of the 1970s made the large firms aware of the complementarity of their skills and the need for a genuine partnership with designers. For instance, the earlier experience of Armani in Cerruti allowed him to develop know-hows in fabrics and tailor-made jackets. This know-how was fundamental for GFT's development of a new way of designing and making collections. Spurred on by the young GFT's managing director, Marco Rivetti, the licensing contracts with Armani and other designers led to new skills and sensibilities within the large firms. The designers could rely on the wider diffusion of products on both the national and international market, thanks to the large firm's financial and commercial resources.

> Marco Rivetti's philosophy regarding this was fairly clear. 'To work well, the relationship between the industry and the designer has to be mutually supportive. The entrepreneur and the designer have to know how to maintain their respective autonomy while taking account of different needs. The creative person has to have operational sensitivity and the entrepreneur has to know how to meet the creative person's needs. The entrepreneur has to know that investing in image is useful to the firm, but the stylist in turn has to understand that press success is a necessary but not sufficient condition, that making wonderful clothes that do not suit any woman does not serve the customer, the designer or the firm.'

The connection between the designer and the industry requirements was fully realised in Armani's experience, first with GFT and then with smaller firms. Armani succeeded for the first time in going beyond the exclusive ambit of high end ready-to-wear to reach a much wider target. The diffusion collections (intended as third designer's lines in terms of price points after couture and ready-to-wear) started here. Armani was able to maintain his stylistic identity also in the new lines, such as the Mani line. These were made in a sufficient number of pieces to be produced in a series, but they had features that differentiated them from ready-to-wear. It was above all in these collections that the close interaction of the designer and cutting and production techniques achieved their greatest levels in the search for a compromise between high designer content and technical requirements.

The revitalisation of the product that follows from this partnership provides a further stimulus to the development of demand. There was, for example, a return to the grand style of formal overcoat and elegant clothes addressed to special occasions. The same article of informal clothing could be casual and sportive without competing against the formal, but by integrating the offer for different use occasions (free time, the weekend, travel and holidays, and so on). In this way it managed to create a new market space for itself, enlarging the target of reference from just young people to new 'yuppies' and youthful adults.

Thus, it was the new relationship among designers, producers and consumers that underlay the process of development of the clothing industry. This process was, however, able to benefit other specific factors in Italy. These were further strengthened by interaction with the phenomena that have been described, to the overall advantage of the whole fashion system.

4.4.2 The strengthening of the fashion system

The reasons for the success of the Italian clothing industry over competing countries cannot be fully appreciated without taking into account the close relationships between clothing industries and other related and support industries. This is particularly the case of the textile pipeline, the sub-contracting system, the retail system, and the other industries supporting 'made in Italy'.

The textile pipeline
The textile pipeline (yarns, textile finishing industries, and so on) is a strong asset for Italy. It provides support to product innovation which offers it great opportunities for growth. Designers enter into direct relationships with the suppliers of raw materials and semi-finished products on behalf of manufacturing and knitwear firms. They can select products, materials and colours. The textile producers, already in the forefront of technology thanks to their proximity to producers in the textile ma-

chinery industry, acquire a new sensitivity to the finished product and come closer to the needs of the market.

The direct relationship between designers and yarn and fabric producers resulted in new stimuli to competitiveness, productivity and innovation within the whole textile pipeline. The local industrial areas encouraged this.

The existence of specialist chemical firms meant that artificial and synthetic fibres were added to traditional yarns and natural fibres in the production of finished articles, accessories and components (raincoats, sportswear, knitwear, stockings, fabrics, and so on).

The diffusion and development of the sub-contracting system

Sub-contracting in the clothing industry developed in the early 1970s. It was fully able to deal with the new needs for flexibility and specialisation in fashion products. Further, the traditional industrial areas for knitwear manufacturing (Milan, Bergamo, Florence, Arezzo, Modena, Vicenza and Treviso) were joined by others in different regions. Some of these developing firms were not vertical ones (Benetton, Max Mara, Carrera, Gruppo Girombelli, Ellesse, Pantrem Pop 84, and others). Some of them were in developed and established areas of local specialisation (knitwear at Carpi and in the Veneto provinces, underwear in Bologna, casual and sportswear in Ancona, sportswear in Perugia, jeans in the provinces of Veneto and near Teramo and in S. Giuseppe Vesuviano, wedding dresses and children's clothes in Putignano).

In the 20 years following 1971 there was a transfer of productive units and employment from the northern regions to the central and southern ones, thanks to considerable financial incentives and the lower cost of labour. The Italian productive system increased its flexibility through the greater use of sub-contracting in those 20 years, and also sought to improve its competitiveness through transferring production to the lowest cost geographical areas. It was for this reason that Italy did not exploit the chance to produce in countries with low labour costs, unlike other western European countries and the USA. Italy was thus able to make full use of the 'made in Italy' label.

The specialisation of the distribution system

The distribution system in Italy, both in general and with regard to clothing, has always been different to the distribution systems of other western countries. Its characteristic feature is high fragmentation and the strong presence of small independent shops and street sellers. These are served by wholesalers that act as intermediaries with industry. At the retail level, the large distributors were unable to establish themselves even during the booming years, because of legislative and taxation mechanisms. These mechanisms always favoured small retailers. The very structure of Italian cities, with their historic centres and the almost total absence of urban planning impeded the development of large department stores, favouring small retail shops.

instit. foundations [handwritten margin note]

With the growth of demand and the advent of the branded product, distribution began to grow as a supporting factor for the development of 'made in Italy', at least within the country itself.

The variety and increasing quality and image of the products encouraged a lot of very small 'general' clothing shops to specialise in specific types of product and/or customer. During the 1980s the whole country witnessed the spread of clothing and accessory boutiques. In these new boutiques a more differentiated and focalised product offer, and visual merchandisng that was more in line with market needs, were added to the already existing intimate relation between the shopkeeper and the customer.

The growing specialisation of the retail industry allowed firms producing quality articles to 'leap over' wholesale intermediation and thus to move closer to the end consumer. They obtained the distribution margins for themselves, apart from the fact that this also led to the establishment of solid agent networks. The new, more direct, relationship between the industry and retail, and the strong competition among sales points provided another stimulus to product innovation. Information about the needs of end users was increased, as was information about the actions and products of competitors. The sales agents, whose job was to show samples and collect orders in the small and widely scattered shops over the country, also monitored competitors. This contributed to increased competitiveness among the producers who used the same sales points.

Competition, whether at the level of retail or producer, was no longer exclusively based on price. It was also based on the ability to offer differentiated products with a high fashion and image content.

A more profound transformation in the relationship between the industry and distribution occurred with the development of franchising by Benetton. Benetton was followed by very few other producers (its most direct competitor Stefanel, and Max Mara). An exception to the trend was GFT's decision to sell off the Marus chain of retail outlets in order to focus on productive activities.

The role of the other fashion industries

As well as considerable tradition in textile-clothing, Italy has always been able to count on a widespread craftsmanship structure in industries that are 'close' to fashion: hosiery and leather accessories, leather clothing and coats, jewellery, and so on. These are all industries that have always had to satisfy a particularly sophisticated and quantitatively significant demand. This created the preconditions for the internationalisation of the Italian product.

The success of the designer label and the clothing industry both in national and international markets has a knock-on effect on the image of related consumer goods. It has an indirect effect on instrumental goods and semi-finished goods (tanning, leather and gold processing, processing of plastic materials, and so on). While seeking out markets where they can express their own creativity, some of the best known designers began to make licensing agreements with producers in other industries. These agreements were closely connected to fashion (personal and household objects, fabrics for furnishings, and so on).

The increased consumption and importance attributed to the designer label in those years produced synergetic effects on the whole fashion system and on the international image of the Italian system. Demand was also sustained by an economic and social environment (economic recovery, yuppyism, emergent classes, and so on) that was very sensitive to external values and status.

The result of this complex process of interaction between demand variables and the offer was the unprecedented increase in the rate of consumption. This put Italy among world leaders for the percentage of income spent on clothes compared to total private expenditure.

The international success of the Italian fashion

The drive to exports by Italian firms was developed from the early 1980s onwards, after the first signs of a slowdown in internal demand. Italian Lira devaluation made Italian exports more competitive abroad. The internationalisation process of Italian clothing and fashion firms, however, reflects an orientation towards the export model instead of direct investments. The focalisation on the product and the lack of marketing orientation pushed Italian firms to rely on importers and distributors rather than creating their own commercial structures. If this can be understood in the case of smaller firms, it becomes less clear in the case of large companies.

The significant exceptions to this are GFT and Benetton. The former began to build its own subsidiaries in the most advanced countries (Germany, France and the US). The latter was helped by its know-how in franchising and its global vision, to spread its own distributive formula first in Europe and then in the US.

Actually there were fewer reasons to internationalise productive activities. It was hard to find other countries with an integrated, developed, specialised and flexible productive system like the Italian one. Therefore there always was little incentive to transfer production overseas as other European countries did.

4.4.3 An overall interpretation

It is now possible to attempt a brief summary of the development of the fashion industry in Italy between 1976 and 1985. Success can be explained by the ability of Italian operators to take advantage of factors that are unique to Italy. Establishing precise cause and effect relationships among the different determinants of the Italian 'model' is not an easy undertaking, and is not perhaps even important, given that almost all the relationships among the determinants are reciprocal interactions.

Some elements, however, have had a greater effect on the Italian fashion system, in terms of differentiation. These are the factors that create a national competitive home base, according to Porter's well-known model:[13]

- An extremely sophisticated final *demand*, not just in the high end of the market but also in the medium and medium-low range, and that is the constant stimulus for producers and retailers
- The development of a specialised *distributive structure* geared to product and service quality, that can always respond to different needs and channel a considerably differentiated production adequately to the market needs
- The learning potential of the *partnership relationship* between designers (inside and outside the producing firms) and the productive system as a whole (textile suppliers, yarns and components, suppliers, tailors, knitwear firms, furriers, and so on)
- A developed and widespread *productive system* that has become increasingly specialised through the emergence of two fundamental roles: the 'commercial firm' that is market oriented and oriented to product innovation, and the 'producing firm', the outsourcer, that is oriented to production and efficiency
- The ease of *interaction* among all the actors in the supply chain, including the *related and support industries*, due to cultural homogeneity and the geographical proximity of productive areas.

The combination of all these factors contributed to the success in this ten-year period of a model that was not just effective and efficient, but was above all very hard for competitors to imitate. This can be explained, as well as by genuinely national factors, by the dynamics of a model in which each element was strength-

---

13. M. Porter 1990, *op. cit.*

ened by the others so that it resulted in an improvement of individual operators and the system as a whole.

The dynamism of the model can be attributed to the special relation (of exchange and partnership) among the firms within the *cluster*. It can also be explained by their ability to make products with a high qualitative content through working on the whole value chain – from raw materials to stylistic content, and from technology to final distribution to the end consumer.

Within the fashion industries Italian firms were able to anticipate general macro-trends, such as:

- The move from standardised and mass products to more specialised, personalised products with a greater content of qualitative tangibles (quality of materials, comfort, functions, and so on) and intangibles (style, image, status symbol, and so on), the consequent reorientation towards more flexible technologies and processes that can produce small quantities and also renew the product in a very short time
- The move from highly integrated industrial firms aiming at achieving efficiency and economies of scale, towards a 'network of firms' based on the concept of partnership and subcontracting.

Beyond the structural advantages of this model, there were also external conditions supporting Italian competitiveness until the end of the 1980s. In the first place, national and international demand was always larger than the supply, at least in the high and medium-high segments where Italian firms competed. The end consumer was interested in style and image content and the Italian style was perceived as unique and original.

What is more important, however, is the fact that there was relatively little international competition during this period. Some industrialised countries had withdrawn investment from the clothing industry in the 1970s because they thought they would be unable to face competition from low costs countries. Another reason for the withdrawal was that they were behind in terms of product innovation due to a less sophisticated demand and the lack of a fashion system (designers, suppliers, manufacturers, services, and so on). The Italian distribution system, with its fragmentation, represented a strong entry barrier for foreign producers.

The Italian textile industry was made up of small firms whose strength lay in their ability to become world leaders in their own segment through the creation of niches that competitors found hard to attack because of the enormous experience that the Italian firms had built up over the time.

In the second half of the 1980s, however, certain demand and supply conditions challenged the supremacy of the Italian model. Loss of competitiveness could also be attributed to the relative myopia with which the firms tended to respond to change. The myopia was fundamentally due to the same causes as Italian success in the earlier stage – the considerable and almost exclusive focus on the product did not allow for the development of a solid business culture or managerial know-how. According to a top manager with long experience in the industry:

> 'The product was seen as almost a miracle, as if everything depended on it alone. This was what lay behind the inability to see the business as a whole in all its components – the product itself, production, distribution, suppliers. The firm is made of all of that'.

Relying on Porter's diamond model, *Figure 4.3* summarizes the determinants of Italian success in fashion related products and industries.

FIGURE 4.3   **THE COMPETITIVE ADVANTAGE OF ITALY IN FASHION**

FIRM STRATEGY. STRUCTURE AND RIVALRY

The crisis of the large business and the rise of subcontracting

Flexible production in localised areas and specialisation (industrial districts)

Small sized firms, family businesses

Rivalry among domestic competitors (inter-personal rivalry)

FACTOR CONDITIONS

Historical tradition in craftmanship

Historical industrial tradition in textiles (Biella, Vicenza, Como)

Entrepreneurship

Climate (strong seasonability)

Art heritage

DEMAND CONDITIONS

Many sophisticated consumers (sensitivity to new trends, taste, style, high income spent in apparel)

Selective, specialised and demanding distribution (boutiques)

High mobility among social classes

SUPPORTING INDUSTRIES

Synergies along the entire textile-clothing and leather footwear pipelines

Competitiveness of the accessories sector (glasses, ties, scarves...) and the machinery sector (textile and footwear machines)

Tradition in haute couture and industrial design

Fashion publishing and fashion trade fairs

International tourism

Source: the authors.

PART THREE

Managerial processes in fashion companies

5.1 The features of fashion products

The value of a product is not in itself, but it is related to its ability to meet a specific set of needs. Needs can be material and only related to the product's functional attributes, or they may be tied to the consumer's psychological and socio-cultural motivations and thus related to the product's intangible values.

According to Henzel[1] (*Table 5.1*), there are two ways of interpreting a product. The first defines the product as it is and deals with physical attributes; the second defines the product in terms of what it evokes and deals with more intangible and symbolic aspects.

To the fashion concious consumer a fashion product (not only clothing but also accessories, cosmetics, jewellery, sometimes even cars) has a significance that goes beyond its functional features. It often becomes an instrument for communicating an 'attitude or a lifestyle' or for making a statement. Fashion has been

---

1.   P. Henzel, 'Imprese di moda e marketing: la semiotica come aiuto nelle decisioni', in R. Grandi (edited by), *Semiotica al marketing*, Franco Angeli, 1994.

TABLE 5.1   **CONCEPTS OF THE PRODUCTS**

THE PRODUCT AS IT IS	THE PRODUCT AS WHAT IT EVOKES
The product as use	The product as magic
The attributes	The product recalls its origins
The products as appearance	The product as essence
The product as certainty	The product as questioning
The product as related to nature	The product as a symbol
The product as only reality (it can only be useful)	The product's surrealistic aspects (it can be absolutely useless)

Source: adapted from Hetzel, 1994.

defined as a visual language with its own communication codes[2] that hark back to semantics. In this sense a fashionable product could be defined as a cultural product, or as a product with a high symbolic intensity. As such, the product is consumed through an act of symbolic interpretation.

Not all products of the fashion system, however, can be regarded as communicative media or cultural products. Some fashion products merely satisfy basic functional needs while others satisfy intangible needs that are located in the higher part of Maslow's pyramid of needs (needs of status, well being, self esteem). It is therefore necessary to provide a classification of fashion products in order to present better the issue of demand segmentation. What is proposed is an old-fashioned but still valid general classification of consumer goods from the American Marketing Association[3]. According to this classification, goods

2. In the words of Fred David (1992) a code can be defined as "*the binding ligament in the shared understandings that comprise a sphere of discourse and, hence, its associated social arrangements... A clothing style is a code as it draws on the conventional and tactile symbol of a culture....but... the meanings evoked by the combinations and permutations of the code's key terms (fabric, texture, color, pattern, volume, silhouette and occasion) are forever shifting or in process.*"
3. The first formulation dates back to M.T. Copeland, 'The relation of consumers' buying habits to marketing methods', in the *Harvard Business Review*, April 1923.

can be divided into three categories. They differ by frequency and level of consumer involvement in the purchasing process, by degree of differentiation, and by product cost.

- *Convenience goods*: these are substitutable goods, they are bought regularly, their price is not high and the purchase process is not difficult. The consumer goods used in daily life fit this category: detergents, mineral water, soap, petrol, and so on. They are also called commodity goods
- *Shopping goods*: these are goods that do not satisfy immediate and tangible needs like convenience goods. They rather satisfy psychological or affective needs. They generally have a high price, reduced purchasing frequency, scarce substitutability and a long, difficult and emotionally involving purchasing process. The consumer does not have all the elements needed for deciding, and must carry out a search and an evaluation of alternatives. Substitution occurs because the goods are regarded as 'obsolete' even when they still meet functional needs. They include furniture, cars, and consumer durables
- *Speciality goods*: these are goods with specific physical or intangible features that make them unique and exclusive. They satisfy highly specific and selective needs. Like convenience goods, but unlike shopping goods, the consumer can satisfy his need when it arises, and the purchase is not, therefore, difficult. The distribution of this category of product is selective and the cost is generally (but not necessarily) high. Giving examples of this category is not easy because every product can fit into the category as a function of subjective considerations. A car, for example, according to its brand, price and positioning may fit the category of speciality goods for one individual and shopping goods for another. Therefore the speciality category crosses over traditional product categories and refers to the specific attributes of the single product.

According to the authors of this classification, products in the fashion system would usually fall into the shopping category, insofar as they are problematic goods. However, given the current complexity of products and offer systems in fashion, we think that this three-part classification can also be reproduced within fashion itself.

Products within the fashion system can be considered as convenience, shopping and speciality, without regard to the specific category of merchandise.

- *Convenience.* All differentiable products that satisfy primary needs, are the object of repeat purchases, and are not subject to fashionability. This could include unbranded or private label products from popular stores with a low fashion content and low price. It also includes products that may not necessarily have a low price but that are basic and not affected by fashion, such as the men's blue shirt or the classic blazer
- *Shopping.* Branded products with a price premium, and the prevalence of intangible and emotional attributes over tangible ones, fit this category. Besides differentiation, shopping products are comparable among themselves and are selected after a process of evaluation that involves the attributes of the product, the offer system, and the price
- *Speciality.* Unique products, or those that are regarded as such by the consumer. Uniqueness can be given by the product features (completely new style or materials, or much better performance than competing products), or by the world evoked by the brand. Fashion clothes or accessories that carry the name of a *couturier* or designer can be considered speciality goods, as can classic and timeless accessories (the Hermès Kelly), but also products offered by a mass brand that become desirable objects for some market targets.

The distinction between these three product categories is also important for understanding the different competitive logics existing in the fashion market. The *convenience* product, being a commodity, has to be managed as a service to the client/consumer (availability of sizes and colours, deliveries on time, replenishments, and so on) with attention to the price/cost effectiveness. The *shopping* product has to create emotions and a shopping experience: therefore it requires a strong market orientation. The *speciality* product is managed with a strong orientation to the physical product, its quality and exclusivity. As one moves from *speciality* to *convenience*, there is a progressive decrease in the importance of the intangible aspects of the product, and an increase in consumer power and rationality in the purchasing process.

If a product succeeds in the upgrading from the *shopping* category to the *speciality* category the firm usually gains extra profits and competitive uniqueness. Offering speciality products is the dream of all the firms in the fashion system. In reality, many products are destined to be subject to a continuous process of comparative evaluation. Only a few products escape some element of substitutability. The segmentation and positioning strategy, which we will discuss in a later section, have the purpose of selecting the best market target for understanding its needs and offering products perceived as unique.

Given the approach that has been chosen throughout this book, the above considerations are all significant for goods in the *shopping* and *speciality* categories, that is for products with sign-values (as opposed to use values) and a short life cycle.

5.2 Industry segmentation and business definition

A successful strategy differentiates the firm from its competitors providing it with a unique positioning. This uniqueness is tied to the firm's ability to offer a specific segment of customers a particular set of benefits. Each strategy imposes choices. A firm cannot offer the whole range of benefits that the market might desire. It has to focus on just some, and to offer them in a unique way. It often happens that firms' inability to make choices leads them to compete for the same customers through the same offers. Industry segmentation forces the firm to identify its own competitive positioning within the industry. In nearly every industry there are distinct product varieties, multiple distribution channels and several types of consumers. Segments are important because they have differing needs: an unadvertised basic shirt and a designer shirt are both shirts but are sold to different buyers. Understanding the particular environment in which the firm operates is thus the first step to segmenting demand and analysing the firm's positioning and its brands. According to Porter's well known "five forces" model, an industry can be segmented into distinct competitive environments when differences in products, customers or product end-use change one or more of the five competitive forces.[4] An industry segment corresponds to a specific product-market-technology combination. Within each industry segment the firm has to pursue a specific strategy in order to compete.

The concept of industry segmentation is wider than that of demand segmentation. Where demand segmentation concerns the identification of different demand needs that correspond to different marketing plans, industry segmentation concerns differences in the configuration of a firm's whole value chain in response to a specific product-market-technology combination.

The fashion system is made up of numerous industries (textiles, clothing, knitwear, leather, accessories, and so on). These in turn can be further sub-divided into different competitive segments. Each firm can decide how to compete, or position itself, within each segment. Therefore, there is a *structural* or *external* process of industry segmentation, that is valid for all the firms competing within the segment. There is also a *strategic* or *internal* process aiming at defining the single firm's competitive space within the segment. In what follows we will be concerned, above all, with the structural segmentation of the clothing industry. This is the most important and complex industry, and most of what will be said can be applied to other industries in the fashion system. After dealing with structural segmentation, the issue of defining the firm's competitive space will be developed.

---

4. The boundaries of an industry or segment of an industry are defined by five competitive forces: customers, suppliers, competitors, potential entrants (mobility threat), and substitute products (substitution threat). The disposition and interaction of these forces determines the intensity of competition within a segment of the industry and its structural profitability. See M. Porter, *op. cit.*

The segmentation of demand is a part of this. Finally, Chapter Six deals with the issue of strategic positioning within a certain competitive segment.

5.2.1 The structural segmentation of the industry

With reference to Abell's approach[5] to industry segmentation we segment the clothing industry grouping three macro-criteria together – technology, product end-uses and groups of clients. Further criteria can be defined within these macro-criteria (*Figure 5.1*).

A further segmentation criterion for the clothing industry, transversal to the three above, is the price band. This will be analysed later.

FIGURE 5.1   **STRUCTURAL SEGMENTATION OF THE CLOTHING INDUSTRY**

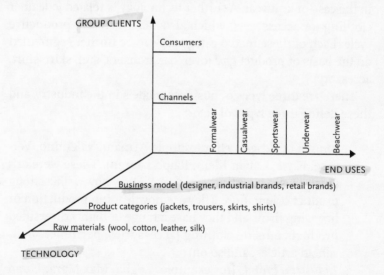

Source: the authors.

5.   D. Abell, *Defining the Business. The Starting Point of Strategic Planning*, Prentice Hall, 1980.

Technology

Technology can be strictly defined as the state of knowledge related to productive processes and goods that are produced, or in the wider sense as methods of performing the business's economic processes. We consider technology in the wider sense, as the dimension that describes how the functions researched by the customers are satisfied, and the possible alternatives. In the case of clothing, segmentation criteria within technology can be product category (category of product and raw materials used), or the business model (type of know-how that is incorporated into business processes and the offer system - craftsmanship, designer, industrial, retail, and so on).

Considering the product, a first distinction concerns the two technologies that are a feature of the clothing industry, textile production (orthogonal and knitted fabric) and knitwear (knitted clothing, including hosiery). The two sectors have different production cycles because of the different nature of the raw materials that are used – fabric in the case of textile clothing, yarn in the case of knitwear. A further technology is related to leather clothing (or accessories) which also has a different productive cycle. Each of these macro-categories can be further segmented on the basis of product *type* (overcoat, trousers, suit, skirt, shirt, accessory).

There are three types of business models in the industry, and these define three types of actor:

1. *Maison* or *designers* (for example Armani, Valentino, Versace, Ferrè, Calvin Klein, Ralph Lauren). These were originally based on artistic and design know-how, with a strong product orientation. They are now leading production or licensing firms and they have a range of highly diversified products outside clothing (accessories, perfumes, household articles, and so on)

2. *Industrial brands* (for example, Zegna, Max Mara, Hugo Boss, Fila, Diesel). Their know-how is both industrial and commercial, and they are strongly market oriented. They have a very well-developed range of products, and are positioned in different market segments

3. *Retailers* (Italian examples include Benetton and Stefanel, at the international level the Spanish chain Zara, the American chains Gap and Banana Republic, and the French Decathlon). They manage retailing, have commercial and sales know-how, and are often able to organise their own supply chain through external manufacturing.

Product end-uses

End-uses describe a product's functions and final destination. In clothing, for example, the main categories of end-uses are external clothing, underwear and beachwear. Materials, shapes, structures and finishing processes can be different according to product end-uses; in this sense there is a strong relation between a certain end-use and a certain technology/manufacturing process. There is a further segmentation option based on occasions of use. Unlike functional end-uses, occasions of use is a market oriented criterion becoming increasingly important for segmenting the offer. Formal occasions of use are thus distinguished from informal ones. As demand becomes increasingly sophisticated, occasions of use are further segmented. Formal occasions include both those of the working-day and those of the evening ceremony. Informal occasions include urban free time and leisure wear for weekends while sports occasions include both passive sports and active sports.

Client groups

The industry can be segmented on the basis of client groups: intermediate clients (trade channels) and the end customer.

- *Intermediate clients*: a first criterion for segmenting distribution is the distinction between a direct and indirect channel. The former create a direct relation between the industry and the end consumer without any commercial intermediation. Sales are managed through mono-brand stores/boutiques, mail-order catalogues and electronic commerce. The latter includes specialised actors in commercial intermediation. They distributes the final product and offer various types of service. It can be further segmented according to different elements. A first criterion, for example, distinguishes between generalised distribution and specialised distribution (by merchandise category or occasions of use). Two further criteria are distribution format and ownership model. The former is defined by a set of elements, including: specialisation, location, sales area, width and depth of assortment, price level and customer service. The ownership criterion distinguishes between independent stores, chains, and franchising[6]

- *End consumers*: consumers can be segmented on the basis of several variables. These include the traditional demographic methods (age, gender), geographical (area of residence), socio-economic (social class, income), or more innovatory methods, psycho-graphic (life style), purchasing behaviour or, the current focus of the industry, mental categories.

A typical segmentation approach in the fashion system mingles end-uses and client groups, obtaining as a result two large segments within external formal wear: menswear and womenswear.

Menswear is characterised by long and continuous productive cycles, very little product differentiation, limited fashion content. Margins are quite small; therefore companies usually implement volume strategies.

Womenswear, on the contrary, is very differentiated and the fashion content (and thus product seasonality) is a key element. It is the most important segment of the industry. Industrial firms sub-contract to specialised suppliers to increase flexibility and reduce time-to-market. Profitability can be very high due to the fact that firms can differentiate their products according to several dimensions. Where menswear is dominated by medium to large firms, vertically integrated, womenswear, at least in Europe, is a very fragmented business, with a variety of competitors from large firms to small specialised firms and ready-to-wear *maison*.

Price

The price band criterion cuts across both merchandise and market criteria in the structural segmentation of the industry.

In fashion generally, and external clothing in particular, five price bands are commonly recognised: *couture, ready-to-wear/de-*

---

6. For more on the topic of distribution see *Chapter 9* of this book.

signer, diffusion, bridge and *mass.* This segmentation particularly applies to the womenswear market. The menswear market follows the same pattern, although it is divided into slightly different segments. The various price segments are defined as multiples of the average market price level. This type of segmentation goes beyond simple price value to the point of designing within each segment different business models with specific key success factors. Moving from the ready-to-wear segment to the mass market reduces the importance of intangible factors such as creativity and innovation, perceived quality and the intangible content of the product system, in favour of tangible factors such as the cost/volume ratio, supply strategies and distribution.

Couture, also defined as high fashion. The final price is not comparable to any market price as this is more craftmanship than business and each dress is considered a piece of art. *Couture* is nowadays less important compared to the past. It still offers beautiful made-to-measure clothes addressed to very selective, international customers (not more than 2,000 customers world-wide). But prestigious couturiers with tailoring skills hardly exist any more. The entrepreneurial model has moved from the fashion house centred on the great *couturier* to the multibrand companies competing in the high end of the market. These companies consider couture as a creative laboratory and communication medium for supporting the wider and more profitable business of perfumes and accessories.

Ready-to-wear, also defined as *prêt à porter* or *designer,* is a segment whose average price is between three and five times higher than that of the average market price. The ready-to-wear business had its origins in the 1970s in Italy as a result of the partnership between designers and manufacturing firms. Its distinguishing character is the presence of a designer who manages the creation and development of the collection and controls the communication strategy. Also competing within the segment are a few small industrial brands, very creative and exclusive, that are perceived as fashion houses even if they do not have a designer. Ready-to-wear collections are sold at a high price and offer a strong creative content according to the designer's taste. It is a seasonal business, with the display of at least two collections each year. The segment is becoming global in terms of actors, channels, targets; the key success factor for competing is the designer's reputation which is a mix of creativity, image, opinion makers, marketing and good relations with international store buyers. Investments in communication are much higher than in other segments: getting press recognition is central for the designer's success. The main channel of communication is the *fashion show*, a very expensive means of promotion held during the traditional fashion events. Another successful way to gain media attention is lending out clothes to celebrities. It is important to distinguish, considering the high end of the market, the difference between the ready-to-wear segment and the *luxury* segment. Ready-to-wear is essentially 'fashion' clothing, therefore a seasonal product strongly related to its time. Luxury goods are timeless products, mainly accessories (jewellery, accessories, pens, perfumes), very exclusive and unique. The business press, reporting on market shares, profitability and price-earnings is used to considering fashion brands and luxury brands as competing in the same business. This vision has been driven by the fact that the luxury market, once a very specialistic market niche, mainly local and exclusive, has nowadays become transversal to product categories, global and more accessible with respect to the past, also as an effect of company diversification and globalisation strategies. Yet it is important to note that the luxury brands core business is, or used to be, in activities and products other than fashion clothing. Many luxury firms, above all French ones, (Hermès, Chanel, Louis Vuitton, Cartier) established their own offer of products with a very high level of prestige and image that are still classic and timeless. Their entrance into fashion ready-to-wear can be interpreted as an attempt to use the communicative potential of seasonal clothing collections to renew and update their brand image.

Diffusion (price two or three times that of the average market price). The second and third lines of designers are positioned here, as well as some collections from prestigious industrial firms. Key success factors are almost the same as for ready-to-wear, since *diffusion* came into existence as the designer brand' extension to wider market segments, traditionally occupied by industrial brands.

Bridge (price one and a half to two times that of the average market price). The bridge is a segment that came into existence in the American market, as an initiative by department stores to offer a product that would act as a "bridge" between the mass market and the first and second lines of designers. Premium industrial brands compete against each other, as well as the lowest designer lines. The critical factors for success are related to the ability to serve the market at the right time with the right style. Image and time to market are more important than creativity.

Mass (the average market price). As one goes down the price bands, products become increasingly basic and less differentiated. The broad mass market can be further segmented into the better and moderate segments (above all for menswear). Yet, price positioning below the bridge segment does not really exist: differentiation is based on other elements, such as the price-quality ratio, retailing and communication. Volumes do matter, and therefore distribution and brand reputation are also important. Unlike other fashion segments, the mass market follows the competitive patterns of other consumer goods – only communication follows the fashion pattern. The more affordable branded lines are to be found in this segment, as well as retailer's private labels and unbranded goods.

Table 5.2 summarises the main features of the fashion market segments.

5.2.2 The fashion business definition

After having listed the main criteria for segmenting the clothing industry it is now possible for the firm to define its own competitive space within a specific segment. The objective is to identify a segment of opportunity where the firm's resources and

TABLE 5.2   **THE MAIN FEATURES OF FASHION SEGMENTS BY PRICE BAND**

	MASS MARKET (THE GAP)	BRIDGE (MAX MARA)	DIFFUSION/PAP (ARMANI)
Key success factors	Price/service	Brand/style	Designer label/creativity
Client-trade	Modern distribution Specialised channels Wholesale	Specialised channels	Boutique Concept store
Strategic variable of the supply system	Volumes and assortments	Time to market	The Designer label
Store and retailing style	Large areas	Specialisation	The designer label concept

Source: the authors.

know-how could best be employed.[7] The approach followed to industry segmentation, the dimension considered as dominant (technology, end uses and customers) and the degree to which these dimensions are further disaggregated, are the key points of the strategic decisional process.

Firms generally follow two approaches for defining their competitive space in the clothing industry. The first of these is a traditional approach that starts from the product and is technology-driven. The second approach, more innovative, is market oriented.

In the former case the process starts with a definition of the end-uses, the merchandise and type of industrial process, before arriving at a definition of the firm's end consumer (*Figure 5.2*).

For a long time, firms in the fashion system were tied to a product and technology orientation when defining their competitive space. This model allowed them to obtain a lot of commercial success.

---

7. On the subject of industry segmentation and the creative definition of business see D. Abell, *Managing With Dual Strategies. Mastering the Present, Preempting the Future*, The Free Press, 1993.

FIGURE 5.2.   **DEFINITION OF THE COMPETITIVE ENVIRONMENT ACCORDING TO TECHNOLOGY CRITERIA**

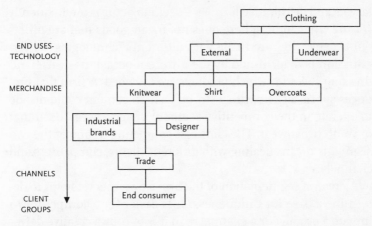

Source: the authors.

Although the product is still central to the fashion system, the competitive environment today seems different. Increasing competition and the growing power of retailers have drawn more attention to the needs of the intermediate and final client, and this has resulted in a stronger market orientation. Further, opportunities for radical innovations on products and technologies are very limited and do not often occur in the industry. The introduction of the mini-skirt or the use of technological materials in clothing or accessories were product or technological innovations that belong to the past.

One recent example of product innovation, which allowed the creation of a new market space in the shoe industry, is related to the Italian Geox brand. The firm came into existence in Montebelluna in the province of Treviso, Northern Italy. It began as a small shoe company, Pol, that produced substantially undifferentiated sports shoes. During the crisis of 1990 the owner, Mario Moretti Polegato, invented and introduced the first 'breathing' rubber sole, and this would revolutionise the way rubber-sole shoes were manufactured. The invention concerned a new material that had been developed in the USA by NASA for astronauts. It was a 'breathable' membrane inside a rubber sole. The market potential was immediately enormous. About 80% of shoes produced in the world have rubber soles.

If opportunities for technological or product innovation are few, innovations in market categories – occasions of use, consumer targets and distributive formats – seem to occur more frequently (*Figure 5.3*). Clothing here does not mean goods that are different because they are made with different technologies. Differentiation is determined by the different occasions of use and dressing styles for which products are intended. A firm that produces sports jackets with a strong fashion content could decide to operate in the competitive segment of sportswear, or in that of youth urbanwear. The choice of competing in one of the two segments means dealing with different clients, competitors and channels.

A creative segmentation of the firm's own market helps to determine a base for uniqueness. It is easier for a competitor to imitate a product or a channel than it is to copy a creative definition of the business itself, and this creativity is usually extended through all aspects of the firm.[8]

FIGURE 5.3   **DEFINITION OF THE COMPETITIVE ENVIRONMENT ACCORDING TO MARKET CRITERIA**

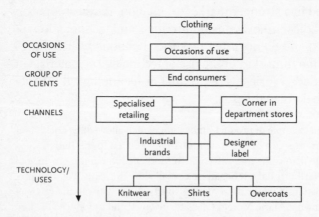

Source: the authors.

---

8. On the topic of the relationship between the competitive environment and strategic innovation see C. Markides, 'Strategic Innovation' in *Sloan Management Review*, Spring 1997.

A *creative definition of competitive space. The Swatch case*
The watch industry was subject to strong competitive pressures in the mid-1970s. The price fall of 1976 and the development of electronic technology had caused a deep crisis in the Swiss industry. The Swiss share of the total value of the world market for watches (net of movement volumes that remained stable) went from 56% in 1952 to 20% in 1980, while the world production of watches increased from 61 to 320 million items. Swiss producers had to give up the medium segment of the market and concentrate on the luxury segment. Despite the fact that Switzerland had introduced the first electronic watch in 1976, the new technology was progressively developed and dominated by American and Japanese producers. The technology made many of the craftsmanship skills that had been built up in Switzerland over the centuries obsolete. It also required large production volumes if advantages were to be taken from economies of scale and experience. The situation of the industry, which exported more than 90% of its production, was worsened by the rise of the Swiss Franc compared to the US Dollar at a time when the American market was the most important export market. There were many failures, mergers and acquisitions in the industry following the crisis. In 1978 Ernst Thomke became the managing director of ETA[9], a Swiss maker of watches and movements. Morale in the firm was very low because of the continuing losses and redundancies. The team working on product development, mainly made of technicians and engineers, was doubtful that they could ever match the Asian competitors in technology in the price range traditionally served by the firm. If he was to initiate a successful turnaround, Thomke needed not only to control costs, but also to motivate his people with an innovative and challenging project. He decided to launch a completely innovative watch, for the growing segment below 200 Swiss Francs. The watch had fewer parts (51 compared to 91 for a normal quartz watch), many of the outside parts were plastic, production was fully automated and very advanced, and the costs of production were low. Product quality was very high because the watch could not be re-opened once it had been built, except to change the battery. Despite this, it was decided not to emphasise functional performance at the launch, but to stress the brand and the world of reference. At the start of 1980 ETA did not have a marketing department, and external consultants were used to follow the product launch. On 1st March 1980, Swatch (an abbreviation of Swiss watch) was introduced on the domestic market with a run of 235 watches. By 1986 15

---

9. ETA was a subsidiary of Ebauches SA, a manufacturer of movements that was controlled by ASUAG (General Corporation of Swiss Horological Industries Ltd.). ETA came into existence in 1931, and in 1979 its turnover was 1,212 million Swiss francs. It also controlled brands such as Eterna, Longines and Rado.

million watches had been produced. Swatch achieved a 19% share of the segment in 1987 globally. It had become a cult in 1989. Thomke's success was the result of an absolutely innovative vision of the watch industry. This had previously been dominated by technicians and engineers, and the industry was product oriented and segmented on a price base. Instead of being a device for telling the time, the watch could be conceived as a clothing accessory and given intangible values. In sum, the question was: "Are we competing in the watch industry or in the fashion accessories business?" Swatch was positioned as a unisex accessory for 18- to 30-year-old 'fashion conscious' consumers. Many people outside this segment bought the watch, however, and this contributed both to enlarging the market and increasing the turnover. The product's technical attributes, such as water-resistance, shock-resistance and accuracy, were all less important than the association of the brand with positive emotions such as 'irony', 'joy" and 'fun'. The price was fixed at a level that allowed for spontaneous and repeated purchases so as to ensure the high margins that were necessary for the huge advertising investment. As a fashion accessory, even if positioned in the same segment as watches of mass-market brands (Timex and Casio), Swatch used different sales outlets. No drugstores and mass distribution like its competitors. Instead it was sold through department stores, boutiques and jewellers, with very careful visual merchandising. Attractive margins for distribution and intense sales staff training, combined with completely innovative advertising, ensured the unique positioning of the brand.

Defining the firm's competitive space starting from a market criterion (occasions of use, lifestyles), has become necessary in the fashion market. Combining the 'end-uses and occasions of use' with 'consumer groups', as shown in *Table 5.3*, provides a more accurate definition of the different competitive options that a firm could achieve in positioning. Each competitive space has different critical factors for success.

It may be much more difficult and risky for the firm to build its own space on the basis of the end consumer, given the variability of the fashion market. One of the solutions that firms are turning towards is to monitor consumer behaviour where it occurs – in the sales point. As will be seen later, distribution is acquiring a central role in characterising brand identities and competitive models in fashion, and is increasingly seen as the starting point for building a winning entrepreneurial formula. The

TABLE 5.3   **DEFINITION OF COMPETITIVE SPACES ACCORDING TO MARKET CRITERIA**

Customer groups / End uses and occasions of use	Men		Woman		Kids	
	young	adult	young	adult	newborn	junior
External clothing						
workwear						
casualwear						
sportswear						
Special occasions						
underwear						
beachwear						

Source: the authors.

consumer looks for retail outlets that reflect his needs, whether these are for emotion or service. Focusing on distribution means analysing a relatively limited number of places where consumer behaviour takes place.

5.3 Demand segmentation

Business literature is full of books and articles about the marketing of consumer goods and services, but there are very few about fashion marketing. There are several reasons for this. Above all, the rapid obsolescence of the fashion product often means that standard American marketing concepts are not applicable. This is because they were conceived for consumer goods in the *convenience* category, which have medium to long life cycles. Secondly, given the importance and autonomy within fashion firms of designers and creative teams (which often control also the communication activities), marketing departments lose two "Ps" in their marketing mix (product and promotion). Up to a few years ago it was hard to find a structured marketing function in the fashion business because the designer or the product man/woman, (who is often also the entrepreneur) deals with the strategy for the market, the product and communication. Management thus only deals with sales management, operations and logistics. Another characteristic of the industry is that the design of collections often occurs *before* market research. This is unlike other industries where product policy follows the the definition of the firm's market strategy. There is, however, a very great need for a marketing strategy that goes beyond managing the marketing mix to become a marketing orientation of the whole firm. The increasingly fragmented market requires it, as does the fashion system, where many firms are facing the problem of the qualitative consolidation of growth and entrepreneurial succession.

The need for a fashion marketing strategy is important also for other reasons. First of all there is the fact that almost all consumer goods are subject to the influence of fashion and to a shortening of their own life cycle. As a result firms are looking for new approaches and tools that allow them to identify the social changes that will affect consumer behaviour within their own competitive environments, and thus to generate new market opportunities. Rethinking traditional segmentation and positioning from the viewpoint of fashion could therefore be useful, not just to fashion firms, but also to firms in other areas.

There is an important implication deriving from the fact that fashion products perform the function of a "semiotic code.[10] Every fashion product is context-dependent and has a socio-cultural source of inspiration. This aspect makes fashion firms the interpreters of the evolution of society and its symbolic language. Therefore sustaining the competitive advantage of symbol-intensive firms depends on their capability of interpreting evolving symbols in society and of transferring them into seasonal collections, retail spaces and advertising campaigns.

---

10. For more on this, see J. Baudrillard, *Il sistema degli oggetti*, Bompiani, 1972.

A brief examination of the relationship between fashion and Western society from the 1960s will help to introduce the specific issue of demand segmentation.

5.3.1 The evolution of fashion consumption

The 1960s and 1970s

After the Second World War the situation of the consumer market, which was substantially similar throughout all Western markets, reflected the characteristics of society. There was a polarisation of consumption between the highest end and the mass market. The higher class demonstrated its own status through the conspicuous consumption of luxury goods. Paris *couture* remained the centre of fashion for women's clothes, while English tailoring was the centre of men's clothing. The masses however, turned to substantially undifferentiated industrial clothing, and this was produced by a manufacturing industry organised along American production methods. Production was in series, and there was very little development of different styles.

The development of fashion lies in the 1960s and is connected with two events affecting consumers– the youth revolution and the emancipation of women.

It was young people who gave the first push towards the segmentation of clothing. Before the 1960s young people had no special clothing. Adolescents simply stopped wearing children's wear and started dressing like adults. The youth revolution made a statement about young people's autonomy by looking for a system of signs that would characterise it. The hippy movement opposed bourgeois values and Western ortodoxies in the late 1960s. Clothing was the first area to feel the effects of the revolution. Clothing for young people began to take form in the 1970s, and this was destined to carve out a place for itself in the market as an autonomous sector that could be further segmented (jeanswear, sportswear and casualwear).[11]

---

11. For more on the youth clothing industry see E. Prandelli, S. Saviolo, "Verso il prodotto relazionale", in *Economia & Management*, n. 5, 1995.

The increase in wealth encouraged buying propensity during this period. A new kind of woman emerged, independent and career-minded, and this woman wanted clothes and a look that suited her needs. These are the years of the crisis of French couture, and the crisis of the large firms in Italy due to trade unionisation. The clothing industry began to gear itself towards flexible and differentiated production, carried out by small firms in industrial areas. These firms were able to respond to the new demand. Ready-to-wear came into existence in this context, from the marriage of industry and the *designers*. Ready-to-wear resulted in greater differentiation within the industry, and prepared the way for the de-massification of consumption and the industrialisation of the 'fashion' concept (previously the exclusive domain of the French *couturiers*). This was fully achieved in the 1980s.

The increased segmentation in demand and supply corresponded to an increase in the number of clothing retail outlets. It is known that a greater differentiation in the offer determines the need to differentiate commercial assortments, and this results in the fragmentation of distribution.

The 1980s and 1990s

Since the middle of the 1980s up to the present the phenomenon of fashion designers has burst onto the scene. There was also a progressive move towards modern and organised distribution, both for single brands and multi-brands. Italian and American designers used their labels to offer lifestyles and worlds of reference. The market could be represented like a pyramid, with a number of price segments that reflected the segmentation of social classes. Italian designers in particular dictated trends, and thanks to the booming consumption after the crisis of the 1970s, the nouveaux riches sustained the growth of the designer labels. Capitalising on their reputation designers began brand extension strategies through licensing agreements. Diversification was looking for new market segments where people showed aspirational purchasing (for example, young people who could not buy a designer dress could buy a designer perfume or accessory).

The end of the 1990s

This was the beginning of a new era. Consumer society was no longer like a pyramid, but took on variable shapes – the *hourglass*, which emphasised the disappearance of the 'average' consumer and product in favour of the high end and the mass market, and the *rhombus*, which showed the reduced rigidity of segmentations.

The consumer society was now looking for personalisation and individuality. Unlike previous decades, subjectivity and sociability were no longer opposites, but part of the same dialectic. The individual first valued his or her own personality, and then searched for others who were like him. Clothing was still a symbol of identity, but a 'confederated' identity that expressed many identities as a function of many life occasions. The product and the market were no longer central. What counted was the individual and his self-image. There were still trends, but these were mixed with memories and personal creativity. Facing an explosion of options, the consumer learned to judge, to become his own designer and professional buyer, and had no time to waste on those who did not understand him. His search was increasingly for products that had meaning and spirit, that could create emotions. The consumer wanted *relational* products. The first firms to perceive this change in the market stopped using traditional segmentation and used 'collective mindsets' instead. The aim was to come up with new offer concepts that could combine the emerging 'sensitivity' with the new 'life occasions'.

The change in demand also made firms *listen* to the market in a new way. They moved from observing needs towards anticipating them. Knowing what was happening on the *street* was fundamental for them. From the time of the Paris *couturiers* up to the end of the 1980s, it had been the *couturiers*, the designers and the stylists who had offered their own vision of style to the street. Now it was the street itself, specifically youth sub-cultures, that suggested creative ideas to designers. The designers studied them to conceive the styles of the future. There was talk about *bubbling up*, the rise of individual and isolated phenomena from the street to the attention of the masses. This is the case of extreme sports, techno and electronic music, piercing and ethnic fashions.

If the visible manifestation of trends was increasingly started in youth culture, the key to understanding this culture lay in understanding the mental states, the collective thought, values and beliefs that were motivating individuals to behave in a certain way. The word 'trend' has less meaning nowadays if it is not used to describe a relationship with culture, with social groups, and with market segments. *Focus groups* have less value today in gathering information and stimuli about trends. What counts nowadays above all is knowing the consumer well and the authenticity of the offer that uses the right words, music, messages and atmosphere for its own target. Making authentic offers requires knowing how to look for what is new, or what is considered trendy and right for the time and the specific target – in short, what is 'cool'. Many of the emerging roles in fashion have a 'search' characteristic – they are called trendscouts, cool hunters, and anthropological expedition managers. These business roles are the mirror for the new realities.

> The most recent revolution in youth fashion concerns the hip-hop phenomenon. Hip-hop is more than just a segment. It is a global culture with its own language, clothing style, and above all its own music. It is also a form of art that includes deejaying, rap, break dance and the metropolitan graffiti of the New York suburbs in the 1970s. Although it was born in black American communities, the hip hop 'nation' of today is a mix of Afro-Americans, Asians, Hispanics and whites. The most important thing to these young, but not always young, people is sharing a language and a style. They represent a group with strong purchasing power that can foresee 'the new'. They are not seen as just trendsetters, but real masters in the art of interpretation. Firms that want to get closer to this market, and to young people, have to complete their own marketing mix with so-called street promotion. The object is to make the brand appear as part of the culture. The huge advertising campaigns of the past are simply over. Firms have to go out onto the street and take over events in order to approach their own target. Boss jeans, for example, sponsored seminars for teenagers in urban communities. The aim was to introduce them to music producers and make them understand how to act as entrepreneurs in an industry of independent artists. Also Diesel's music project aims at finding the best talent in five musical genres - Electronic, Drum'n'Bass, Hip Hop, Scratch DJ and R&B/Garage.

In the new context it is neither the product nor the price nor the image which is central: it is the corporate and brand vision, intended as an attitude, a set of ideas and beliefs. This shift towards the dominance of brands and logos over the product and manufacturing together with the branding of music, sports and even people has been strongly criticized by many, among them the well known "No Logo" by Naomi Klein. To offer a final opinion over the matter is really hard, due to the complexity of the issue. If it is undoubted that some American corporations have become virtual companies managing only marketing research and advertising budgets, it is also true that most European brands have maintained their commitment to product quality and manufacturing excellence. Furthermore the shift of production from Western markets to the Far East has involved both human rights infringements and economic development. What is certain is that the fashion system is a mirror of society and fashion brands are business entities not entitled to rule over regulations and political issues.

5.3.2 From traditional segmentation to segmentation by mental categories

Demand segmentation places consumers into 'homogeneous' groups in terms of their needs and reactions to marketing initiatives. This process allows for identifying and analysing the specific needs of the so called *target* or *segment*. In fashion in particular, segmentation helps to define, season by season, the specific features of the offer system with respect to the general market trends. Segmentation can be regarded as artificial and weak since the formation of segments relies on theoretical assumptions. In practice, different groups move from one segment to another, or are impossible to segment.

The description of segments is, however, a compromise that allows for matching the product with the needs of a group of customers.

There is no single way of segmenting the market for a product. There are many segmentation variables, and each firm has to use the best mix of them to meet its own needs and those of the market. Although there are many different approaches to segmentation, all of them have to meet certain basic requirements. They have to offer a precise definition of each segment, so that these do not overlap (requirement of the minimum variance within segments, and the maximum among segments). Secondly, the segments must be reachable by the firm economically. Finally, each segment must be targeted by a specific marketing mix[12]. As the market changes, so segmentation criteria have to change too. They must follow the market on the one hand, and on the other they must follow the opportunities offered by technology. The recent development of communication systems (the Internet), for example, allows single individuals to be reached through a micro-segmentation approach. The consumer is looking for a pluralism of lifestyles and must be targeted through a combination of segmentation tools.

> There are no longer wide movements in youth culture, like punk. Nowadays there are social groups, and these are subcultures that have niche tastes and lifestyles. A significant example is the hundreds of specialist youth magazines that relate to very small segments. The firms that intend serving the youth market have to tune in to these niches. The time of quantitative marketing studies is over. The proliferation of virtual worlds means that the consumer is becoming increasingly more elusive in the mass, but increasingly more accessible in the niche through new tools such as the Internet.

A view of the main approaches to segmentation is given in what follows. This will show the particular features these approaches have in the case of fashion.[13] There are two segmentation macrocategories, and these depend on how the grouping of customers is carried out. These macro-categories are *descriptive* and *behavioural* segmentation. The objective of descriptive segmentation is to describe the individual without regard to his purchase or consumption behaviour. Geographic and demographic criteria

---

12. By marketing mix we mean the combination of decisions about pricing, trade channels, product features and communication.
13. The part analysing the traditional segmentation variables was carried out with suggestions from E. Valdani (edited), *Marketing*, UTET, 1995, p. 66.

of segmentation are used here. Behavioural segmentation groups customers on the basis of their way of thinking, buying and consuming.

Descriptive segmentation
This type of segmentation considers the *individual in general*, on the basis of widely available objective data and statistical information. The two main criteria of this segmentation are geography and socio-demographics.

Geographical segmentation divides the market into different units – countries, regions, provinces, cities, even suburbs. Geographic segments usually correspond to official boundaries. The assumption is that the characteristics and thus the needs of the individuals vary as a function of place of residence. Although this is a traditional and well-established criterion, original applications of it are more popular nowadays, such as that of Garreau.[14] Garreau suggested segmenting the US on the basis of cultural boundaries instead of political ones, thus showing nine 'nations' in which local communities share similar cultural values.

One particularly interesting geographic segmentation method is based on the anthropomorphic characteristics and socio-cultural characteristics of the population. Anthropomorphic characteristics allow for segmenting the market on the basis of height, average size, and drop. The populations of Northern Europe, for example, are averagely taller and have different sizes and drops than the populations of Southern Europe. Socio-cultural characteristics show attitudes towards the colour and use of certain fabrics (natural rather than synthetic ones), buying habits, and dominant retail formats. Combining the anthropomorphic and socio-cultural characteristics of the population gives seven international macro-segments. Europe is usually divided into two geographical areas: the pan-German area (Germany, Scandinavian countries and Eastern-central), the Latin area (Southern and Mediterranean Europe, and Britain). Asia can be divided into three sub-regions: Japan, the countries of Southeast Asia and Australia, greater China (China, Taiwan and Hong Kong). The American continent divides into North America (the USA and Canada), and Central and Southern America.

14. Regarding this, see J. Garreau, *The Nine Nations of North America*, Anchor Books, 1981.

Socio-demographic segmentation divides the market into groups that share variables like income, age, gender, profession, and family life-cycle stage. The underlying assumption is that consumer behaviours are influenced by these variables. Income is associated with quality products in many markets, including the fashion one. Markets are thus divided into a high, average or low range, and these refer to the income of the different segments.

The socio-demographic variables need to be combined one with the others and they also need to be integrated with other criteria. Although they are very easy to use, and are fundamental for identifying the characteristics of different segments, they do not reveal the motivations that make consumers behave in a certain way. Behavioural segmentation does throw light on these motivations.

Age remains a fundamental criterion for segmenting the fashion market, but the construction and interpretation of segments is very different to the past. The classic age segmentation distinguishes between: kids (5-13 years), adolescents (13-20), young people (20-39), adults (40-65), and old people (over 65 years). Additional segmentation methods have now been developed, among which generational marketing[15]. Starting from the premise that mass marketing is giving way to mass confusion this strategy is supposed to reach consumers right where they live, demographically, socially, and psychologically, thus rendering mass marketing *passé*. A generation is defined by dates of birth, a cohort by important external events that occur during its formative years. In the US, for instance, people born between 1930 and 1939 are often labeled the Depression generation, but those born between 1912 and 1921 are the Depression cohort, since they became adults between 1930 and 1939. In reality, a plethora of names exists for some generations.

What is shown below is an example of one of the most current methodologies on the international scene[16].

- Pre-teen (from 7 to 13): very young but precocious, highly sensitive to fashion and novelty. They come from families that have higher purchase power than in the past (double income), they have few brothers, they

---

15. Strauss W., Howe N., *Generations: The History of America's Future, 1584 to 2069*, William Morrow & Co., 1992.
16. Adapted from *Viewpoint*, n. 6, September 1999; *Street trends, The Sputnik Mini-trends Report*, Harper Business, 1998; T. Polhemus, *Street Styles*, Thames and Hudson, 1994.

tend to have group identity with their age group, they are ambitious and want to imitate young people who are older than them by a few years. This is a very fragmented market

- Teens or net generation (from 14 to 25): they grew up with technology and electronics, they look for everything that is new, they are independent, strongly oriented to consumption but also very mobile in their lifestyle and therefore require products that can follow them. This is a very changeable and trendsetting market
- Generation flex (from 25 to 40): also known as generation X, this was the first post-modern generation. It has experienced important changes in social life (the disappearance of political ideologies, the increase in divorce, new illnesses, flexible work), it is made up of cynical and untrusting consumers who are value-oriented and do not pursue a precise lifestyle
- Boomers (from 40 to 55): the '60s generation, oriented to well being, health and career. It is made up of strong, refined consumers who redefined the life stage formely known as "aging"
- New senior (from 55): given greater life expectancy, this is the generation that will represent an important market in the next ten years in terms of dimension. It is characterised by consumers with young attitudes, strong purchasing power, who are active and independent, oriented to products that fit their specific needs (clothing, travel, fitness).

Some authors put the pre-teen generation, teen and flex groups together into a macro-category known as the visual generation. This group of young, post-modern consumers grew up in a world dominated by the media. It is very sensitive to visual symbols and communication. As symbols nowadays form lifestyles and collective identities, it is necessary to study the symbols rather than political belief, cultural level, or purchasing power, in order to understand this generation. It is a difficult generation to classify by known stereotypes since the purchase and consumption behaviour of the individuals carries the marks of the free choices that make styles, symbols, messages. The anthro-sociologist Ted Polhemus defines the young people in this group as 'style-surfers' or 'symbol surfers'.
At the other extreme of the market are the new seniors. They belong to a segment that will have the greatest demographic strength in the new century, and they are very different to the senior markets of the past. The new seniors are young in spirit, and they will appreciate firms that can lever this characteristic.

Behavioural segmentation
This type of segmentation considers the *individual as a consumer*, and attempts to go beyond descriptive factors to find causal factors that can be used to build market segments.

The main criteria for segmentation are based on purchasing behaviour, lifestyles and benefits.

Segmentation by *purchasing behaviour* is centred on the knowledge, attitudes and reactions of the individual in product purchasing. The purchasing process concerns the evaluation and selection of a product-service-brand combination by the buyer. The individual-buyers are divided on the basis of three variables – user status, occasion of use, and brand loyalty.

With regard to user status, consumers can be grouped into the following categories - non-user, potential user, new user, habitual user and former user.

Occasion of use relates to the purpose or context of use of a specific product, without regard to the consumer's characteristics (this criterion is widely used in fashion, as said in 5.2.1).

The third variable defines different segments on the basis of the level of loyalty towards a product or brand - consumers with strong loyalty towards one brand only, towards two or more brands, occasional loyalty, or not loyal.

Psychographic segmentation considers *how the individual lives.* Lifestyle is a multi-dimensional concept that acquired a great success in many industries. The underlying assumption is that the consumer buys a product reflecting his characteristics and behaviour, both as an individual and in relationship to the reality he lives. For the purposes of demand segmentation, lifestyle has been identified through the *psychographics* approach. This is based substantially on three elements – activities carried out (profession, hobbies, holidays, sports, and so on), personal interests and opinions on various aspects of society (politics, culture, education, and so on).

Psychographic segmentation differs from demographic segmentation because individuals with the same personal details may have different psychographic characteristics. Psychographics is a method that is more tied to the analyst's experience and intuition than to quantitative measures. Despite this, it has been very successful in consumer goods industries. A market for psychographic researches exists in many countries, where lifestyle analyses are regularly produced and diffused.[17]

Benefit segmentation considers *what the individual wants*, with regard to the values and benefits he or she is looking for from the product or brand. The assumption is that someone who buys the same class of products is driven to do so by the search for similar benefits of the same intensity. In the field of cosmetics, for example, possible sets of benefits for a lipstick, could be: long-lasting, lip-drying protection, colouring, and so on.

To define a segment, every set of benefits can be traced to demographic variables (young-adult consumers, of low-high education) and lifestyles (reserved-exhibitionist). Benefit segmentation is used above all for communication campaigns. The advertising tool allows the firm to make the connection that is rarely made by the consumer, between expected benefits and product attributes.

A fundamental criterion in the fashion industry concerns the perceived importance of the fashion content compared with other values such as price and brand prestige. Combining attitudes towards fashion with socio-demographic variables results in three macro-segments - affluent consumers, value oriented consumers and fashion victim consumers.

- Affluent consumers are those who buy a particular product for reasons of status or exhibitionism. They are generally well-off adults or young adults, they tend to be classic in their way of dressing, and they are very brand oriented and fairly brand loyal
- Value oriented consumers are mature and canny, they look for value in the offer as the right mix of price and perceived quality. They belong to the average income segment (but not necessarily), and they are transversal with regard to age
- Fashion victims are usually young consumers. They are fashion concious, and they buy the brand to show that they belong to a certain social group rather than a social class like the affluents. They are not brand loyal and they are transversal with respect to income, although they are willing to spend

---

17. The best known psychographic research companies on the Italian market are Future Concept Lab and GPF & Associati. The best known on the French market is RISC (Research Institute on Social Change). The American market has the 'guru' company Faith Popcorn and the Sputnik network.

The geographic distribution of the three segments is not homogeneous internationally. Affluent consumers are particularly concentrated in Asia and the Middle East, and value oriented consumers in Europe. Fashion victims seem more distributed internationally, and this confirms that young people are increasingly creating a global segment.

From market segmentation to market anticipation

Becoming is by now the only fixed point for modern consumers. Modern individuality is flexible, multidimensional, and it emerges as the aggregation of daily choices rather than as the result of rigid and fixed lifestyles. Lifestyles are not considered as predefined, collective behaviours, but as concepts of the product that are available to consumers and firms in the modern geography of consumerism. Thus personal identity depends increasingly on the characteristics and number of lifestyles that are adopted. In the face of this, the traditional segmentation model has to be replaced by a market *construction* approach that can anticipate consumer needs. The most advanced firms thus go from psychographic segmentation based on lifestyle to segmentation based on *mind set*.[18] The unit of analysis is no longer the individual, but the mental category and behaviour that occurs on the different life occasions.

The fashion firm has to move close to many behaviours through a relational and participatory model rather than an authoritative one. The offer system has to create a sort of friendship with the final consumer. The purpose of this is not just to satisfy current needs, but also to suggest new ways of using the product. There are firms that co-design their product with their customers, allowing a free choice of sizes, colours, accessories and materials. Therefore, it is necessary to move from marketing of territories with its origins in military art (targets, segments, positioning), towards a marketing of flows. Everything here has to be invented, and space must be made for experimentation and for offering consumers whatever they want if they can only imagine it.[19]

---

18. Street Trends, *The Sputnik Minitrends Report*, Harper Business, 1998.
19. M. D'Andrea, in F. Morace, *Metatendenze. Percorsi, prodotti e progetti per il terzo millennio*, Sperling & Kupfer, 1996, p. 272.

6 The process of strategic positioning

6.1 The basic theory of positioning

After segmenting demand and selecting the desired market segments, the firm has to position itself within the market. Positioning choices[1] are the most important element of the competitive strategy. They are the guiding criteria for developing a marketing mix that is intrinsically consistent, as well as consistent with the development of the environmental context.

Despite this, many firms' advertising or merchandise and distribution choices show that there has been no positioning project, or a change of it from season to season. Positioning is not a discretionary choice for firms, but a necessity to avoid market confusion.

---

1. The term 'positioning' first appeared in marketing literature in 1969 (Ries and Trout). In strategic management, Porter introduced the idea of strategy as positioning. Porter founded the Positioning School in 1980. The concept goes back to the times of Sun Tzu (400 BC), however, who published a treatise on the art of war which was the first manual where the concept of strategy was suggested as positioning.

Positioning involves placing the product or brand system within a defined system of perceptions of the selected target. The objective is to generate lasting and sustainable differentiation between the firm and its competitors. In this sense it is possible to talk about a move from a *convenience* or *shopping* approach, towards a *speciality* one, that is the creation of a basis for uniqueness in the market. Positioning is not performed in the market but in the consumer's mind. It is carried out through a series of actions that give the offer system a unique semantic space. Perceptive factors play a fundamental role in the consumer's evaluation and choice of a product or brand. Products are perceived as a set of tangible and intangible attributes, each one of which has a different relative importance (degree of attribute presence) and a given intensity (presence). Differentiation makes sense, but differentiation costs of are only worth paying if the consumer perceives the differentiation and considers it as determining. In fashion particularly, where the consumer buys emotions rather than tangible elements, understanding the importance of the product's perceived features is fundamental. Given the symbolic nature of the fashion product, it could be said that competition takes place among *messages* rather than among *products*.

Positioning is traditionally carried out with reference to a number of factors, and the firm chooses the most important of these for its own target:

- *Product attributes*: physical and tangible product features, such as the materials used, durability, resistance, care over details, and so on. In the case of clothes, it is often difficult to differentiate the product just on the basis of physical or functional attributes. Removing the label from ten pairs of jeans or ten pairs of shoes would make it difficult to recognise the brand of the producer. Further, given the difficulty that the non-expert consumer has in understanding the value of materials, finishing and construction, it would also be difficult to attribute a price to those products. Functional and performance characteristics are easier to attribute in other industries: for example, cars, consumer durables and services

- *Benefits* or *values associated with the product*: they refer to those intangible values expressed by the product that are meaningful for the target and are mainly expressed through communication – seduction for Versace, exclusivity for Hermes, durability and strength for Caterpillar, irony for Diesel. The consumer seeks benefits, not attributes, even if he or she does ignore the relationship between the expected benefit and the product attribute
- For *specific functions or occasions of use*: in this case the product is positioned with respect to particular occasions of use, often out of traditional ones. An example might be sports jackets for formal urban occasions, or the item that can suit different occasions
- With respect to *benchmark competitors*: the positioning of competitors is both a limit and an opportunity for new positioning. It is a limit because it is very hard to to take possession of some attributes or values already covered by competitors, unless clear incremental advantages are being offered. It is an opportunity because the firm can try to innovate old and static market positions. The innovative positioning of Diesel compared to the market leader Levi's in the jeans industry can be seen as an example of this.

Positioning in fashion is usually based on *dressing style*. Although the clothing expresses the values of an individual, the dressing style matches different ways of defining the clothing need. Dressing styles are defined on the basis of the dominant social identities and lifestyles and represent a continuum from classic to contemporary and avant-garde.

Table 6.1 shows three established dress styles for women's clothing. These correspond to specific consumer benefits and features of the firm's offer.

The positioning of brands within the clothing industry is achieved through the so called *dressing style-value matrix*. This was originally introduced in American distribution in the 1980s. It was then adopted in Italy, first by the COIN group and then by Gruppo Finanziario Tessile. This matrix allows for translating market trends into consistent positioning strategies, and for the evaluation of competitors. Dressing style is on the horizontal

TABLE 6.1 **DRESSING STYLES AND CHARACTERISTICS OF THE OFFER SYSTEM**

	CLASSIC/ TRADITIONAL	MODERN/ CONTEMPORARY	AVANT-GARDE
DRESS FUNCTION	Dress for covering	Dress to be interpreted	Dress to be exhibited
SYSTEM OF SIGNS	Seriousness	Essentiality	Recognizable
STYLISTIC CODES	Materials and details	Shapes	Colors, accessories
LIFE OCCASIONS (CORE)	All	Day time	Special occasions
PERSONALITY	Classic	Up to date	Eccentric

Source: the authors.

TABLE 6.2 **THE DRESSING STYLE-VALUE MATRIX IN WOMENSWEAR**

	CLASSIC	CONTEMPORARY	AVANT-GARDE
DESIGNER	Valentino	Armani, Calvin Klein	Jean Paul Gaultier Martin Margiela
DIFFUSION	Burberry's Boss Women Valentino Roma	Armani collezioni, Ferrè studio, Max Mara, Strenesse	D&G Cheap and Chic
BRIDGE	CP Company	Emporio Armani Max&Co, Charactere	Diesel Style Lab
MASS	Benetton	Stefanel	

Source: the authors.

axis (classic/traditional – contemporary – avant-garde), and market segmentation on the basis of price bands on the vertical axis (designer – diffusion – bridge – mass). The firm can formulate a product, distribution and communication strategy within each grid that is consistent with the positioning that is sought in terms of price and dressing style. *Table 6.2* shows the positioning of some womenswear brands on the Italian market.

Positioning is based on distinctive differences that have to be:

- *Meaningful for the target*: if the positioning follows market segmentation the profile of benefits that the target expects would have to be known. Otherwise, there would be a risk of 'shooting in the dark' and this would mean there would be no customer loyalty or learning process within the firm

- *Communicable*: no positioning, no matter how clever and innovative it is, can be successful if it is not effectively communicated to the target. The product cannot speak. Communication requires that the positioning is easily recognisable, simple, and clear. There are quite often inconsistencies between product features and the image that is expressed through communication in fashion. This is because positioning is not clear, or not clearly perceived by those responsible for communication (the advertising agency). The move from expected benefit to perceived attribute is not automatic in the consumer's mind. Thus, positioning can only be achieved through an effective communication

- *Profitable*: the costs of creating differentiation and the bases of uniqueness (differentiation costs) have to be lower than the price premium that the final customer pays for differentiation. At least in Italy, the costs of developing samples and collections, the costs of fashion shows and the pricing process have been greatly ignored. The costs of the collection are usually only taken into account at the end of the season, and prices are usually defined adding the desired mark up on costs without any reference to the market and to competitors. This practice could be tolerated while the market was growing and the increasing margins absorbed a firm's inefficiencies. Now that the market is not growing, all the product variety generating costs should be evaluated as part of the firm's whole market strategy.

Positioning the brand in a new segment. The Levi's Tailored Classic case

At the beginning of the 1980s the American jeanswear leader, Levi's, was facing market saturation in the American jeans market. The management wanted to explore the possibility of using the Levi's brand to enter a new, strongly developing, segment – formal menswear. The segment of young male adults who were oriented towards classic and quality clothing (known as 'classic independents') was in relative growth in the US. This was compared to the 'price shopper' (price and basic product oriented) and 'trendy casual' (fashion oriented) segments. A new positioning strategy for the new segment was formulated – a high quality product with a 'tailor made' image, a price premium, and distribution through department stores. Focus groups tested the project, and these resulted in a positive evaluation of the physical product, but a negative perception of the Levi's brand associations with formal clothing. 'I would feel awkward saying that my tailored suit is branded Levi's, because Levi's is mass market jeans,' said one interviewee. The management decided to go ahead anyway. The objective was to 'convince the market' of the offer's soundness. It was decided to launch the new product, Levi's Tailored Classic, in 1982, and to support the launch with a strong television promotion. The project was unsuccessful, and after a few years Levi's was forced to withdraw.

What had gone wrong? The firm had not listened to the market or understood the new segment. It had thus run into problems of competition, price and image, and for its part, the market had refused to legitimise the historic brand identity of Levi's in the new territory. The gap between the identity of Levi's in five pockets jeans and formal wear was too great, as shown in *Table 6.3*.

TABLE 6.3   **THE LEVI'S IDENTITY AND CLASSIC-FORMAL IDENTITY**

LEVI'S BRAND IDENTIFIED VALUES	CHARACTERISTIC OF THE NEW SEGMENT
Wild West	Conformism
Casual	Classic
Perceived quality: duration e resistance	Perceived quality: tailoring details
Occasions of use: leisure time	Occasions of use: workwear

Source: the authors.

The firm also made a mistake in positioning on distribution, selecting the department store as a channel. Department stores work on the basis of profit per square metre, and this meant that Levi's had to progressively reduce its price in order to increase volumes. Its communication media, television, was also wrong. It failed to reach the selected target (classic independents), which was more oriented to reading magazines.

6.2 Positioning and value of the offer system

The firm and brand positioning relates to consumer perceptions of the value created by the entire offer system. Indeed the consumer considers the product as embodying several attributes and qualities, all affecting value. The value associated with an offer system in the case of problematic goods like fashion, results from several features: the product, the price, the firm, the retailing space, all interacting among themselves as in *Figure 6.1*. Perceived value results as a difference between the offer system perceived quality and the price. Where this difference is positive there will be value for the consumer.

The first group of value drivers concerns *product features*. A distinction can be made between:

- Tangible attributes (physical, functional and performance)
- Intangible attributes (style, image, value elements and emotional benefits sought).

The second group of value drivers concerns *features of the offer system* other than the product. These include: retail strategy (formats, layout, visual merchandising, assortments), the level of

FIGURE 6.1   **VIEW OF THE VALUE CREATED BY THE OFFER SYSTEM**

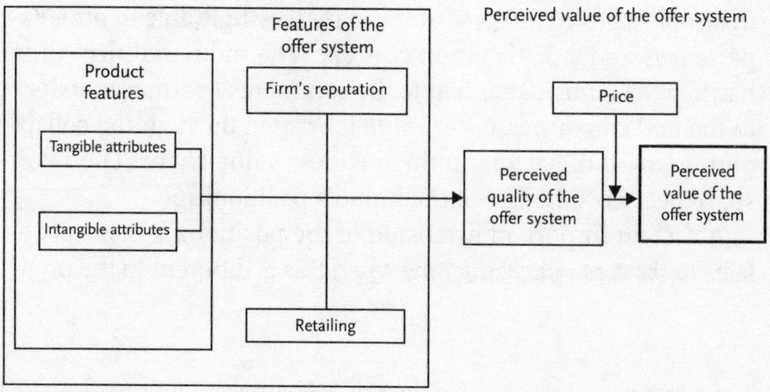

Source: the authors.

service provided in the store (replenishment, tailor-made and after-sales service), and the firm's reputation (prestige, reliability, innovation and credibility). By putting together all the information that is available to him, the consumer will be able to form a judgement about the quality of the offer system, its ability to satisfy the benefits that are being sought.

The final element concerns the consumer's *perceived value*. As already mentioned this is the difference between the perceived quality of the offer system and the price that is asked.[2] If pricing is not correct, perceived quality is not enough to justify the purchase. The critical issue is that while the price is always certain, the quality of a fashion offer system is the result of a subjective judgement of the consumer's that is affected by many individual factors.

The emphasis on perceived value places the consumer at the centre of strategic thinking, rather than the competition. This encourages firms to plan new ways of satisfying the consumer and solving his or her problems. Further, the perceived value approach allows for pushing beyond the product characteristics themselves, so that the product is like a 'work in progress'. Other elements of the offer system can be progressively added to it in the consumer's mind, and the firm may not be able to control these, or may not pay attention to them, with the result that it loses the desired value.

An important extension of the concept of positioning concerns *distributive positioning*. Distribution is increasingly less interested in simple sales of the product, and increasingly able to offer experiences and a distribution concept. The industrial firm thus has to pay as much attention to the commercial partner as it does to the end consumer. Offer value is created through the collaboration of all the actors in the business value chain. The retail space becomes the test of the brand's positioning.

A second important extension of the positioning concept relates to *the corporate positioning* when this is different to the prod-

---

2. For more on the topic of see W. Chan Kim, R. Mauvborgne, 'Strategy, value innovation and the knowledge economy', in *Sloan Management Review*, Spring 1999.

uct/brand positioning (corporate brand versus product/line brand). The concept of corporate reputation is increasingly important as a guarantee of the entire commercial offer. It is more than brand image. Reputation is an asset and it is built through reliability, service and credibility. It is a value that extends from the market to the network of suppliers, up to the financial community and anyone working with the firm.[3]

6.3 From product positioning to brand positioning

Up to now the discussion of positioning has taken no account of the differences between the product and the brand. In reality, the brand is increasingly the pivotal factor in fashion strategies. The brand has moved from an ancillary position to becoming an asset and a value driver for the whole business. Further, the brand emerges as the area of convergence between production, distribution and consumption.

Brand management is nowadays a very complex process. It is designed to assemble and maintain a mix of tangible attributes and intangible values over time. These attributes and values are significant for the customer and they make an effective distinction between the *identity* of the brand on the market and other competing products. A better understanding of the brand and its role with regard to the product starts from the correct definition of the term 'brand'. Kotler[4] gives one of the most quoted definitions of the brand. Kotler's definition was taken up by the American Association Committee on Definition in 1960. It says that a brand is 'a name, term, symbol or design, or a combination of these, that is intended to identify goods or services from one or more sellers, and to differentiate it from those of competitors'. This definition, despite its acceptance and diffusion, does not reflect the whole strategic potential associated with the brand in current competitive contexts. The brand definition that

---

3. For more on the concept of reputation in fashion, see C.J. Fombrum, *Reputation*, Harvard Business School Press, 1996, p. 231.
4. Cf. P.M. Kotler, *Marketing Management*, Prentice-Hall, 1997.

is used here is the following: 'the aggregation, within specific signs of recognition, of a complex of values, associations, expectations, to which customers attribute a value that goes beyond the technical and functional attributes of the products that are identified by the brand itself'.[5]

According to the definition that has been suggested, the concept of brand thus seems to consist of two elements:

- A *material element* that relates to the brand's system of signs (name, logo, colours, pay offs and advertising jingles). These have a primary role in identifying the brand and products associated with it, as well as guaranteeing the quality/performance of the products. These brand functions reduce the consumer information and selection costs in a complex competitive environment
- An *intangible element* that relates to the *associations* evoked by the brand in the consumer's mind. The relationship between the brand and consumers has 'perceptive' connotations that refer to the consumer's generation of a mental representation of the object in question (brand image) which summarises both the tangible elements (the physical characteristics and functions of the product) and emotional factors (the material and symbolic contents).

The art of branding originates from semiotics as the brand constructs a meaning in the mind of consumer. One definition interprets the semiotic nature of the brand as 'the set of discourses about the brand among all the subjects involved'.[6] If this is true firms cannot have control over brand positioning unless they control brand identity as this is perceived by the market. The concept of brand identity has only been fully examined in the literature recently. Kapferer, a brand management expert, defines it in this way: 'It starts as a meaningless word related to a product and then, year after year, the word acquires an autonomous meaning that is determined by communication and products

---

5. Cf. C. Zara (editor), *La marca e la creazione del valore di impresa*, Etas, 1997.
6. A. Semprini (edited by), *Lo sguardo semiotico*, Franco Angeli, 1997.

from the past. Over time brand identity defines an area of legitimate possibility...'.[7]

6.3.1 The relationship between brand and product in fashion

The brand becomes a strategic lever for differentiating the offer and making the firm's competitive advantage sustainable. This is particularly the case with fashion products, where symbolic and evocative elements dominate over technical and functional ones. By its very nature, fashion is linked to a short-term time horizon, the *season*, and this has led firms to put a strong emphasis on product oriented strategies. Nowadays, however, products are substantially *homogeneous*, and stylistic innovation is limited to a few large international brands, while an adequate quality/price ratio is taken for granted within almost all the market segments. The consumer and distribution express an individuality and identity that is increasingly independent from the industry. The modern consumer, according to his or her lifestyle, considers as leaders a few products and brands within a specific market segment. Distribution selects a few strategic industrial suppliers at an international level. Both the consumer and distribution require a long-term relationship with the firm. This relation cannot be based upon the product, which is subject to change as it is to fashion. Brand identity allows for the creation of a bridge between the short and long-term period, between the product and the market. The ability to create a lasting, self-nurturing relationship with the consumer depends above all on the strategic management of the brand. The distinction between brand and product becomes fundamental. Products are what the firm produces, but the brand is what the consumer buys. Further, while products have ever shorter life cycles, the brand can escape the effect of time and represent a lasting asset for the firm.

The brand is even more than a marketing variable; brand management is a strategic process that begins before the marketing plan has even been formulated. Brand management involves all

---

7. J. N. Kapferer, *Strategic Brand management*, Free Press, 1992, pp. 38-39.

the resources and functions of the firm being focused on one strategic objective – differentiating the firm's offer by supplying an ideal combination of tangible and intangible attributes to a specific group of consumers. In this way the product is no longer the result of seasonal creativity alone, but the consequence of a consistent business strategy.

6.3.2 Defining brand identity

The brand is a phenomenon that is in constant development, as a result of the conversations that are held about it.[8] A brand emerges as related to a product; through communication strategy and product diversification the brand is gradually endowed with attributes, images, associations, all forming a certain identity. Therefore, over time brand identity develops from being *product attribute* to representing a firm's *economic asset*. This development pattern is not spontaneous, but is the result of specific strategic interventions. These can be divided into three stages (*Figure 6.2*).

FIGURE 6.2   **THE EVOLVING BRAND-PRODUCT RELATIONSHIP**

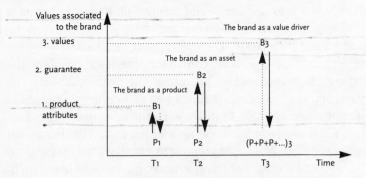

B = brand P = product (P+P+P...) = groups of products

Source: adapted from Kapferer, 1992.

---

8. A. Semprini, *op. cit.*

- *Stage T1: The brand as a product.* At the beginning, brand power is limited to distinguishing a firm's product from those of other firms, through a system of signs (name, logo, and so on). During this first stage the products contain the elements of differentiation, and they give significance to the brand. Thus, in the words of Kapferer, a brand = a product = a promise

- *Stage T2: the brand as an asset.* Over time, and as the result of actions taken by the firm, the brand acquires its own personality, different from the product. The brand, acting above all as a guarantee, represents the reason for the consumer to repeat the same purchase. Brand identity is associated with a complex of benefits that go beyond mere product attributes. Line extensions start here (i.e.from womenswear to accessories). The brand represents an asset for the firm

- *Stage T3: the brand as a value driver.* The brand relationship with the product is reversed; the brand communicates an autonomous identity, this also increases the potential for extension in new product categories. The extension may be related or unrelated. Examples of this process of extension are Benetton (from sports clothing to motor sport), Swatch (from watches to spectacles, telephones and cars), and Virgin (from records to airlines and soft drinks).

The huge success of the Nike brand was based on the happy intuition of its founder, Philip Hampson Knight. He understood before anyone else that sports shoes had become a commodity, and that brand image or shoe style had to be the pivot of the business offer, given that it was difficult to differentiate one shoe from another. Knight borrowed the concept of the seasonal collection from the world of fashion, and brought out new styles every season. Even best selling models like the Air Jordan were given new colours every three months. It was reckoned that on average Nike brought out a new model of shoe every day.[9] Brand identity was built on the concept of sport, which the entrepreneur regarded as 'American culture but in a world language'. Intense sponsorship of successful athletes connected the brand with the everyday world of young consumers and the values

9. R. Lane, 'You are what you wear', in *Forbes 400*, 14 October, 1996.

evoked referred to the athletic ideals of determination, individualism, sacrifice and, above all, victory. It is not by chance that Nike is the Greek goddess of victory.

The emphasis on brand management and the building of strong identities, that is the move from stage T1 to stages T2 and T3 of the brand development path, is already a priority within mature markets where products look almost undifferentiated to consumers. The soft drinks industry, airline services, the car industry and insurance services are all examples of industries where products have exhausted their communication potential and brand identity became a point of reference for the consumer. It is more difficult in fashion to make a clear distinction between stage T1 (product attributes) and stage T3 (values) during the process of brand identity building. When a brand is born (or repositioned) it can directly enter the value stage (T3). Designers labels do this, where the brand is immediately associated with the designer 'world' and taste, and are able to support a wide range of products. In the case of jeans, where products are not really differentiated, the brand almost exclusively communicates values (a recent example is Diesel or the Japanese brand Evisu).

The process of brand identity building also depends on the type of actor who owns the brand. Every brand owner in the fashion world has a precise brand mission that depends on the actor's own characteristics and know-how:

- *Specialised industrial brand*: the brand belongs to an industrial firm with a credibility that is tied to a distinct product know-how. Brand identity comes into existence as a result of product attributes and manufacturing skills. Ermenegildo Zegna, an Italian premium brand competing in the high end of the menswear market, has strong skills in wool spinning and weaving and is well known as one of the producers of woolen fabrics and elegant men's suits. The company never extended the brand to womenswear as the original brand identity was related to the concept of masculinity and acted as a guarantee of tailored details.
- *Fashion house with a designer*: in this case there is a *griffe* (=

designer label) with a credibility tied to an area of taste and to the designer's creativity.[10] Extension to different product categories (from clothing to accessories, cosmetics and homewear) is a natural development for a designer brand whose competence is associated with style and not to manufacturing skills

- *Retail brand*: brand identity is linked to the ability to offer a retailing service that starts with the sale of retail concepts, and finishes with 'experiential shopping' and 'relational sales'. The retail brands are nowadays the most fought over actors in the competitive arena of the fashion system, and there are very different brand identities – a specialised identity for end uses in the case of the sport inspired brand Decathlon, and the refined Anglosaxon world of travel that is evoked by the Banana Republic stores.

In the move from sales-oriented distribution towards concept-oriented distribution, the retail brand and the distributor's private label are two fundamental strategic levers. Modern distribution keeps in its assortment a few leading industrial brands for each category, a few private labels, and perhaps some industrial brands with a good price positioning, and there is a progressive elimination of weak industrial brands. These often become the subcontractors for private labels. This trend has an important implication. Multi-brand industrial firms should concentrate their resources so as to carry just one brand to the top of their own category, instead of dispersing resources into several, barely differentiated brands.

---

10. In the high end of the fashion market there is sometimes confusion between the word griffe and the word brand. The concept of the griffe is associated with the creative sign of an inspired mind. The world of griffes is thus the world of creation, of something unique that cannot be reproduced. The brand, on the other hand, does not come into existence as a unique work, but is part of an industrial series. Griffes can become brands, but brands cannot become griffes.

6.3.3 Brand identity levers

Brand identity is never defined through a single business decision. It derives from the interaction of many dimensions, within and without the firm. For fashion firms, brand identity defines itself in relation to four elements of the business system – the firm's history, stylistic identity, visual identity and retail identity.

History is one of the most valuable assets belonging to a brand: Guerlain (1829), Zegna (1910) and Levi's (1853) have a fundamental role in defining the brand authenticity and standing. History also discloses the original know-how on which the brand grew and built up a credible positioning. A brand obtains its legitimization and potential for growth from the know-how that the market attributes to the firm. The antique Hermes's saddlers have developed today into a wide range of luxury accessories, all associated with craftsmanship, skilled employment of leather and the concept of travel. History and know-how are the starting point, and often also the basis for the building of a credible brand identity.

Stylistic identity is determined by the stylistic codes that are a permanent character of the firm's products, as well as the development of the seasonal offer. These codes can relate to forms, materials, colours, details and also types of product (the colour jumper for Missoni, soft colours and relaxed cuts for Armani, and nylon for Prada). The stylistic codes are particularly important in market segments where the product is central.

Visual identity is defined by the permanent communication codes that are a feature of the firm's communication, and that make it unique and recognisable. Until recently communication was 'ancillary' to sales for fashion firms. Communication was mainly reduced to product advertising in specialised magazines. The result was communication homogeneity and overcrowding, and it was difficult to distinguish between different brands. Communication has to move away from the product; it needs to have a strategic role and communicate the firm's positioning. Brand identity is different from brand image. Image is associated with the reception of a message, and this is influenced by external signals. Brand identity refers to the act of transmitting image and communication codes. It is thus a message from the sender.

Retail identity became increasingly important in the 1990s. This was partly because of the development of distribution in innovative forms, and partly because of the progressive vertical integration of many industrial brands. Retail identity refers to the way in which the offer system is presented to the market. It is therefore concerned with an integrated system of choices, in the sense of localisation, channel, assortment, sales point communication and level of service. All these are included in the *distributive concept* which should be unique for each brand. *Visual merchandising*, which was previously concerned essentially with communication and promotion at the sales point, has been broadened, starting with information flows. It now includes animation and the design of environments. It thus requires integrated know-how for environment design, marketing and visual communication. Sales point service includes the traditional features of reception and technical assistance for the consumer, but also accessory services such as the exchange of goods, tailoring, home delivery and loyalty cards. Just as the product area should have its own guidelines in terms of stylistic identity, so retail identity should be codified into a manual like those used in a franchising system.

There should be a very strong consistency between retailing, stylistic and visual identity in fashion. Product, distribution and communication strategies have to be inspired, from season to season, by the permanent codes that support brand identity. "Dynamism in permanence" is perhaps the most important concept in fashion brand management together with the the issue of maintaining relevance for new generations.

Armani's identity pervades the whole firm, the environments and the atmospheres, starting from the designer's real lifestyle. The symbolic system is immediately recognisable, whether it relates to products, stores or communication. Thanks to his apprenticeship in industry and later partnership with large manufacturing firms, Armani has been successful in imposing a professional image as a designer who can mediate between market demand and seasonal creativity. From his first collections onwards, Armani was able to interpret the needs of modern women. The Armani style was never imposed from above. It followed the woman, her way of living, and her personality. The Armani jacket has always been recognised for its essential refinement, tailoring, its distinctive shoulder, and a certain style of button. The advertising campaigns make limited use of expressive signs, but they create a very strong link between the language of the model's body and the style of her clothes. The woman in Armani communication always seems more emphasised than the product, in the dressing for success period of the 1980s, in her autonomy and achievement in the late 1980s, and in her affirmation of romanticism and sensuality or her free interpretation of styles as in the 1990s. The designer manages all communication directly. Despite different photographers, models or media, the communication is always recognisable for its harmony of style and taste.

6.4 Positioning and innovation

We already mentioned that the essence of successful positioning is dynamism in permanence. Meeting the demands of a dynamic market leads to a continuous change of the offer system, and this is particularly true of industries with a high rate of innovation. The fashion system continuously faces the problem of the 'organising what is new'. It is thus important to distinguish between strategic positioning and the operational effectiveness of its implementation. Changing does not mean changing strategic positioning. Successful firms carry their positioning forward over time, but through the continuous development and improvement of their operating effectiveness, which means the individual details of the offer system (product, service and communication). A change of competitive position, which is usually a rare event, is only necessary when the fundamental needs and values of the target (the customer) change, or when the technology or offer system are imitated.

 The fundamental problem in fashion is how to make the firm's brand identity co-exist with innovation and change. The profitable, long-term survival of firms depends on the intrinsic fit and match between the offer evolution and the evolution of the collective imaginary, rather than on simply anchoring brand identity to a 'winning' product. Individual products have to evolve as a result of the development of fashion, but at the same time the offer has to remain anchored to the deeper 'meaning' of brand identity. It is clear that the collective imaginary has a longer life-cycle than fashions, even if both are destined sooner or later to fade away. The trick is the ability to make the brand evolve together with the social imaginary of reference.

A correct brand positioning allows for interpreting social change in a way that is consistent with the firm's own target. It is said that fashion changes every six months. Thus, firms which do not have a profoundly rooted and widespread brand identity attempt a *revolution* in stylistic codes and communication. The construction of brand value requires, however, an *evolution* every six months in the firm's stylistic codes and communication, interpreting the development of the market with regard to the firm's own brand identity. This implies that those involved in the product and in creativity are always in touch with the 'custodians' of brand identity. These custodians may be the entrepreneur, the marketing managers, or the brand managers. Change naturally requires a constant process of adapting business know-how. New opportunities can be seized by integrating the current stock of know-how with new ones that have been developed internally or brought into the firm.

7   The process of product and collection development

7.1 Creative and managerial processes in the fashion product development

The seasonal renewal of collections, which has been the element of innovation in the Italian fashion system, was centred on the product. Designers and the product department were responsible for designing and industrialising the product. This also included intervening on commercial and economic variables that were not related to their specific know-how. The creative persons' dominion was even more important in the French model of *haute couture* and luxury ready-to-wear. Therefore for a long time the stylistic and aesthetic value of the physical product dominated over other variables such as market segmentation, pricing and service. Nowadays this kind of dominance survives within those few international firms that are able to create and impose new fashion trends. For firms that are not part of this élite, however, the need to make the product orientation fit with market orientation is urgent. This is why there must be a continuous search for a balance between the two fundamental components of the product system in fashion. The first component is related to the long-term strategic choices determining competitive positioning and the stylistic identity of the firm; the second component is more related to seasonal themes, and it is necessary for guaranteeing the end consumer a continuous product innovation. The process of product development in fashion can be defined as the integration of two sub-processes. The first of these focuses on the definition of aesthetic components, and is dominated by the creative people. The second is focused on the definition of economic and competitive targets, and is dominated by managers. The seasonal analysis of aesthetic-technical trends (shapes, colours and materials) is usually the area dominated by the creative people. This has to lead to renewing the firm's stylistic codes from season to season, without distorting the firm's stylistic identity.

The interpretation of long-term socio-cultural trends, market analysis (consumer and trade) and analysis of the previous season's sales, however, have to be carried out by commercial or product management. The objective here is to define the entire offer system in terms of brands, the number of collections, merchandising, end uses, and models/variants.

The two processes should be performed in parallel, even if they have to converge in the definition of the seasonal collection whose aim is to integrate aesthetic creativity and commercial strategy.

Having a strong positioning and being oriented to market needs allows for filtering and interpreting trends in an original way, and it avoids the domination of pure aesthetic logic. In firms that do not have designers with strong personalities, focusing on product results in a levelling of the offers. On the other hand, the interplay of management and creativity creates an interdisciplinary area of extreme richness, that is the essence of the fashion system. Regarding the product development process, the management of creativity should be able to create a system that is consistent at different levels – short term versus long-term, aesthetic versus commercial variables as indicated in *Figure 7.1*.

At this time we want to propose a definition of some key terms, particularly the difference between fashion, style and design. Where *fashion* is trendy, fosters change and progress and faces

FIGURE 7.1   **CREATIVITY AND MANAGEMENT IN PRODUCT DEVELOPMENT**

	SHORT TERM	LONG TERM
Aesthetic variables	Stylistic themes of the collection	Stylistic identity
Competitive variables	Collection Architecture	Corporate and brand identity and competitive positioning

Source: the authors.

the future, *style* isn't trendy, but, as observed by Polhemus (1995), it is inherently conservative and traditional, making use of permanent stylistic codes and decorations. The example of primitive societies is illuminating. The tattoos of the Maori and the tattoo patterns of some African peoples all serve to resist change and to mark membership in a social group. A style is a distinctive form or quality, a manner of expression[1] that can apply to clothing (crew neck versus turtle neck or denim versus gabardine), cars (convertibles versus station wagons), art (pop art versus art deco). Within a specific style, decorations, patterns and texture may change; individual interpretations of the same style are called *designs*. When a style becomes popular many different designs of that style can be produced. A style does not become a fashion until it gains consumer acceptance at any given time.

7.2 From the analysis of trends to the definition of creative concepts

The need to make seasonal trends structural and consistent with the timing of the textile pipeline is a key point in fashion. The top of the pipeline, with its very extended working times, has to make the new materials available on time to meet the deadlines of the manufacturers of the final products. In this sense, defining trends in fibres and yarns is fundamental in order to pro-

---

1. Schmitt B, Simonson A., *Marketing Aesthetic*, The Free Press, 1997, p. 84.

pose a direction to designers in the clothing business. If the trend identifies the direction in which fashion is moving, it is the market that decides whether the trend is widespread and medium term, or can only be exploited for a single season. Understanding the degree of a trend's permanence is thus the most delicate and risky aspect for fashion firms. These firms operate within general institutionalised trends, and they have to find the proper route for each of them that is also consistent with their own stylistic identity and brand positioning.

The process of trend forecasting is nowadays formalised by well defined actors and institutions. Rather than originating from intuition and crystal balls, seasonal trends emerge from a well defined process of research and information sharing, and from the interpretation of individual firms.

General fashion trends emerge from the interaction of three actors in the textile pipeline:

- *Bureaux du Style* are the first to start. Mainly based in France, they identify emerging general trends likely to have an effect on the textile industry in the following years. They work as groups of sociologists, designers, producers and materials experts and collaborate with national and international opinion leaders to produce and sell information about general trends. This information becomes available in *Cahiers du Style* which cover different areas (colours, yarns, cloths, print designs, and so on)
- Fibre producers and/or the international secretariats for natural and synthetic fibres. They carry out their own research and/or interpret the suggestions from Bureaux du Style. They manage information about trends as a service to their own customers. They are thus the first producers to give information about fashion trends as they have to design their product 24 months before it comes out on the market
- Product Fairs for semi-finished goods (yarns and textiles) such as Pitti, Premiere Vision, Interstoff and Moda In Tessuto. Fairs are the final stage in the process of seasonal trends development, as well as the occasions for gathering,

comparing and discussing trends from the Bureaux du Style and fibre producers. Trends displayed at textile Fairs become input for the lower stages of the pipeline (clothing producers). Textile firms contribute to emerging trends with their own interpretation of general trends, as a way of presenting their own sample collections of yarns and textiles to their clients.

Seasonal trends are strengthened in the commercial relationship between the different actors of the pipeline. The producers of yarns and textiles interact with their own opinion leader manufacturer customers to finalise the features of the seasonal offer. It is at this stage that general trends are finally incorporated into a finished product.

An important stage in fashion trend forecasting is the identification of *social and consumer trends*. Consumer trend analysis is an additional tool for research based on the identification of mega trends in society that sooner or later can result in fashion trends or can affect the future behaviour of fashion clients. These trends originate from evolutions in social values and identities. Further, the increasing integration of industrialised economies means that these trends are increasingly common to different countries. Consumer trend analysis is an empirical rather than a scientific analysis and is focused on the observation of social and cultural phenomena. At the international level, there are some well known trend experts who regularly publish trend analyses that fall halfway between sociology and marketing. They include, among others, the Americans Naisbitt, Toffler and Popcorn, the French RISC institute, and the Italian institutes GPF & Associati and Trend's Lab.[2]

Fashion firms can receive many suggestions from the outside, but it is only an ongoing process of internal research that transforms external inputs into original and innovative products.

---

2. Significant texts on trend analysis have included: J. Naisbitt, *Megatrends*, Warner Books, 1982, and *Megatrends 2000*, William and Morrow Company Inc., 1990; A. Toffler, *Future Shock*, Bantam, 1970, *Third Wave*, Mass Market Paperback, 1991, *Powershift: Knowledge, Wealth and Violence at the Edge of the 21st Century*, Mass Market Paperback, 1991.

Usually fashion firms can count on two sources of internal research:

1. Exploratory marketing research
2. Exploratory technical research in the product-style area.

Exploratory marketing research draws on many sources, and these can be divided into two groups:

- Trend analysis. This allows medium and long-term market forecasts of a socio-cultural nature to be made. They relate both to society as a whole and to the specific business target. Few firms develop medium and long-term socio-cultural research as an internal activity. They usually purchase consumer trend researches that are carried out by external professionals (psychographic researches)[3]. To be effective, this research should be anchored to those socio-cultural features that are more interesting for supporting the single firm's positioning
- The second group of sources concerns relationships with actors in the competitive system. Industry fairs, visits to customers and suppliers, and the systemic analysis of competitors are important sources for analysing market trends and testing the market positioning of the firm.

Research in the product area is not limited to receiving inputs from marketing. It usually goes forward with its own exploratory activities. As in the case of marketing, exploratory product research is fed from aesthetic-technical areas:

- Technology: machinery, finishing processes, specialised fairs, industry representatives, and technical journals
- Market: specialised fairs, style consultants, magazines
- Product: developments in yarns and textiles, colouring agents, products for finishing.

---

3. Regarding this, see 5.3.2 of *Chapter 5*.

A designer with a strong personality will generally not adhere fully to market trends, but will develop them in an original way. Designer research follows routes that are not classifiable. Sources of inspiration come from history, from art, from architecture, and from nature, and over time they are collected within personal archives that represent a valuable asset for the firm.

FIGURE 7.2   **THE EXPLORATORY RESEARCH PROCESS IN FASHION FIRMS**

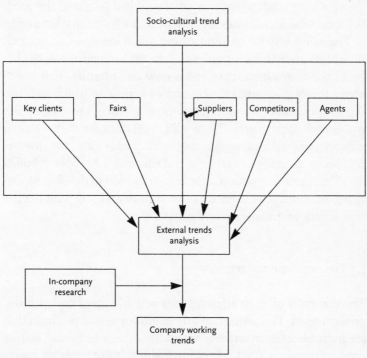

Source: the authors.

Overriding seasonal trends can give a firm an image of creativity and innovation, but we have to remember that general trends are accessible to the whole market and risk making products alike. Further, unlike the past when trends were clear, the market is increasingly unpredictable, complex and contradictory. Fashion cycles themselves are much more variable nowadays.

In order to cope with several trends firms tend to increase the variety of their offer, generating heavy costs in terms of quality and service. At the opposite extreme, however, a detailed customer observation may not be enough for understanding the market. Asking the end user, or even the intermediary, what he or she needs means creating a product that is already old and out of fashion. The fashion system needs to anticipate the market, and it is just this need that underlies the conflicts that are typical of fashion firms. Such conflicts involve the commercial areas, which tend to push for what sold last year, and the product area, which cultivates an anticipatory view of market needs.

The safest way for creating strong brand identities, is one that interprets both fashion trends and the end consumer on the basis of the firm's distinctive know-how and identity. This is not about forecasting what the consumer wants, so much as offering the consumer the development of a concept that he or she has already appreciated. The development of exploratory research on social and fashion trends at company level eases the interaction between creative, marketing and commercial people. It builds up a corporate learning platform from which to develop inputs and guidelines for the entire offer system and it represents the real source of distinction and innovation.

7.3 The seasonal collection

The company offer in all industries is made up of one or more product lines. The concept of line identifies sets of products that are homogeneous in terms of functions, occasions for use and/or product category. The key word in fashion is not 'lines' so much as 'collections'.

The collection is based on the season. Just like the line, the collection is a set of products grouped according to different criteria. Historically, the collection comes from French *haute couture* where the *couturier* usually presented a limited series of completely new models every six months.

Renewal in *haute couture* involved all the models, while modern collections are the result of a mix of models with different purposes. Some are totally renewed from one season to the next, and others are just carried over with small changes. This mix between renewed and continuative items in each collection changes as a function of the positioning of the brand. The renewed part, or fashion, is greater in ready-to-wear women's clothing and minimal in men's sportswear. It is also clear that the role of managers and creative people varies as a function of the composition of the collections. Creative people's involvement is greatest in the fashion part and least in the more basic and continuous part.

A firm that makes fashion usually works on three seasonal collections at the same time. It analyses the sales results of the *past* season, monitors the progress of the *current* season, and designs the collection for the *following* season. If one imagines an Italian fashion firm in February 2002 one would find the different departments working on the activities shown in *Table 7.1*.

TABLE 7.1 **A FASHION FIRM'S ACTIVITIES AND TIMING**
(in February 2002)

FIRM DEPARTMENT	ACTIVITIES AND TIMING
Operations	Delivery collection for Spring/Summer 2002
Sales	Selling collection for Autumn/Winter 2002
Marketing	Analysing sell-in and sell-out results of Spring/Summer 2002
Product design	Designing collection for Spring/Summer 2003

Source: the authors.

The clothing firm starts three to twelve months before the presentation of the collection to the trade. European companies generally present two annual collections (spring/summer – S/S, and autumn/winter - A/W). These are preceded and followed by pre-collections, flash collections, sales and end of season collections. American retailers, on the other hand, produce up to 24 small collections a year in order to renew their merchandise in the sales point on a flow delivery basis. They also have permanent sales within the store in order to encourage the turnover of goods.

The largest part of the collection of a designer firm follows fashion trends and is renewed on a seasonal basis. The creative concepts of the collection are usually defined by one or more designers who may act as:

- Entrepreneur designers who work exclusively under their own name (Armani, Valentino and Calvin Klein)
- Well known or even less well known designers who design for established brands (Lagerfeld for Chanel, Tom Ford for Gucci, and Galliano for Dior)
- Freelance designers who work as consultants, generally for more than one brand.

Thanks to the originality and success of their own style, the *entrepreneur designers* have created integrated fashion empires under their own names. French designers started first, Italians followed in the seventies, American designers entered the fashion system in the eighties; nowadays their names are associated with a wide range of products often far from the original core business, from accessories to cosmetics and home textiles. As they are entrepreneurs, the designers are involved not only in style, but also in selecting materials and accessories, in communication and store design. They are usually supported by licensee companies that produce and distribute the collections on the basis of a licensing agreement. Recently some entrepreneur designers, mainly Italians, have acquired majority stakes in their licensing companies in order to gain a stronger control over the entire value chain. Both Armani and Dolce & Gabbana, for instance, decided to acquire their manufacturing companies.

The *stylist designers* generally have very strong and creative personalities, and their role is to renew and upgrade the style and image of a brand or label that is already successful. Usually named as design directors or fashion coordinators, they have an important role within the business, because they are responsible for making the brand identity evolve. If these creative figures do not identify with the historic identity of the brand, and decide to bring their own identity to it, the brand equity that has been established over the years can be destroyed. Thus awareness of the stylistic codes associated with a brand is important, as is the careful selection of the creative figure who is to be entrusted with its renewal.

> The historic Maison Dior entrusted its identity to two very different stylist designers in the 1990s. The first of these, Gianfranco Ferrè, was an entrepreneur as well as a designer, and he managed to interpret the historic elegance and femininity of the brand. He also brought it up to date through his own experience as a ready-to-wear designer. John Galliano, on the other hand, was an inspired creative talent who had little experience of ready-to-wear. He did everything in his own way, and this was very different from Ferrè's contribution. Recently Dior decided to renew its identity, again trying to connect to the emotional values that were attached to the brand when it started: revolution in womenswear. Therefore new and eccentric designers were brought in, trying to make a classical and conservative company evolve.

Freelance designers are the perfect solution for those firms willing to keep a direct control of the product development process. These designers sell a seasonal creativity that is generally limited to offering creative inputs or partial suggestions for the collection. There are, however, successful freelancers who can suggest creative projects for the product, image and positioning.

Managing consistency between seasonal collections and long term stylistic or brand identity depends on the designer as well as on managers. In the case of designer entrepreneurs, the fit should be ensured by the fact that style, product and image are guaranteed by a single person who brings together the roles of entrepreneur, designer and communications manager.

In the case of stylist designers and freelancers there is the problem of making these people understand the brand's stylistic and visual codes and involving them in the firm's creative process. The firm's awareness of its own stylistic codes and competitive positioning and its selection of designers should facilitate this integration.

Stylistic identity as an opportunity and a bond: the Missoni case

The Italian fashion house Missoni became famous in the 1960s thanks to an unmistakable style – highly coloured knitwear with lines, squares and designs that could be freely combined. These patchworks of uncoordinated pieces could be 'put together' into patterns to make a jumper with geo-metric patterns match a jacket with different coloured lines. It was a dis-tinctive style, with a very recognisable product. It was necessary to renew the product in the 1980s, and in the 1990s the firm went into crisis. Total black and minimalism were very far from the Missoni style. Retail mini-malism wrong-footed the small firm that was forced to invest heavily in the opening of flagship stores. A process of 'cleansing' was started, and the style of the mono-brand boutiques followed the general trend (cleanliness, white, few clothes on display). The colours remained, but the ranges were changed, as were the designs, the matches, the modelling, and the mate-rials (leather acquired a more important role). Although the jumper still had geometric patterns, it was now combined with a single-colour jacket, and the 'put together' look was challenged. The attempt was to encourage modernisation of the style without giving it up completely. Missoni was not credible when it ventured beyond its own style, because it entered ter-ritories that did not belong to it in the mind of consumers. This is how the difficult subject of stylistic development arises, the possibility of acquiring new spaces without losing the historic roots that underlie brand identity.

7.4 Rationalising variety and variability of the product system

7.4.1 The costs of variety and variability

The variety and variability of the seasonal offer are the distinc-tive element of the fashion system. Variety means the numbers of product references in terms of both the finished product and the individual components (models, fabric and sizes) of a col-lection. Variability means the degree of innovation from one sea-son to another. As already mentioned, with respect to fashion-ability, apparel can be divided into roughly three categories: *fash-ion items* with a four months' selling season; *seasonal items* which are in stores for approximately six months and *basic items* that have a selling season of one year or longer. In the past the growth in variety was the fundamental tool for fuelling sales. This was done by entering different segments or by offering the same tar-get a mix of products that could meet different needs. Many spe-cialised firms turned towards line extensions, and sometimes even towards product/market diversification, developing a total look concept outside their own clothing industry. All this led to a considerable and uncontrolled extension of the product mix at different levels (number of brands, collection lines, product families, models and textile-colour variations). This meant that making samples was very complex, and the later management of sales, production and delivery was even more complex. In order to analyse the impact of variety and variability on the offer system it is necessary to consider the relationship between these two factors and another three economic variables – costs, service and level of risk.

The critical importance of costs

There is a trade-off in any productive system between product variety/variability and unit costs as indicated in *Figure 7.3*.

FIGURE 7.3   **PRODUCT VARIETY/VARIABILITY AND THE EFFECT ON COSTS**

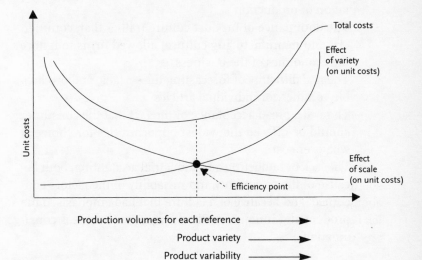

Source: the authors.

The product's operating costs can be grouped into two large categories. There are costs related to volumes and to the scale of activity, and there are the costs related to product variety and variability. Where economies of scale apply[4], the average unit costs reduce by a certain percentage for every doubling in the scale of activity. The costs due to variety, however, reflect the greater complexity and longer time periods of all the design and production stages. An increase in product variety necessarily leads to an increase in average unit costs. The total costs due to the scale of activities and to variety represent the product total cost. There is then, at least in theory, an efficiency point at which the mix between the volume and variety of each article allows for minimising average unit costs.

In the fashion system, and particularly in the Italian model, not much attention was paid to this economic dimension. There were several reasons for this:

- The strong market growth and the increasing margins of the 1980s hid a greater product variety that led to progressively higher costs because of the increased fragmentation of production
- The dominance of product culture (rather than commercial and manufacturing culture) allowed firms to ignore the economics of the business
- The real difficulty of forecasting the saleable and producible volumes for individual articles
- The widespread acceptance of the fact that the consumer should be offered the widest opportunities for choice at whatever cost
- The lack of budgeting and industrial accounting, both because of the complexity and variability of the factors concerned, and because of a culture that had emphasised the product and innovation above any other business consideration.

Although the explosion of product variety and its consequences for costs occurred low down in the pipeline, among the produc-

---

4. A firm's average costs may remain constant, or rise or fall as its output expands. If they fall the firm is said to have economies of scale. Reasons for economies of scale are a specialisation of labor, experience, dimension and location of the production plant.

ers of finished articles, it was transferred upwards to the producers of textiles and yarns.

> The owner of a large Italian textile firm said: 'In the past we always gave a lot of freedom to designers and to the product manager, so that we could offer our customers the greatest choice. We never evaluated the return on the large investment that had been made, above all in the development of samples. This was part of our culture of service to the customer, but nowadays there are no longer the margins for continuing like this. The excessive costs and, I would add, the waste, of this way of producing, are no longer repaid by the customers. We have also seen that many of our clients in the clothing business take advantage of our creativity for the development of their collections, and then have the fabric that we suggested produced elsewhere, at lower costs and quality.

Many Italian firms had reached *breaking point* as a result of the trend to increase variety, with no evaluation of the commercial, productive or logistic implications. The uncontrolled explosion of product references led to reduced economies of scale and increased variety costs. It created a productive system that was very inefficient. More worryingly, the system had little chance of improvement.

The critical importance of service

The growth in complexity related to variety also has an impact on the length of the product life cycle, and consequently, on the level of service that is offered.

> The owner of a leading Italian firm selling sophisticated sportswear with a strong product variety, says: 'The success of our formula (variety) caused us a lot of trouble. We could no longer deliver on time and the fabric inventories had become unmanageable'.

Thus, even when collections are successful despite their costs, firms often do not manage to deliver on time or in a co-ordinated way with respect to the product mix that is required. Foreign retailers in particular have always complained about this. They have earlier scheduling than Italian distributors, and they are anyway used to a higher level of service. Nowadays, however, it is clear even to the traditional Italian store that if a good product does not arrive on time this will result in lost sales.

Another complaint from distribution regards the manufacturer's difficulty in delivering according to seasonal deadlines or to item co-ordination requirements.

Finally, arranging replenishments very close to the sales season (the so called *flash collections* that come before the traditional season), or even during the season itself, is becoming an increasingly important element for selecting the best suppliers.

The real challenge for producers nowadays is not the product content (aesthetic quality, the materials, the product range, and the fashion content) as much as service and timing above all in the mass market and in the bridge segments.

Uncertainty, working times and risk

The progressive variety and variability of collections leads to increased costs and longer delivery times. It also increases the risk of buying fabrics and yarns; they call it *blind buying* to indicate the sourcing of inputs before knowing what inputs will be effectively used in the collection. These purchases are generally made through advance orders that are made even before the collections have been designed. Without such advance orders, however, it would be difficult for textile suppliers to deliver on time.

Orders based on estimates from the first weeks of sale allow for correcting *blind buying*. They have to be made quickly, or they will automatically cause a delay in production and trade deliveries. This problem of the management of uncertainty has a different impact on different products in the textile-clothing pipeline. Firms operating in the womenswear, especially in the ready-to-wear segments, have the greatest difficulty, above all with regard to woolen fabrics, because of the longer and more complex productive cycle. The problem is less urgent in menswear and cotton clothing (jeans, sweaters, and underwear), because of the reduced variability of the offer and the longer time to market. Countries specialised in certain products/productions (for example the US with casualwear and Germany with menswear) do not face the complexity that is a feature of the Italian model. The need to preserve the offer variety and variability requires the identification of managerial methods for rationalising them. Fashion firms should pursue product innovation but at the same time thay have to be able to control costs and manage the level of service.

7.4.2 Product and market orientation

The creative people take for granted that a successful product from the past collection has to be eliminated or changed to create a new reason for the consumer to purchase. The commercial view, on the other hand, tends to keep certain items and designs that have been successful in the past as these are seen as less risky.

The truth is half-way. The fashion industry cannot be completely dependent upon the market needs as the consumer wants to be surprised and excited by creativity; on the other hand, free creativity without any marketing constraint is not profitable. A middle way has to be found, in order to create a greater integration between the creative and managerial parts of each firm. A balanced approach that starts from a knowledge of the customer and his or her purchases.

Analysis of the best selling products or of key clients, at the top and bottom of the textile pipeline, shows that a high share of turnover is often due to a small percentage of products/customers. Clothing producers usually have a large customer portfolio in terms of outlets. These require wide sales networks that are both hard to manage and expensive. But only a few customers secure continuative orders of large amounts. Moreover, the high turnover of sales points is a problem that afflicts many producers, and there is often no way to solve it. Thus, the difficulty of providing a good service to the best clients is due in large part to the need to offer a degree of service to many less important and less loyal clients.

The marketing director of an Italian knitwear Company says: 'We have a very selected clientele. It consists of the best-known retail outlets in the largest cities throughout the world. Despite this, out of about 400 customers, our core base is not more than 50 to 60. Unfortunately, we only occupy a marginal space for many of them compared to the total knitwear offer in the retail outlet. Our objective is to become exclusive suppliers of the best retailers.'

The advantages of focusing on key customers also becomes clear higher up the pipeline.

The commercial director of a wool-mill says: 'We recently carried out an analysis of our 300 customers throughout the world. We discovered that 30% could easily be eliminated, because the costs of the relationship (contacts, samples, references, and so on) were greater than the income generated. The 15 to 20 most important customers, however, have the real possibility of producing 60-80% of our turnover. This will depend on our ability to offer an appropriate range of products and a service for the development of the collection, that we are not currently able to guarantee because of the excessive fragmentation of our customer portfolio.'

As well as improving the level of service, focusing on key customers also makes it possible to rationalise the offer. This is rightly considered one of the critical issues of the industry. This process has to start at the retail outlet, and is then passed on to the producers of the finished products and progressively up the pipeline. A correct segmentation of the trade and end customer, together with clear positioning, lead to the definition of a collection that is neither too wide nor too deep. On the contrary, when the width and depth of the collection are used to 'shoot in the dark' in the absence of an accurate definition of the consumer, trade or producer targets, the result is a poorly judged offer, and one that is ineffective on the market and inefficient from the productive and logistic viewpoint.

The commercial manager of a medium sized clothing business says: 'When definitive choices are made about the collection this always ends up with a higher number of variants than the objectives that were identified at the beginning. This happens partly because of the anxiety about leaving something out that might sell, and partly because of the pressures from creative people. The problem is that these decisions are often taken on the basis of the owner's personal taste rather than on the basis of a rational plan.'

A firm producing quality knitwear that had licences from many designers wanted to increase the sale of its own brand. The firm decided to include new lines that would carry it into new market segments. At the same time a medium-high priced line was introduced, and a decidedly cheap one to satisfy requests from the largest sales agents. The operation was a huge failure although the owners had been convinced that they were about to cover a market segment that was much larger than the previous one.

These examples show that depth rather than width of collection is the important issue, particularly in fashion. Given the presence of many small businesses that are very specialised in individual segments of the market, the clientele, which is also increasingly specialised, demands the possibility to choose among many offers within one well defined type of product. Collections that are too wide often do not have a distinct character with reference to specialised competitors.

Offer rationalisation does not necessarily lead to giving up product variety. Firms willing to meet market needs are used to developing a wide variety that matches the firm's market positioning.

Thus, the firms that want to be *product specialists* should act on the number of models and fabric-colour variants. Conversely, those that prefer to be *generalists* with a total look offer, should be able to offer a combination of co-ordinated themes, focusing on the number of collections and on product categories.

A leading Italian clothing firm producing women's underwear tried several times to enter the men's segment. It focused on strong brand image and retailing synergies. The limitation and qualitative unsuitability of the collections in terms of product types and fabrics, did not allow it to wrest leadership from the main competitor which could rely on an incomparable depth of range.

Greater offer rationalisation without sacrifice to product variety can be achieved through modular collections.

A manager who had just joined a large Italian manufacturing firm realised that the management of the huge number of product codes was very complex. One of the causes of this complexity was that there were 18 types of jacket, which had considerable effects on costs of production and delivery. This did not seem justifiable to the manager. After various fruitless attempts to convince the product men that the 18 basic models of jacket could be easily reduced to 3 or 4, the manager decided to play a trick. 'I cut out the label of various models and laid them out on a table. Then I asked the product managers to find their own. Most of them could not recognise it, and they had to give in to the evidence that their reluctance had no plausible explanation.'

A further rationalisation of the offer is possible by means of *tuning* the collections, that is bringing them closer to the specific demands of the key clients. By directly involving customers who are opinion leaders in the initial, intermediate and final stages of collection development, it is possible to eliminate codes/articles that do not offer great benefits in sales but do contribute to an excessive and unproductive impoverishment of the offer. This has considerable implications in terms of costs, quality and service. Although the most obvious effects of rationalisation can be seen in the finished articles, rationalisation is also reflected in the higher stages of the pipeline.

> The owner of a wool-mill in Italy says: 'An analysis of the relationship between the fabrics that had been developed and sales showed the following data. The product area created approximately 2,000 variants of fabric, but only about 1,000 variants were shown at the Idea Biella Fair. Only 500 were able to sell at least one item, and the percentage achieving satisfactory sales was even lower. All this represents enormous waste. We decided to continue analysis of the sales and costs of the different variants in order to find a solution to the problem. The objective was to come to Idea Biella with a smaller collection but one that had a greater chance of being sold. This requires a very close relationship with those of our customers who were already important in the initial stages of collection development. In this way we will not only put the needs of our customers first, but also carry forward the development of commercial relationships, and this will produce great benefits in terms of customer service. It is inevitable that our customers will also be pushed to rationalise their offer, and this can only improve the flow of the whole pipeline.'

7.5 The process of developing collections

The need to rationalise the variety and variability of the offer system should lead firms to give a structure to the process of developing collections with a precise definition of timings and resource needs. In what follows, the development of seasonal collections will be described and analysed. It is a process made up of significant activities whose main managerial problems will be shown. The stages or significant activities are:

1. Definition of the collection guidelines
2. Definition of the collection plan (the collection's architecture)
3. Execution of the collection
4. Presentation of the collection.

The definition of collection guidelines

The definition of guidelines should lead to the general features of the collections. The definition of the objectives of the collection is carried out by the product/style department together with the commercial people. The starting-point is the final analysis of the sales of previous collections for the same season. This is obtained by gathering information on *sell-in* (sales to trade customers) and possibly *sell-out* as well (sales to the end consumer). The quantitative information (customer statistics, markets, ABC analysis) then requires to be enriched by qualitative elements collected from the sales force (agents, retailers) and/or directly from customers. Other information that is often left out of account (complaints, returns, defects, remainders, and so on) is also very important for providing the full background of past results. Financial analysis is also important through the construction of accounts for each collection.

The marketing skill is to produce guidelines of the features that are closest to the consumption attitudes of the end consumer. This is done through market and competitor analyses, as well as the prospects for distribution in different markets. Analysis of final sales and marketing reports should result in decisions about the selected customer segments, the channels and geographic markets, positioning with respect to competitors, and the resources that are available and those that should be developed.

The product area contributes to the definition of the objectives of the collection, not from the viewpoint of the collection's architecture or structure – these are part of the collection plan –

but from the viewpoint of seasonal stylistic codes. Seasonal codes concern fashionable patterns, materials, colours, details and also types of product. They have to evolve seasonally as a function of the development of fashion, while remaining consistent with the long term stylistic identity of the firm.

The relation between seasonal codes and stylistic identity is particularly important in market segments where product creativity is fundamental, and thus in the high end of the market.

> Stylistic identity for the Gianni Versace label has always been linked to a concept of 'Mediterranean' baroque. The permanent codes that have been used to represent his style and identity are Greek geometrical decorations, the mythical jellyfish, and the colour gold. The style has its justification in Versace's own background, the Italian region of Calabria. Also the designer of Dolce and Gabbana used permanent stylistic codes that originate from their motherland, Sicily: black, lace, seductive blouses and hot atmospheres from lazy and sunny villages where beautiful young women relax in the shade of the Indian fig tree.

> Prada's success was due to the invention of a minimalism that lacked the intellectualism typical of the most avant-garde designers, and thus very easy of access to the wider public. Both for accessories, the core business, and for clothing, Prada adopted stylistic codes that were linked to simplicity of lines, technical items and research on materials.

The guidelines that are drawn up at this stage should be included in the collection plan, which deals with the number and types of collections and deliveries[5]. This is built on the basis of the main occasions of use, end uses and product types, and is very closely tied to the competitive advantages and distinctive features of the collections.

The collection plan
Once the general inputs for the collections have been outlined both from a stylistic and marketing perspective, the next move

---

5. A delivery, in fashion terminology, is a collection that is identified by a specific season/occasion of use/merchandise that is displayed on a particular date to the sales force. A clothing collection of any size is generally subdivided into more than one delivery in order to stress the different components of the whole offer system.

is the building of the collection/deliveries plan. This provides a qualitative and quantitative definition of the variety structure with reference to different elements such as fashion content, occasions of use, merchandise and price band. It may be useful to use some *matrixes* (collection matrix) based on occasions of use, price band, drop, designs, variants, and so on. This approach aims at controlling the total number of articles in the collection. The *matrixes* (*Table 7.2*) are thus a planning tool that defines the structure of the collection in terms of innovation and variety.[6]

TABLE 7.2   **AN EXAMPLE OF COLLECTION MATRIX IN WOMENSWEAR**

	FASHION			BASIC	
PRICE BANDS	workwear	dailywear	special occasions	dailywear	leasurewear
HIGH-END	n. of items				
MEDIUM TO HIGH					
MEDIUM					
MASS					
					n. of total items

Source: the authors.

According to firm positioning and product range a single collection can cover different occasions of use and price bands, or the firm may decide to devote one collection to each occasion of use and price segment.

The occasions of use, a typical market category that was analysed in *Chapter Five*, can belong to three general categories: day/work, special occasions/evening, free time/weekend (*Table 7.3*).

The creative person should not work on the definition of collection structure, and the manager should not interfere with the

---

6. For more on the operating tools that support the development of collections, see P. Varacca, 'Lo sviluppo delle collezioni nel sistema moda: logiche e strumenti operativi', in *Economia & Management*, n. 6, 1993.

TABLE 7.3   **DEFINING OCCASIONS OF USE IN DEVELOPING COLLECTIONS**

DAY TIME	SPECIAL OCCASIONS	LEISURE TIME
Workwear	*Ceremony*	*Casual*
Office	Weddings, social events	Week-end
Business trips	Cocktails	Friends
Formal occasions	*Evening*	*Sportswear*
Lunch-dinner	Theatre	Passive sport (walking, cruising)
Events	Parties	Active sport

Source: the authors.

contents in terms of seasonal stylistic codes, models and colours. It is important that the collection plan also clarifies the degree of seasonal renewal (fashion versus basic products) that the firm wants the collection to have. A high degree of innovation involves greater workloads in the following stages of the manufacturing process (product industrialisation, testing, production launches). An increase in workloads must be checked in advance in order to ensure production capacity and respect of timings.

When defining the offer structure, a recent development is the criterion of the timing of delivery to the sales point. This criterion is aimed at favouring a better sell-out according to the seasons. Based on deliveries are the so called *colour stories*, or sets of co-ordinates for the products, characterised by:

- A specific occasion of use (daywear, casualwear, and so on)
- A specific season for sale/consumption (end of summer, autumn, winter, winter cruise, pre-spring, spring, summer, and so on)
- A stylistic match of the models, fabrics and colours.

Colour stories have to be delivered to the sales point as such, in just one delivery. This is for the following objectives:

- To reduce to the minimum the time that the product is in the shop, so that what arrives systematically is what can best be sold at that time

- To encourage continual renewal of the product in the sales point, and thus the return of the customer, through the systematic arrival of new product packages (approximately every 15-20 days)
- To maximise sell-outs thanks to the greater matchability of the items and the greater degree of assortment that is the result of the products' shorter periods in the sales point.

The design and sale of colour stories also allows for the following objectives to be achieved:

- It guarantees greater product characterisation and identity in the sales point
- It reduces the possibility that agents or retailers will put the offer together 'to please themselves' (the so-called 'buying as a single product' of collections that were instead designed as co-ordinates or matchables)
- Satisfying the needs of differentiated delivery times for different markets, and offering the possibility of differentiated delivery dates for a certain number of colour stories (market A: foreign, opinion leader, tourist area; market B: other customers)
- Encouraging a better timing of the purchase of textiles and productive activities.

The execution of the collection

After the definition of the collection plan the execution phase starts. It provides for the organisation of many activities that are often performed chaotically. These activities are concerned with the operational stage of the development of the collection, the production of prototypes and sample collection and the definition of timing. The timing is very important: defining a real programme of activities, instead of a simple calendar means that is necessary to define the standard workloads of the resources, and to estimate the needs of the resources generated by the collection plan on the basis of this. The advantage of using tools like a properly developed collection plan and an activity based plan is that it leads to easier control of the progress of the collection.

As a result there is a higher probability of reducing delays and costs, both as regards the collection and production, and a higher probability of making a suitably full collection.

Sometimes it is not easy for product management to convince the creative staff of the need for this planning, as it is considered a limit on their capacity for expression and on the time needed for developing stylistic ideas. However, the current needs of the market impose increasingly stringent working times. As a result, planning improvement is now a necessity that cannot be ignored.

Presenting the collection

Once the sample collection has been defined, the purpose of the presentation of the collection to the trade and to the sales network is to refine the collection's match with the market demand. A growing number of firms also involve particularly significant clients (key clients) in this. As further additions or reductions to the collection are defined here, the way these decisions are taken often means that they have great weight in the outcome of the whole development process. Unfortunately, lack of time does not allow for carrying out the necessary checks. This increases the risk of later difficulties in production (defects, re-workings, rejections, returns, complaints, and so on).

The method of developing the stylistic offer varies according to whether the firm stresses a high level of innovation or greater qualitative reliability and service. In the former case the process is characterised by the greater autonomy of the creative people over marketing. In the latter case, working with clients is an important competitive tool. The making of customised and exclusive offers is also frequent in this case, as is the use of personalisation on the basis of client demands. Exclusive offers and personalisation both require close collaboration from the early stages of design onwards. The contribution of clients to highly innovative offers is usually only sought at a later stage, for the screening of the definitive collection.

The choices about the width and degree of innovation of the product system are crucial for different industries. For firms in the fashion system, this is particularly important. They develop at least two collections a year, and often broaden and renew their product lines in order to seize market opportunities. As already indicated in earlier chapters, the offer system in the fashion industry, and particularly within the clothing industry, is very complex. This is partly due to the *physical and technical features* of the products (cloths, models, finishing and accessories), partly to *destination of use* (functions, end uses and occasions of use) and partly to *dressing style* (classic, modern, avant-garde). The complexity is also the result of the degree of innovation of the distribution service in the whole offer system. There is thus an imperative to rationalise the process of collection development. There must, however, be awareness of the need to safeguard creativity and inspiration. These are the two essential elements; without them fashion would not even exist.

A rational approach to collection development should allow for allocating tasks and responsibilities to the different parts of the firm that are involved in the activities that range from the first creative stimuli up to the presentation of the collection/sample collection. The analysis of single activities should reveal the main shortcomings in working times, costs and quality, and should also identify the most appropriate tools and methods for improvement. The ultimate objective is to create collections that both meet market expectations and are in line with the requirements of the supply chain.

Figure 7.4 presents an overview of the entire product development process.

7.6 Organisational implications

A development of collections aimed at rationalising the offer structure and a willingness to enhance the firm's creative dimension and innovative skills also require an upgrade in organisational models. The cultural dimensions of the fashion firm, its creativity and management, have to be integrated with business knowledge during the process of product development. Business knowledge relates to the product, the market, sourcing, technologies, distribution, logistics, and planning and control.

FIGURE 7.4 **THE PRODUCT DEVELOPMENT PROCESS IN FASHION**

Defining collection guidelines
- Reporting on past seasons (margins, ABC analysis, sell-in-sell-out, deliveries, replenishments, inventories, problems with suppliers)
- Marketing analysis (competitors – trade – end-consumer)
- Defining objectives, number, strategic positioning of collections (end-uses, occasions of use, price bands, degree of innovation)

Defining the collection plan
- Defining the collection plan (collection matrixes, deliveries, color stories)

The execution of the collection
- Timing and scheduling
- Building the collection (prototypes and samples)
- Internal tests

Presenting the collection
- Presenting the collection to sales network
- Presenting parts of the collection to key clients and opinion leaders

Considerable improvements in the rationalisation of this process can be obtained at two levels:

- Internally, through the creation of *interfunctional product teams*
- Externally, through the development of a *pipeline partnership*.

Interfunctional product teams
In the most advanced firms the primary functions of directing and checking the progress of collection plans are entrusted to the product team. The key components of the entire organisational structure are contained within product teams: product manager, commercial staff, industrialisation managers, purchasing and sourcing area, production and logistics. The co-ordination of product teams can be entrusted either to the prod-

uct area (product manager or fashion/design director) or to the marketing and commercial area (brand manager, marketing manager). Generally, firms with a greater product and innovation orientation prefer that the process remain in the hands of the product-style area, so as not to risk an excessive levelling of the offer as a result of commercial inputs. These firms are usually fashion houses and firms with a strong brand identity. Conversely, firms with a positioning in the mass market, or that attribute more importance to the market, favour the role of marketing, sales or retail within the team. What counts most is to create a common language and approach to organising the collections, evaluating contributions from all the different components of the firm. The most important activities of the product team are the initial and final ones. Regarding the initial ones, a shared analysis of the previous collections and of current trends should be the basis for defining guidelines, collection plans and timing. These become qualitative and quantitative objectives and time targets to which all the business areas have to make a contribution. With regard to the final activities, an agreement has to be made about whether the choices are consistent with what the team has approved. Product teams represent a good opportunity for comparing and enriching interdisciplinary experience.

In the first place the different business areas become used to developing business objectives that everyone can identify with, and this is especially true of the creative people who are less accustomed to this. Secondly, product teams allow a learning process where everyone can make his own contribution to improving the management of the product development process.

Product teams do not overlap the other business functions. Rather, they are mechanisms for the co-ordination, direction and control of the most important process of the fashion business. Outsiders such as opinion leaders or strategic suppliers, are often integrated into the product team during certain key stages of the process, such as the approval of the architecture of the collection and the approval of the definitive collections. This reinforces the internal awareness that progress is being made in the right direction, in relation to both the needs of the market and the needs of the productive system.

The pipeline partnership in product development

A more complete rationalisation of product development presupposes not only that components are highly integrated within the firm itself, but that there is also integration with other actors in the supply chain. This creates the conditions for strengthening the competitiveness of the whole 'business pipeline' to which the firm belongs. This is the only way to achieve the different objectives that were mentioned earlier:

- Considerable reduction of product development costs
- Reduction of manufacturing costs, thanks to better industrialisation and better volumes per item
- A better ratio between the offer variety and the offer market target
- Better level of service, thanks to the consequent reduction of times in product development
- Lower costs of product distribution, for a reduced dispersion on the market
- Closer sharing of results with the firm's own suppliers-clients.

The strategies for rationalising the offer system that have been presented up to this point show the need for closer and more intense information – sharing between the different links in the pipeline. The only structured and reliable information that is often exchanged today is information connected with orders, and this results in a delay of information about the determinants that have generated the orders.

The objectives of strengthening the reliability and rapidity of information within the pipeline can be summarised as:

- The transfer of information designed to minimise uncertainty and to reduce working times in the different stages of product development, logistics, production and distribution
- The transfer of know-how designed to make the cross-fertilisation of knowledge more systematic and lasting. The cross-fertilisation process today is mainly informal and based on personal connections.

This implies changing relationships between firms. These often have a short-term relation based on opportunism and conflict rather than collaboration. Putting this model into practice imposes certain conditions:

- The awareness of all the actors in the same pipeline that they belong to an integrated value-creating system
- The belief that the pipeline success is the condition for the success of the individual actors who work in it
- The need for a strategic leadership within the pipeline
- The sharing of a strategic orientation, of values, of the way of perceiving and managing the business.

Only the partnership model, as opposed to the market model, allows for developing relationships that are based on trust. It is trust-based relationships that allow for a more effective and efficient exchange of know-how and experience, and this is extremely important in industries that have a strong intangible content and have time constraints such as those based on fashion.[7]

---

7. For more on the subject of inter-firm relationships, with particular reference to the concept of networks or firm networks, see H. Hakansson, J. Snehota, *Developing Relationship in Business Networks*, Routledge, 1995.

8 The operation and logistic process

The complexity of the offer system, with its variety and variability over time, makes the productive-logistic process especially important in fashion. Although back in time the textile-clothing industry was oriented towards efficiency in manufacturing, this changed with the introduction of the seasonal collections in the 80s. The orientation on product renewal resulted in neglecting the impact of innovation on the supply chain (industrialisation, sourcing, manufacturing, deliveries, timing and service to the customer). Offer differentiation was regarded as so important that it justified any inefficiency in costs or timing. The increasing pressure of competition, changes in consumption models and in distribution structures, have required a rationalising of the productive and logistic cycle while respecting the differentiation of the offer.

In the past the productive and logistic cycle, the supply chain, was regarded as an 'execution machine' that could fulfil any designer's desire and fancy (although there was no possibility later on of industrialising that fancy). Nowadays, however, there is a tendency to create greater integration between the collection development processes and the supply chain. The purpose of this is to favour the advanced resolution of problems that may rise in industrialising and producing the collection. The recent development of information technologies in production, logistics and retailing helps to support the management of complexity, but most firms have still to reconsider both methods and tools in supply chain management. This chapter will cover the fundamental stages of the operating process in the clothing industry. It will also emphasise the most important subjects regarding other business processes (the development of collections and the commercial process).

A general overview of the process of product development and the critical effects of product variety on the supply chain are anticipated in *Figure 8.1*.

FIGURE 8.1   **EFFECTS OF VARIETY ON THE SUPPLY CHAIN**

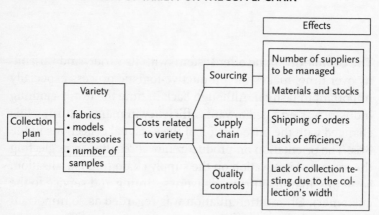

8.1 Codifying materials

The following types of articles are managed in the fashion system:

- Basic materials (yarn, fabrics)
- Accessories and consumption materials (linings, buttons, zips, clothes-hangers) that are used to complete the product

- Finished products (manufactured articles, knitwear and finished accessories)
- Semi-finished products to be used for a well defined finished product.

Every article is codified, usually with an identification made up of several elements. This identifies the main characteristics of the product (*Table 8.1*). One code identifies the model, line, and the year and season to which it belongs. Other codes identify the original merchandise category and the colour variant.

The finished product code is thus a set of different parts whose mix is defined in the sample collection. Sizes, drop, height and variants are not managed through the product code because these do not show the model although they are essential for identifying the finished product where materials are transported. Sizes, drop, heights and variants are used with the product code to give the details of the product, and this always shows the year and season when the article was made.

TABLE 8.1 **CODIFYING THE FASHION PRODUCT**

INDUSTRY	CODE 1	CODE 2	CODE 3
Apparel making	Kind of model/line/season	Fabric	Color
Knitwear	Kind of model/line/season	Type of yarn	Color
Leather goods	Kind of model/line/season	Type of skin	Color

Source: the authors.

Size

Size is a typical element in the clothing and shoe industries. Every finished product, and often a semi-finished one as well, has a scale of sizes that identifies the possible measures for every article. Sizes have different measurement scales in different countries (for example, size 12 in the US corresponds to size 42 in Italy). Knitwear also has a 'variable' size, and this indicates how much the garment can be enlarged through stretching and ironing. For instance there can be orders for size 50 and a stock of 48/variable 50 in the warehouse. There is a scale of measurement for some accessories as well (buttons, labels and zips), and this is in terms of diameter, length or weight.

Season

As said earlier, the fashion system has seasonal products, and seasonability depends on the each geographic region. Further, the fashion firms can also present shorter seasons or 'flash' collections that are usually tied to particular events (for example New Year's Eve or carnival). There is a sample collection of products for each of these events. This feature distinguishes the fashion industry from other industries that have a seasonal element, like food where the products remain the same from one year to the next. As already mentioned, fashion products can be divided the following way, depending on the season:

- Seasonal fashion products that relate to one season in one year
- Continuous products that are offered for several years, usually for the same season.

Designers have led the way in increasing the seasonality of their goods and retailers have given them strong support as a steady flow of new merchandise onto the shelves attracts customers.

Economic performance for fashion firms is calculated over the season (including end of season sales) rather than on the solar year as in other industries. The season allows market results to be obtained on a quarterly or monthly basis without having to wait for the end of the year.

8.2 The making of prototypes and pattern books

The process of product development, as already explained in the previous chapter, starts with designing and developing the seasonal collections. Once the designers have defined the models, the next step is making a *planning specification* where classes of products are assigned a sales forecast. A forecast is also made of the consumption of materials regarded as critical enough to be purchased 'blind'.

Some technical details are then defined for every model in the collection. A first *bill of materials* is used to make preliminary sales projections for the season and for the consumption of materials that have to be ordered for production.

The starting point is the *prototype bill* (or samples). This is a very simplified, single-colour and single-size bill of materials. It provides indications for making the sample, and above all cost indications. It is used for deciding whether to put the sample in the collection or not. Once the collection has been defined, the real *bill of materials* comes next. This describes the materials and production methods for a certain model, and it requires a specific reference for all the components of the models in the collection.

8.3 Production cycles

Once the bill of materials for each model has been defined, it is then possible to define the *production cycle*. This, together with the bill of materials, indicates the skills, methods and production times of the article. Production cycles have to be defined at various levels. A cycle normally refers to one model, but sometimes greater detail is required (one cycle for size, colour or variant), or less detail (one cycle for line). Every cycle is made up of successive production stages, and productive progress depends on these – the unit of measurement, however, has to be clear from the start. The planning specification that was made at the beginning of the process is associated with a preliminary and very general planning cycle. This only examines the critical stages of production (typically cut and manufacturing), and it is used to determine the number of items to be worked on at each stage. The requirements of the various internal departments and external suppliers where the work will be done are planned at this time. Specific characteristics/skills should be identified for each supplier/internal department:

- Product category (trousers, skirts, coats and accessories)
- Cutting type, which identifies the materials treated (leather or silk)

- Stages of production that have to be managed (cutting, manufacturing, ironing)
- Work capacity per single stage (usually expressed in number of articles per unit of time for external suppliers, and in time per article for internal department)
- Sourcing of materials (the firm itself, bought on commission, or by third parties)
- If any, management of suppliers for materials or accessories.

A further aspect is the planning and management of the production capacity from external suppliers, in order to have all the information about available productive capacity (not used or booked) at a certain period of time. This is especially the case where work is done through sub-contracting. The system is thus enabled to know which supplier is ready in terms of skills and available capacity.

Producing prototypes does not require production cycles. Scheduling will take place before the launch, and this will assign every sample collection list to a standard production cycle, in order to calculate the quantities of material required, and the production necessary for each stage. Scheduling will also order the batches of materials that have to come from the warehouse and external suppliers in the various stages of manufacturing. Where the conditions for launch are not optimal, it is necessary to arrange an alternative bill of materials and production cycle.

The costs of the collection are also calculated during this stage, on the basis of information in the records about costs, the average cost of materials, accessories and semi-finished goods per supplier and per year/season[1]. These are calculated by estimat-

---

1. The term "cost" is used in different contexts (and by different individuals) with different meanings. Some of the most fundamental and important types of cost are total cost, variable cost, fixed cost, average cost, direct cost, common cost. Each term is applied to a separate and distinct concept. *Total cost* is the sum of all costs incurred by the firm to produce any given level of output--that is, the sum of the firm's variable and fixed costs. A *fixed cost* is invariable with the level of production, thereby not changing in the short run. A *variable cost* changes directly (but not necessarily proportionately) with the level of production. *Average total cost* is the total cost of producing a given quantity of output, divided by the total number

ing the amount of material that has to be purchased during the season. The *standard cost* corresponds to the item's *industrial cost* (all the item's direct cost plus the share of common costs that are attributed to it). This standard cost has to be independent of the method and place of production, and is obtained by taking into account forecast consumption in bill/cycle of production and weighting the average costs of materials/accessories and manufacturing for the mix of suppliers and the mix of cycles/bill.

8.4 Sales

The sales stage now begins. More will be said about this in *Chapter Nine*. The firm uses its commercial network to present the sample collection to customers. The sample collection is the list of products that are on sale during the season:

- Models that have been produced *ad hoc* for the season, described in the sample collection list
- Basic products, with possible mixes of materials and colours for the season
- Finished products bought by other firms that will only be put on sale
- There must be a sales price for each model in the sample collection. The sales price is usually the total of standard costs plus a mark up. The mark up is calculated by taking into account the following features of the market to be served:
  - forecasted sales
  - costs of freight and sales
  - commercial policy

The price list can be by model, by model/fabric, by model/fabric/size, and the cost of a variant is generally a specific surcharge. If a model can be produced in more than one material there has

---

of units produced. A *direct cost* can be specifically attributed to the production of an individual service or product, without requiring the use of allocations to separate it from costs incurred in the production of other services or products. *Common costs* are incurred when production processes yield two or more outputs.

to be a price list for each group of materials. Finally, the price list has to have a period of validity and it must be possible to translate it into different currencies.

Once the customer has seen the sample collection, he or she sends the order that identifies the quantity/models/sizes/colours required, and the relative conditions in terms of prices, deliveries, payments and possible product personalisation or consignment variations. When the order is received by the producer the materials needed for manufacturing ordered goods are usually booked.

One of the sales network that is most used is that of agents. They obtain orders through standard softwares installed in their personal computers. When the order portfolio is sufficiently established, a check is made that the fixed minimums for production have been reached, and orders for models that have not reached this minimum are cancelled. Throughout the year a distinction is made between two different kinds of order. Sales campaign orders are made at the beginning of the season and relate to a complete mix of sizes/colours. Re-assortment orders are made during the season and are necessary for replenishing mixed sizes/colours after sales.

8.5 Production and logistics

The seasonality of production in the fashion industry makes long-term planning impossible. It is impossible to go beyond the current season as there is no sample collection for the next one.

Production is managed in one of two ways, through the warehouse or by order line.

Warehouse management uses the existing portfolio of orders to trace a sales projection, in order to estimate the whole season's orders. This makes it possible to determine the quantities that should be produced and to plan production launches. Products for the current orders and those that have been forecasted are then brought to production, less the stocks and the items being currently produced.

Order line management consists of restricting planning to the existing orders only.

Production launches are very closely tied to the types of fabric used (except for knitwear). Different articles are produced in the same launch, and these can be grouped by model-fabric-colour, by model-fabric, or by model-cut (for example a coat), irrespective of whether the production is per order line or per warehouse. Defining the correct quantity to produce is done by considering the group of order lines that are to be produced out of stocks in the warehouse and articles that are already in production. Then a launch test can be carried out, which consists of:

- Checking the availability of materials. This is generally the fabric, as this is the most important material in the first stage of production, that is cutting
- Checking the availability of resources. Once it is clear what order lines can be produced on the basis of the standard production cycle, the individual production stages can be identified, and external suppliers or internal departments can be assigned to each of these
- Calculation of requirements, how much material will be needed to complete production.

Now the production launch can be made. External suppliers and internal departments have to be sent clear and detailed documentation about the models, sizes and colours to be produced. The high reliance on third parties, and their craft-related size makes this stage of information transmission particularly important for successful production development. A production job order can come back to the firm in one or more stages. Then there is quality control and delivery to the warehouse.

The filling of the warehouse with finished products is a circular process in fashion. It is full at the peak of each season's production, but between one season and the next it is practically empty. For this reason warehouse management is frequently left to third parties. The consignment plan has to define what to deliver on the basis of customer orders, and this depends on the type of production undertaken. If the production was carried out according to order lines, then the warehouse is organised into customer boxes. A check has to be made on the costs of delivering products to the customer when a specific percentage of the whole order has been made. If, however, production is organised by product, the warehouse is organised into article boxes. The firm has to decide which customers should receive the merchandise that is available on the basis of commercial priorities. Delivery routes have to be optimised in both cases.

Shortening the pipeline and increasing efficiency with Quick Response

Nowadays most textile and clothing firms are experiencing benefits from the implementation of Quick Response (QR) techniques to their supply chain. Typically, QR includes building partnerships between customers and suppliers and having the ability to share inventory and sales information to the benefit of both partners. The goal is to be able to reduce inventory, reduce working time, and build strong collaborative relationships among business partners. Many people think of QR only in terms of electronic data interchange (EDI) and electronic transfer of information. However, true QR demands an infrastructure to support flexibility and agility in addition to the ability to exchange information electronically. Numerous articles[2] have been written on the advantages of Quick Response for both basic and fashion goods. The common denominator between articles and studies is increased profits for everyone in the chain. If the right goods are on the right shelves at the right time, the consumer will buy them. There is naturally a long list of more specific benefits that can be measured, for example:

- Increased sales and market share
- Increased inventory turnovers
- Increased gross margin
- Fewer out-of-stock conditions
- Fewer markdowns
- Less overall inventory
- Reduced chargebacks.

Table 8.2 presents some basic elements of a QR approach in the case of apparel producers.

---

2. Hunter A., *Quick Response in apparel manufacturing*, The Textile Institute, 1990; Kincade D. H., Cassill N.L. & Williamson N.L., "Quick Response Management System: Structure and Components for the Apparel Industry", *Journal of the Textile Institute, 84, 1993*; Riddle E., Bradbard D., Thomas J. & Kincade D., "The Role of Electronic Data Interchange in Quick Response". *Journal of Fashion Marketing and Management, 3. 1999*; Lowson B., King R., King R., Hunter A., *Quick Response: Managing the Supply Chain to Meet Consumer Demand*, John Wiley & Sons, 1999.

TABLE 8.2   **APPAREL QUICK RESPONSE - BASIC ELEMENTS**

• Consumer style testing, point of sale tracking and post season analysis of consumer/retail sell-through, turns, stock-outs and forced markdowns
• Involvement of key retailers and fabric suppliers in style design (CAD), editing and forecasting
• Working with key retailers and fabric suppliers in development of retail sales and receipt forecast adjustments and working times
• Sharing retail order entry and availability information with fabric suppliers and fabric order and availability information with retailer
• Master schedule capacity utilisation planning integrated with forecasts, forecast corrections, fabric order and cut plan
• Block scheduling of production flow
• Full use of technology for short cycle sewing, finishing and price-ticketing
• Rapid internal movement of goods from cutting to sewing and sewing to apparel distribution center or store
• Cut planning from fabric supplier inventory records and rapid receipt and processing of fabrics into cutting
• Shorter seasonal calendar with more compact design/sampling schedules and smaller initial orders
• Quality assurance sampling to permit direct receipt of fabrics and shipments of finished apparel

Source: Hunter A. (1990) p. 56-57.

9.1 The sales process

There are two operating approaches in the fashion industry, and in particular in clothing:

- The *programmed* approach where firms produce only that part of the offer that has already been sold. This has the following stages: building of the seasonal sample collection, presenting the collection, acquisition of orders, production launch and delivery. This pattern allows the firm to minimise unsold stocks that would be out of fashion the following season
- The *running* approach where firms produce the offer that is planned for the season on the basis of sales forecasts. It is only later that production is sold. This pattern has the following stages: production planning, production launch, sales and delivery. It guarantees a much more rapid delivering time compared with the programmed approach, which is the only possible method in the case of fashionable collections. The running approach does not differen-

tiate substantially from the business approaches in other consumer goods.

The two approaches exist side by side in fashion firms, as the offer systems contain both fashion and running/basic products. Clearly the predominance of the fashion orientation over the running one depends on the positioning of the brand and the firm.

Given this premise, the objective of the sales process is to obtain customer orders as quickly as possible. Within the programmed approach, the order represents the starting point of the productive and logistic process (purchase of raw materials, transformation and delivery). In the running approach, however, the order is only the information from which the distribution process starts.

The programmed approach is, as has been said, more diffused in the fashion system. Here the sales process starts with the presentation of collections to the sales network. The sales network is made of show room managers or commercial managers (area managers, key client managers and agents). Product and commercial managers display the whole seasonal offer (themes, technical features, price bands and level of service). The objective is to illustrate the concept of the collection in terms of target, positioning, selling proposition to all the people involved in sales. This is very important since the tangible and intangible contents of the collection risk being left to one side, or simply ignored, in the many steps before the product reaches the end consumer.

There are usually two shows for the sales force. The first of these is more spectacular, and the objective is to transmit the image of the collection. The second show is more technical: the product and collection managers explain, item by item, the reasons for the choices of specific textiles and colours, and the assortment options of the various items.

Once the collection has been presented to the sales force, there then follows a series of stages – budgeting, presentation of the collection to customers, order acquisitions and the management of after-sales service.

The budgeting process

Defining the sales budgeting generally takes place before the collection is presented to customers. The sales budget is usually defined by product line/brand and by geographical area. It is an important occasion for giving the sales network responsibility for their specific results. If the sales network is to be motivated it must be involved in the definition of objectives. The firm's commercial management and the sales network discuss the 'potential' for each geographical area as part of the budgeting process. This is an evaluation of existing and new clients interested in the line/brand. The objective is to define the medium-term actions (from one to three years) that have to be implemented for every combination of line/brand/geographic area. This is how market oriented firms build up a detailed customer database for each area; customers are rated on the basis of their past orders/sales potential as priority 1, 2,3... Usually for fashion companies the number of customers is very high, even though only a few of them contribute greatly to turnover. For this reason it is fundamental to create a customer database, in order to select the most suitable line/brand mix for a particular area. The budgeting process is much easier if existing customers and new customers are already identified with their sales potential. Where this is not the case, budgeting becomes pure imagination, or risks being left wholly to the agent/representative who may not be fully aware of the commercial strategy of the firm.

Presenting the collections to customers

The trade customer sees collections in the firm's showrooms and through the sales network.

The *sales network* in Italy came about because of the high degree of fragmentation of the fashion distribution. The sales network is the most traditional sales structure. It is based on representatives and agents. These people, who are not employees of the firm, may work for one or more firms with a commission on sales. Agents work through direct contact with customers (these may be retailers or also intermediate manufacturers in the case of the higher stages of the pipeline), from whom they take orders. The smallest and most traditional customers are visited directly by the agent. Sales to large, structured customers generally take place in the show room managed by the agent. The problem of this sales formula is linked to several factors:

- The increasing width and variety of fashion collections means that it is increasingly necessary for the agent to make a selection of the offer to be presented. If the agent receives no guidance from the firm, there is a risk that this selection will be made on the agent's personal decision
- The agent usually considers the customer as his own asset, and is only rarely willing to supply all customer information to the firm, connecting the product to the channels that are most suitable to the brand
- The concentration and sophistication of distribution means that the role of a commercial intermediary is less and less important, but it also requires the development of sales people who are well integrated in the business culture, and who understand relational marketing, the product, and the management of service. The agent cannot, and should not, be a creative person, but he still has to understand the creative culture and language of the firm if he is to carry these features to the lower stages of the pipeline.

For all these reasons the leading firms are now moving towards selling though the firm's showrooms or through direct sellers who specialise in product types (knitwear, accessories or coats), or customer types (boutiques, department stores or specialist chains), or geographic areas.

Selling through the firm's showrooms is the most advanced method. They allow all the products in the collection to be shown under the direct control of the firm. The showroom is visited by customers during the sales campaign. This usually takes place during the fashion shows and trade fairs period. The showroom is a simulation of a shop/setting, and it allows for an immediate evaluation of the suitability of product assortments. This suitability seems an imperative given the complexity of collections and the importance of global co-ordination (the product and visual merchandising) within distribution.

The order acquisition process

The sales campaign varies from firm to firm. It can cover a quarterly period for which the sales network is given a weekly budget. It is worthwhile checking the attainment of significant qualitative and quantitative objectives even after the first few weeks. This kind of checking is increasingly necessary for the rapid identification of market trends and for planning purchases on the basis of them. The sales process is very closely related to the sourcing of materials (fabrics, accessories). To guarantee delivery times that meet the current needs of the market, given the long working times that are a feature of the textile pipeline, some of the purchases and production have to be made "blind" – without any certainty of total orders. Leading firms manage this structural uncertainty through an accurate customer segmentation. This allows for projecting orders from the first few weeks and estimating total needs up to the end of the campaign. This requires a *fine-tuning* among progressing sales and production planning. It implies not only the use of very sophisticated information systems, but also a sales structure that is integrated with the firm.

The management of after-sales service

Evolving distribution and retailing formats requires collaboration from the agents and the firm's sales force. This assistance generally consists of checking the quality of assortments and deliveries, of providing support for sales point activities (visual merchandising), re-plenishment during the season (of both running products and infra-seasonal ones), and the replacement of defective items. It means creating the conditions for moving from a sell-in logic (sales oriented to trade customers) towards a sell-out logic (sales oriented to the end consumer). Service management therefore implies a closer customer and seller relationship that can be used as the basis for developing knowledge and a very strong relationship based on trust. This relationship is fundamental for the development of an offer system that is more oriented to the market and to commercial policies that match specific customer segments. This is a further reason why independent sales networks are increasingly unsuited to the current competitive environment.

9.2 Seasonal presentations and fashion shows

The fashion show is a characteristic feature of the industry, and its origins go back to the Parisian *high couture*. The fashion show was transferred to the clothing and accessory industry in the last thirty years. There are two types of fashion show:

- *Image fashion shows* are held in the centres of world fashion (Milan, Paris, London and New York). They take place about five or six months before the season of consumer sales. They are designed for the buyers from the most important international distributors, for the specialised and general press, and for opinion leaders. Fashion shows are now theatrical events that have a high return in terms of image, where the presentation of the product has lost some importance. In the last ten years the role of top models and the presence of celebrities have often captured the attention of the media. Many of the clothes presented have an exclusive image function and they are not presented in the showrooms for sale. All these factors have called the status of fashion shows into question, considering also the high costs of the shows. French shows are particularly expensive because they have always been a pure and inspired stylistic exercise and a communicative event that no longer has anything to do with the commercial situation of the brand. But fashion shows attract journalists and favorable reviews attract top retailers: this is the fashion game
- *Retail shows* are a typical feature of countries where distribution is developed, as in the US. The public at a retail show is made up of final customers, usually opinion leaders. The objective is to achieve direct sales to customers of the articles that are ready. Collaboration between the producer and the retailer is important in this case as well. They work together to offer a correct presentation of the product characteristics, and above all to achieve a good sell-out.

9.3 The distribution strategy

A crucial aspect for fashion firms concerns the choice of distribution channels. As has been emphasised several times, the distribution channel and the sales point are the fundamental elements in building brand identity. This is because the consumer does not perceive the product as an island, but as part of a wider offer system in which the retail space is also an important feature.

Until recently, many European and Italian firms in the fashion system used a multi-channel distribution (direct and indirect channels). This, however, presented problems related to the consistency of the offer system as this was perceived by the end consumer. Indirect channels do not allow for effective control of the brand's marketing mix in the way that direct channels do. The information flow from the market is also much more immediate when the firm that owns the brand also manages distribution. Conversely, the indirect channel offers the industrial brand the chance to compete with its competitors within the sales point. This is an important opportunity for checking brand positioning.

During the 1970s and 1980s firms grew through their use of indirect channels and distribution to independent retailers (through boutiques and department stores). The distribution strategy was aimed at identifying and serving those segments of customers that were most suited to the offer system. This was predominantly done through indirect sales networks. Many firms also used wholesalers, and this allowed them to obtain large sales on a reduced variety of models. One of the most important trends in the 1990s was the direct management of distribution by industrial firms. These firms began to abandon the indirect channel as a result of the development of fashion and consumer tastes. Approaching the market was achieved through direct sales networks. Another way of approaching the market was through a vertical integration of the lower stages, by means of franchising chains. This was done above all for designer labels, but also for industrial brands such as Benetton. Franchising allows for direct control of brand positioning in terms of assortments, pricing and image, and it does not require direct financing to open shops. Direct channels, which mainly consist of single-brand shops or franchising, are thus combined with traditional indirect channels, and this creates the conditions for multi-channel distribution. Some people argue that because of the resources and skills that it calls for, retail management is not part of an industrial firm's core business. Others, however, argue that vertical integration allows a stronger brand identity to be created and offers more reliable information about a firm's own market. Coming close to the place of consumption seems an increasing need in modern society, where consumer behaviour is increasingly less understandable through traditional models of analysis.

New approaches in terms of integrated supply chain management include vertical alliances and vertical integration. They allow for improving the quality and speed of response to the market, and thus the reduction of stocks. The vertical partnership forms that have been introduced recently, such as quick response, integrated marketing policies, co-makership, and the development of private labels, have allowed improvements in the logistic, communicative and informative flow of the whole pipeline.[1]

Brands with a relatively wide product range are generally more advantaged by the direct management of retailing. Competition does not focus on the product for brands that are transversal to the target or occasions of use. It increasingly focuses on the whole assortment and the sales point. Specialist single-product brands, however, are more limited in scope. It is harder for them to justify the single-brand retail outlet, both from the consumer viewpoint and from the profitability viewpoint.

---

1. On vertical agreements in the fashion system, see E. Sabbadin, 'La partnership verticale nel sistema moda', in *Economia & Management*, n. 2, 1995; E. Sabbadin, *Marketing della distribuzione e marketing integrato. I casi Marks & Spencer e Benetton*, Egea, 1997; C. Forza, A. Viella (editor), *Quick Response. La compressione dei tempi in progettazione, produzione e distribuzione*, CEDAM, 1996.

9.3.1 Segmenting distribution

As has already been said, the first choice that the industrial firm has to make concerning distribution policy relates to the channel, which can be direct or indirect.

When the firm chooses a direct channel it manages sales to consumers directly. It does this through retail formats (stores, web sites and catalogues) under the firm's brand name. Directly operated (or mono-brand) stores are the most widespread and interesting example of this approach. These can be segmented according to sales area dimension, assortment and location distinguishing between:

- *Flagship store*: these are usually large, owned by the firm, and they are located in prestigious places internationally. They have a wide assortment with a tendency towards the total look, and a sales point image evoking the world of the brand. Shops of this type are not bound by rigid turnover and profitability targets because they are considered as investments in communication
- *Self standing stores*: these are independent stores located on streets, central and semi-central, whose sales area ranges from 50 up to 200 square metres. They are consistent with the brand's identity and policies. They may be owned by the brand or they may be franchises
- *Shops in shops*: these have limited sales areas (from 30 to 120 square metres) and they are located within a shopping centre/mall. They have a more limited assortment and they use dedicated personnel usually employed by the firm. Regarding the end consumer, these stores have to lever both on the retail brand and the industrial brand to attract consumers. In this case the consumer is usually loyal to the retail brand that guarantees him an assortment of selected brands. Being located within the best selling and reputated retailers is therefore a condition for creating synergies between store loyalty and brand loyalty.

The firm with an indirect channel makes use of a number of intermediate services that can be classified according to *distributive format*. The concept of distribution format summarises different features: possible specialisation of merchandise or market segment, localisation, sales area, width and depth of the assortment, price level, and the level of service to the end customer.

There are different multi-brand distribution formats in fashion:

- *Traditional speciality stores*: these have small but deep assortments, branded products, a high level of customer assistance, and a premium price policy. They are specialised by reference to target (men, women or children), or by reference to merchandise (formal clothing, sportswear, accessories and shoes). This format has suffered the most from the integration of industrial brands into retailing
- *Department stores*: the department store is a generalised form of distribution that nearly all countries have,[2] although it is more developed in Anglosaxon countries and in Northern Europe. The distinguishing features are medium to large size, different merchandise departments (clothing, cosmetics, accessories, home furniture,...), a positioning that is not only price-based, and the coexistence of private labels with special areas for branded products. They are generally located in large cities, they have loyal customers, and they represent very important clients to their suppliers
- *Large speciality stores*: these focus on a few categories of merchandise (underwear, sportswear and shoes). They have a wide and deep assortment, private labels and brand products, a trademark policy, and they serve all price segments
- *Popular stores*: they are generalised, and they have a wide but not deep assortment, private labels and unbranded products, low prices and a popular image
- *Discount retailing* and *firm outlets*: both of these formats came into existence in response to the need to create a

---

2. The best known department stores in the world are Bloomingdale's and Macy's in New York, Printemps and Galerie Lafayette in France, El Cortes Ingles in Spain, Rinascente and Coin in Italy, and Harrods in Britain.

channel for selling unsold stocks from earlier seasons
* *Street markets*: they have a wide but shallow assortment at low prices and are very widespread in Southern Europe.

According to Retail Intelligence, the two leading clothing retailers in Europe, Marks & Spencer and C&A, have suffered in recent times as both have lost touch with key customer groups and have struggled to provide successful product assortments. All over the world generalised stores have lost market share to more nimble smaller clothing specialists who are better able to adapt to changing fashions in terms of product and in terms of in-store environment. New players are have also entered the global fashion market in the medium to lower segment with successful strategies, such as Hennes & Mauritz, the rapidly-expanding Swedish-based fashion group, the British Next and Grupo Inditex (Zara) of Spain.

One of the best known large speciality stores in clothing and sportswear is the French firm Decathlon, which came into existence in 1976. Its offer is characterised by a strong brand, high service levels, professional management, the widespread use of information systems and efficient production processes because of international sourcing. The 'satisfied sportsmen' slogan expresses the group's mission which is founded on bringing families close to sport and on customer service. The assortment is wide and deep (30,000 to 40,000 articles for 35 different sports), and it is not organised by brand but by sport. The price of the articles varies from low to medium-high. The sales points are generally on the outskirts of large cities, although smaller shops have also been opened in city centres (the standard size is about 10,000 square metres). Decathlon personnel are trained in sport, and there is also a school within the firm (Ecole Internationale des Métiers Decathlon).

A diffused method of entering multi-brand distribution (mainly department stores and large speciality stores) is through the *corner*. This is a small area (10 to 30 square metres) that is devoted to a specific brand. It has a personalised layout and a co-ordinated offer mix. The corner makes it easier to show the single brand identity and image to consumer within a multi-brand distribution. The corner assortment and merchandising mix is directly managed by the industrial firm, and the end consumer perceives the world of the brand clearly. The corner also creates conditions for the better management of service to the trade (replenishments, flash collections, management of returns). It can do this because it monitors sale-out on a daily basis, and because it maintains a good level of assortment and image. The corner is based on different contractual formulas, and these vary according to the degree of control from the industrial brand. The brand may manage the space completely in terms of assortments, sales staff, sell-out surveys and visual merchandising, or it may delegate all the activities to the retailers. The greater the brand's control, the easiest is the transfer of the firm's own commercial policies to the sales point. This also increases the chance of the consumer to obtain all the information required

One of the most interesting forms is the *partnership corner*. Here the producer and the retailer have an almost equal share in the investment and costs of managing the space, and they cooperate to give each other the information that is needed to optimise sell-outs. The *soft corner* formula is quite common where the retailer has a strong brand identity and an established clientele. This formula allows for the personalisation of the space that is needed by producers, without weakening the retailer identity. Thus, the sales point maintains its own identity even in the presence of strong industrial brands.

The corner is almost mandatory for firms willing to affirm their brand identity, but that are not able to create a network of directly operated stores. This is above all true in those geographical areas where there is a widespread distribution structure and a lot of medium to large multi-brand retailers.

The involvement of the brand owner in managing the sales point changes according to the type of distribution channel used. In directly managed distribution, where the retailer brand and the industrial brand are the same, the firm has to control all the marketing and retailing variables in order to achieve a consistent positioning among all the markets. In indirect distribution, where retailer brand and the industrial brand live side by side, commercial and distribution policies have to be adapted to the demands and specific situation of each channel. In this case as well, however, there is a trend towards harmonisation between all channels (the so called integrated multi-channel management). The purpose of this integration is to avoid possible distortions in the perception of the brand, and competition over the same brand among different channels. *Trade* selection is fundamental in the evolution from a product oriented strategy to a brand oriented strategy. Where there is no direct presence there can be a problem due to the trade filtering of information. This affects how the brands are perceived on the market. Traditional multi-brand stores are not always willing to invest or try out or support new approaches to the customer.

The most recent direction taken by leading firms is to design and present differentiated offer systems (packages) to serve different retail formats – traditional multi-brand stores, franchising partners, *free standing shops* and corners. The advantage of this is a more focused offer, a more rapid assortment and replenishment of the best selling articles, as well as more control of the market through the day to day management of sell-out information.

9.3.2 Towards the concept store

The sales point is going through a profound change. It was once the place or channel where goods were sold that had been produced anywhere. Nowadays, however, customer satisfaction and loyalty also include the place of purchase. The consumer does not perceive the offer system as something built only by the producer. Actually he or she only sees that part of the system that is present at the time of purchasing. As the sales point is the place where brand strategy is fully achieved, the brand cannot ignore the sales point when defining its market strategies. The sales point is thus the point of departure for building a lasting and interactive relationship with the consumer. This relationship is increasingly based on emotional rather than functional aspects in the fashion system.[3] The pre-condition for building customer loyalty to the sales point is a clear differentiation of the brand in

---

3. On experiential branding Pine B. J., Gilmore J. H. *The Experience Economy*, Harvard Business School Press, 1999;, Schmitt B, Simonson A. *Marketing Aesthetics. The Strategic Management of Brands, Identity and Image*, Free Press, 1997.

terms of market positioning. This explains the recent development of concept stores. These are single or multi-brand spaces
within which the sale of products takes place in a distinct environment proposing a concept. Concept stores have strong identities and autonomous capacities to attract customers. The objective of the concept store is not immediate or occasional sales,
but to attract and maintain groups of customers who are search-
ing for an emotional/informational feature apart from purchase
itself. The chance to enter a sales point without being obliged to
buy something directs the final consumer towards a more open
and less 'frightened' relationship with the brand. This establishes
the conditions for a lasting relationship that is founded not just
on sales, but also on emotions and shared values.

> Nike Town stores are large, mono-brand stores where the space used for
> events connected to the Nike world is greater than the space used for the
> sale of products. Nike uses photographs, directors and famous athletes to
> tell the stories of successful people. In this way it creates an environment
> that emphasises brand values – emotion, action and victory. Every Nike
> product is thus charged with these values and attributes, and purchase
> should be the result of a strong relationship between the brand and the
> consumer.

The idea of the *concept store* is thus being added to the traditional *brand loyalty* and results in greater store loyalty. This makes
for a completely different relationship between the retail brand
and the industrial brand. In integrated distribution models, there
is an absolute fit between the two brands. This allows for opti-
mising the role of the sales point. It becomes both a place where
a customer relationship is set in motion, and a channel for expressing brand policies. In this case it is extremely important to
ensure consistency between the identity and positioning of both
the brands that have to share a common vision and a common
target.

Fiorucci: a concept store

The Fiorucci concept store was founded by the Italian entrepreneur Elio
Fiorucci. He was inspired by London's Carnaby Street during the 1960s.
Carnaby Street was the centre of youth culture, and it was full of shops

with ethnic products and highly coloured clothes that would soon be worn by the hippies. Fiorucci opened his store in Milan's Corso Vittorio Emanuele, as a meeting place as much as a place for selling products. This used to be a very traditional part of the city, where shops had sober names like Principe di Galles and Duca d'Este. Fiorucci had a sculptress help him to create a different kind of space dominated by music and colours. It was genuinely revolutionary as there was no concept of informal, street-bred youth fashion in those days. People were astonished and sometimes hostile, but curiosity overcame their misgivings, and the shop became a commercial success in a few years. Fiorucci became a point of reference because of its architectural solutions such as its lack of windows and architectural barriers, and because of its music and people. Some novelties, such as a unisex fitting-room, were later dropped, but the inspiration was a good one – people wanted a place where they could feel free. Fiorucci was also different from other stores because it did not sell just clothing, but accessories, toys and household objects. Italian products were mixed with ethnic and hand-made ones. Over time, other brands joined Fiorucci and, as happens in American department stores, they expressed their own offer system in corners. Fiorucci did not rent out space, however, so much as bring together different articles that were all on the same wavelength under the same roof. This is how the Fiorucci style came into existence. The shop became an enormous container (1,600 square metres) for different products with the same concept. It was a philosophy and taste that can only be partly explained (the colours, the love of shiny materials like coloured plastic, the playfulness, the irony, the dreariness of fashion as an obligation). It was a concept that supplying partners could identify with intuitively, so much so that they were the first to tell Fiorucci that a product was not in the Fiorucci style. The Alessi and Swatch brands, for example, "are Fiorucci", because they refer to the same philosophy and stylistic codes represented by Fiorucci, although they are in different industries. Very serious or expensive products are not part of its world. The brands that are selected provide the product and build the image, and they provide their specialised staff. The people who come in are not made to feel awkward, and the ambience is sensuous (white wood, newspaper photographs on the walls, and perfumes) and at odds with the historic shops of the city centre which lack an emotional atmosphere. The image is also expressed through packaging, labelling, and bags. Fiorucci is the only business that can draw its own logo in a hundred different ways while still preserving its identity, and this is because the concept of change is part of its genetic code.

9.4 The commercial process and marketing intelligence

Market oriented firms have to see the commercial process not just in terms of final sales, but also as part of the wider process of information and marketing intelligence that involves the whole value chain. The creative people and the product area cannot know the needs of distribution customers and end customers. They have to be led by product and marketing managers who are responsible for analysing the market in terms of the mix, assortments and range. The commercial area has to lead product managers on the basis of the needs and feedback that come from the market. The end customer will never see the whole collection in the firm's showroom. He or she sees and forms opinions only on what is available in the sales point. If what the sales point shows is the result of a progressive selection made by everyone in the chain (agents, retailers, store directors), the brand is not able to communicate its own potential, and thus compromises its value and identity.

In an industry where time is crucial, the choice of a direct or indirect channel impacts a particular effect on the quantity and quality of market information that the producer can obtain in reasonable time. Sell-out information in the indirect channel is obtained at the top of the supply chain with a great lag. This information has to be transferred by different subjects (the retailer, the agent, and the commercial department), and it often becomes available when new collections have already been developed.

The direct channel allows the obtaining of better quality information more rapidly. The sell-out of directly managed stores can be read every day. This allows for analysing the best seller and the slow seller products. Seasonal re-assortments can be made on the basis of these data, so that there is a guaranteed assortment that is complete in terms of sizes and models in the sales point. Further, these data can be cross-referenced with data about consumer characteristics, and this sets off a process of very useful learning for the development of both the offer and the brand. The commercial process can thus link with market segmenta-

FIGURE 9.1   **THE INFORMATION PROCESS FROM THE TOP TO THE BOTTOM OF THE VALUE CHAIN**

Source: the authors.

tion and brand positioning to create the conditions for the necessary interaction between strategic choices, the product and the sale process.

New approaches to merchandising

In making product and pricing decisions for individual stores, retailing managers have long relied on their experience. But as a consequence of erratic changes in demand, collapsing product life cycles and an increased market fragmentation, merchandising decisions (getting the right goods to the right place at the right prices at the right times) have become even more complex. It happen quite frequently that a good number of the items customers come to buy are out of stock and a good number of all the goods are sold at marked-down prices.

Assortment planning is one of the key activities of the merchandising function and it occurs throughout the supply chain. In apparel manufacturing assortment planning is conducted by designers, merchandisers and product managers during the product development process (collection plan); by agents or sales representatives as they communicate a collection to potential buyers and write purchase orders for clients. In the retail sector assortment planning occurs when retail buyers determine product offerings, merchandisers allocate goods to individual stores and store managers and visual merchandisers create merchandise display. New merchandising optimisation systems[4] have emerged which aim at revolutionising the retailer's merchandising chain from planning to buying, stocking, pricing and promotion. The value of these applications lies in their ability to provide, first, a more accurate demand forecast; second to improve the retailer's decision making process.

1.   Better demand forecasts: retailers are accustomed to relying on last

---

4.   These considerations are taken from Friend S.C., Walker P.H., "Welcome to the New World of Merchandising" *Harvard Business Review*, Nov. 2001 p. 133-139.

year's sales to determine this year's forecasts but this approach evaluates only what the retailer sold and not what he could have sold had the inventory been available. By analysing historical data the software measures the consumer's response to each key driver of demand such as price, inventory levels, promotions, or seasonability. Therefore, demand forecasts are much more accurate than traditional ones

2. Better decision making: once the demand forecast has been established the software analyzes the effects of adjustments to the demand drivers by which retailers control margins and results (pricing, timing) also recommending actions

If optimisation makes the merchandising process much more rational it is also true that fashion forecasts must reflect trends that are not evident in the historical data. Here comes the retailer's experience and intuition.

Merchandising optimisation solutions are most appropriate for retailers that:

- sell products that have a short shelf life or have uncertain demand
- operate complex processes with many decision making points (i.e. chains that have multiple stores and sell hundreds of items)
- cannot recover easily from wrong decisions, because of seasonability.

10 The communication process

By Erica Corbellini

10.1 The nature of communication

Communicating is such a natural action that it seems clear to everyone. Our life is a continuous exchange of verbal and non-verbal messages. What is surprising is that the act of transmitting a message is not, by itself, communication. For communication to occur, the 'sender builds an internal representation of the external world and then starts a symbolic behaviour that transmits the contents of this representation. The recipient has to first perceive the symbolic behaviour, that is to restore the internal representation, and then builds a further personal internal representation of what it means. This final step depends on access to arbitrary conventions governing the interpretation of the symbolic behaviour.'[1]

This means that communication is the symbolic transmission (medium) of a mental representation (message) between two subjects – the one who transmits (sender) and the one who receives it (recipient). Communication only works if it takes place

---

1. P.N. Johnson Laird, *La comunicazione*, Edizioni Dedalo, 1992, p. 12.

in a specific context where there is a shared set of codes (verbal and non-verbal). The message transmitted by the sender has to be decoded by the recipient according to the sender's purposes. This is only possible if the medium, the symbols chosen to represent the message, has the same meaning for both parties. There is no communication where one of these elements is missing.

Communication is a circular process. This is why it is more correct to use the term 'interlocutor' rather than 'recipient'. 'Interlocutor' makes it clear that the recipient's role is an active one. The recipient becomes a sender through feedback, and thus starts off the communication process afresh.

The effectiveness of communication depends on the clarity of the message and the definition of the target. Communication efficiency is the result of the medium that is chosen. With reference to a firm's communication to the end consumer, the message-medium-interlocutor triangle becomes the product-window-customer relationship, when taken to extremes.

Semiotics is the discipline that 'dismantles' communication, and shows how it works. The semiotic approach came into existence in the 1960s, when there was an increase in advertising campaigns and scientific surveys. Semiotics studies the world of signification and language, and its objective is 'the objectification of the generation and organisation of meaning, independently of the language or form of expression through which it manifests itself'.[2] The semiotic approach teaches those who wish to communicate that those who receive the message are not just passive recipients. They have an active role in decoding the explicit and implicit meanings of the message. What matters in the area of business communication is recognising that brand identity cannot be imposed by the firm, as it is above all something that comes to life in the mind of the consumer.

A firm's communication strategy has to be developed at different levels. The most common distinction is between internal and external communication:

---

2. D. Bertrand, *Lo sguardo semiotico*, Franco Angeli, 1997, p. 116.

- *Internal communication*: this is mainly directed at targets within the firm (employees, shareholders, the sales force, trade unionists, suppliers, and customers with a partnership link to the firm). As a tool for sharing information and for spreading knowledge within the firm, internal communication generates learning processes and creates connections between the different resources of the firm, leading them to reach common objectives
- *External communication*: the interlocutors here are 'environmental systems that are connected outside the firm, among which the firm operates'[3] (intermediate and final customers, opinion leaders, suppliers, public authorities, the labour market, the financial market and providers of capital). External communication can be divided into two macro-areas – communication with intermediate customers and suppliers (business to business), and communication with the final consumer (business to consumer).

If we think of the communication pipeline as a system of activities and roles with a single purpose (the satisfaction of the final consumer), then the distinction between internal and external communication becomes less important. A more important distinction seems to be between *external marketing communication, internal communication, economic and social communication* and *institutional communication.*[4] The issue raises itself of the co-ordination and integration of these different types of communication, which are really four levels of the same concept rather than four separate concepts. At the organisational level this role can and should be performed by the communication function whose responsability is to maintain consistency between all the communication levels. For this to take place communication has to be seen as a process that embraces the whole organisation. It takes the form of a series of messages that express an autonomous meaning, but that are also the elements of an *integrated communication process.* Integrated communication occurs when 'any act

3. R. Fiocca, *La comunicazione integrata nelle aziende*, Egea, 1994, p. 8.
4. R. Fiocca, *op. cit.*, p. 12.

of communication [...] is decided on and executed with full awareness that the variety of tools used for communicating and the interconnection of the effects of communication on various publics make a united and general vision of communication necessary'.[5]

Integrated communication thus refers to a strategic design that provides for the synergetic and scientific use of all the means available to achieve a particular objective. All the communication specialists (public relations, press offices, image and communication agencies) share the same vision – that of the firm. Vision includes internal communication as much as external communication.

Integrated communication is above all necessary for a brand that has to communicate the intangible values of a lifestyle. A brand identity cannot be described, but the brand logo evokes elements that recall a project. The more the perceived project resembles the intended project, the higher is the effectiveness. If all the messages coming out of the firm (external communication) and those within it (internal communication) are consistent, the perception will be reinforced. If the messages are dissonant, however, each type takes something away from the other.

10.2 Communication in fashion

10.2.1 The contents and role of communication in fashion

The basic problem of fashion communication is the difficulty to focus communication just on the product. The fashion product changes every six months, and that is why the firms that communicate best, through establishing a brand image, are often those that offer a more basic and running product (jeanswear or sportswear). In this case brand values can be associated with a specific product (in one famous advertisement it was suggested conducting a funeral for Levi's five-pocket denims. The product is ideally a life-long companion, and this is something that a collection item that changes every six months cannot, and should not, be).

Communicating about fashion is thus not like communicat-

---

5. *Ibid.*

ing about any other consumer goods. Advertising codes have proved themselves inconsistent with fashion codes, because fashion is already a form of communication. Fashion communicates about itself, and is badly served by overlapping messages in another language, such as that of advertising.

Fashion has always used visual tools for communicating – photographs, shows, showrooms, models, displays, videos and sample collections. This is because symbolic elements are more important in the purchase of a fashion item than functional attributes. These symbolic features are more easily delivered through a communication based on images and aesthetic representations: the more refined the communication, and therefore the more 'useless', the more it needs this kind of support. The problem fashion companies have to face is to match the world of communication with the world of the brand, that is finding consistency between brand identity and visual identity.

The role of the communication department within fashion firms varies a lot.

At one extreme there are firms that conceive communication as the management of press relations, particularly with the so-called fashion stylists, deciding what items have to be to photographed for publishing an editorial article or how to dress celebrities in testimonial advertising. At the other extreme there are firms that organise both institutional and brand communication. Here the communication function also deals with financial and corporate communication. This variability is usually related to the firm's size and communication budget (and in the case of multinationals, to whether it is the headquarters or a subsidiary). Some large groups, for example, delegate their press office to external agencies of public relations, while others make an internal distinction between fashion, perfume and jewellery press offices. Others again have a strong internal specialisation, and the head of the press office only deals with fashion editors, while the public relations and communications manager covers the other interlocutors and media.

For these reasons it is not possible to make an unambiguous distinction between the internal and external actors in such activities as public relations and the press office.

10.2.2 The communication pipeline in the fashion system

The firm should control the consistency and synergy of all the messages that are transmitted by means of a single vision that directs the internal and external actors involved in the communication process.

One complex element in fashion communication is that this area involves a broad series of actors and professionals with very different backgrounds. Public relations agencies, event agencies, advertising agencies, press offices, artistic directors, and specialised agencies for artistic sponsorship, are all involved in the search for locations when organising fashion shows.

With regard to actors that are *external* to the firm, a distinction can be made between agencies that have direct contact with the firm, and specialised consultants offering their services to agencies. This distinction attributes an integrating role to advertising and public relations agencies. There are however some specialised actors, particularly influential photographers and art directors, whose own fame means that they have a direct relationship with the firm, and they can define casting and other elements.

Then there are some indirect or direct actors. These include production firms that are called in by the advertising agency to make films, spots and videos. Large advertising agencies played a number of roles in the past, but rising costs have led to a greater degree of specialisation. Thus media centres have become separate businesses whose objective is to achieve greater economies of scale. They have developed direct relationships with the fashion firm. *Figure 10.1* presents the communication pipeline.

The advertising agency

Advertising agencies perform an integrating role within the communication pipeline. Their most important figures are the account manager, the copy manager and art director. The copy manager and the art director are the creative parts of the agency, while the account manager is both a facilitator who brings the agency and the client together, and a project leader who ensures the timely performance of all the stages of the project.

FIGURE 10.1   **THE COMMUNICATION PIPELINE IN FASHION**

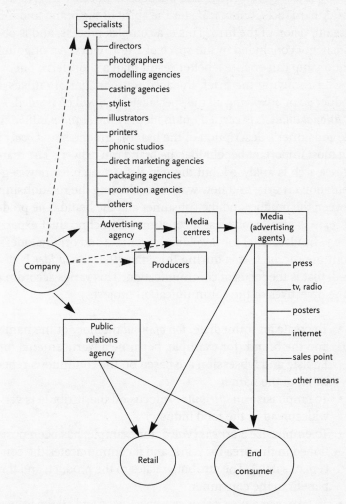

Source: the authors.

The communication project may be a television or newspaper campaign, or it may be an event. The project starts with a briefing, which is a meeting where the customer explains the brand concept to the agency account manager. The message that the firm wants to send to consumers is also explained, as is the target to be reached. This is a very important occasion that the firm has to plan very carefully. The purpose is not just to give the agency hard facts, but to transfer the spirit of the brand and the mission/vision of the firm. This is a complex process, and is obviously not concluded in the space of a few hours. An ongoing relationship can ensure a better result than a short-term one.

After receiving the brief, the account manager organises a product team, involving all the specialists who will be needed. A *situational analysis* is carried out to identify the *brand positioning* (the consumer's description of the brand), and the *brand benefit* (the most important benefit that the brand can deliver). The market research is analysed, but there is also a search for new segmentation criteria, and new ways of evaluating the relationship between the product and the consumer and the brand. The product team is also involved as a consumer. Direct product experience is fundamental for developing accurate and original ideas about the product. It is during this stage that the *ladder* is defined, that is the focus of communication. This varies according to the objectives of the communication project.

- To create an immediate, *top of mind* memory of the name and the brand (for example, perfume advertisements for Egoiste and Obsession are based on the continuous repetition of the name)
- To emphasise an *attribute* . A focus on the attribute is very widespread in the food industry
- To emphasise a *benefit* (Volvo, for example, has been positioned in this area for years, and it communicates the concept of safety). The attribute relates to the product, and the benefit to the consumer
- To take over a physical or symbolic *space*, and all the values related to it (Marlboro, for example, the West, and Merit, sailing)
- To reflect a *value* (Nike: 'just do it'; Barilla: 'home is where Barilla is'; Diesel: 'for successful living'). All the advertisements that evoke concepts like rebellion and irony fall into this category
- To claim a *role*. This is the most difficult area to cover, as it means taking on a mission or role in society (for example:

United Colours of Benetton, not only jumpers but also praise of the multiracial society; Apple, whose mission is to adapt the PC to people rather than the opposite).

The result of all this is the *copy strategy*. The copy strategy is a summary of the strategic thinking that identifies the communication route that will be taken, as well as some of the creative indications.

The *media strategy* is added to the copy strategy. This defines the choice and importance of different media. It is only at this point that the copy and art departments develop the real creative part. Ideas come from both of them at the initial stage.

The result of this work is often tested, not only within the product team, but also with pre-tests conducted with final consumers (focus groups). These obviously only provide a qualitative indication. After having seen the proposal, the client may accept, reject, or require possible changes to it; the commissioning firm often holds a bid between different agencies.

In the case of a *television advertisement*, presentation takes the form of the *story board* of the alternatives that the client firm is asked to select from (the story board is a document made of different key frames that illustrate the key actions of the story, often designed by hand by the graphic designers). Once the firm has made its choice, the agency chooses a production firm on the basis of economic estimates and proposed film directors. When these have been selected, they are presented to the client, and the directors show their own *show-reels* (this is a kind of visual curriculum vitae).

In the case of a *press campaign*, the agency shows its own creative suggestion through the layout. This document is made up of hand-made designs that are then scanned and computerised. They represent the different *subjects* of the campaign (different forms of the message in the same format and pay off – the phrase that defines the basic concept of the communication).

After client approval the agency makes the *executives* (computer documents that define the precise position and colour of each word or object on the page). These will be used for the camera ready copy, to be sent to different magazines.

Fashion designers do not make a great use of advertising agencies. On one hand it is argued that the presence of designers would be too influential. On the other, that the agencies do not have art and copy departments accustomed to the fashion language. In reality, fashion firms and communication and advertising firms are both playing on the same ground – creativity. This would make meetings between designers and art directors turn into clashes of personality that would be too hard to overcome for the sake of finding a common approach. The separation of the two worlds has resulted in a difference of language. Fashion has traditionally regarded itself as 'above' the agencies, and has denied itself the communication potential that the agencies could have offered. The agencies, for their part, have not developed the necessary sensitivity to operate in an industry with different rules to those of consumer goods. There is also the problem of size. Modern advertising agencies are more like factories than creative workshops. Their excessive rigidity and bureaucracy puts off designers who are looking for a personalised relationship.

The language of advertising itself is in crisis. Communication has evolved considerably since the days when constant advertisement "bombardment" was considered sufficient for persuading consumers. For goods with a high intangible content, however, communication has to have increasing contact with other sciences like psychology, sociology and semiotics. This means that advertising has to shift from persuasion towards empathy. Ads work on a variety of different levels including, but not limited to, sign typology, paradigmatic meaning, psychological appeals, emotion, roles, values/beliefs, and knowledge. Again, the impact of an ad comes from the interplay between these various aspects of make-up and the reader's own notions about him/herself and the world. Nowadays both the advertising industry and the fashion industry perceive the need to work closer, but there are still few signs of this change. The advertising world is certainly interested in fashion because it is one of the few industries where communication budgets are not declining. For their part, fashion firms want to overcome the crowding of advertising in women's magazines. They are looking for new directions for their advertising communications.

The last few years have seen the birth of several small advertising agencies that specialise in fashion. These small agencies operate as both advertising and image agencies (management of events). The large agencies, however, still stay behind (except for sportswear or large distribution). There is an increasing tendency for fashion firms to recruit their communication managers from advertising agencies.

Public relations

Managing public relations means tracking all the public actions of a brand, the shows, the presentation of the sample collection, the launch of a new line, the opening of a new boutique, and special events (usually society gatherings, or those related to fund-raising or arts, sports and music sponsorship). The objective is to promote the brand image to final consumers, even if the initiatives themselves are generally aimed at those who work in the industry and opinion leaders. These people talk about the events, and they get talked about, and this should bring the event to public notice.

As fashion firms become increasingly professional in the way they use management, and their communication increases in sophistication, there arises the problem of redefining the role of public relations. Public relations in the era of integrated communication cannot be left to individuals with contacts in the upper classes who just organise parties. The boundaries between public relations people, stylists and consultants are more and more fluid. The public relations role in the strict sense often includes some consultancy work nowadays. This includes organising photographic sessions, styling and direct mailing. Some people think that the future will be for large integrated communication agencies. Their specialisation will make them more efficient and professional. Others think that the public relations function is already the 'business card' of the firm, and that the role will not be entrusted to outsiders.

The press office

A press office uses press releases to interact with fashion journalists about the publication of material related to a product, a collection, or even the financial performance of the firm. The press office therefore has to know 'who does what' in the press, and it has to be able to talk the same language. Press releases have to be drawn up in a certain way, with a heading, a body of text, and a tail. Sometimes the newspaper typesetter, for technical reasons, cuts either the heading or the tail. It is therefore necessary that a press release is written with a balanced centre. More important still, clearly, is the press office's ability to send a message that is consistent with the philosophy of the firm. This means that the press office has to absorb the firm's culture and the concept of the brand. The consistency with brand identity should not only concern the message, but also the medium and the context. The paper on which a press release for a designer's label is written will be glossy, while ecological paper will be used for a younger brand. Employees in the press office of a jeanswear firm will have very informal behaviour, while a French fashion griffe will behave very formally.

The press office uses the press review to measure the result of its own work, both quantitatively (in terms of the number of times the message has been sent out) and qualitatively (for example, how many papers have mentioned the collection positively, and how many negatively). These evaluations are necessary for future actions and for personalising these to suit specific interlocutors.

Communication is not made only by technicalities; there is a strong relational element that often makes personal knowledge of the interlocutors necessary. Journalists, for example, are invited to showrooms to see the collections because the product has emotional elements that cannot just be transmitted through the written word or through photographs. The message therefore becomes a live event, and it also develops thanks to the relationship that is built up with the interlocutor.

The emphasis on the relational aspect has clearly some drawbacks. Sometimes the press office in a fashion firm is reduced to the performance of public relations activities. It is also true that many complain about the 'vices' of the industry but also do little to improve the situation. If communication is not supported by clear and accurate documentation, looking for a 'short cut' is inevitable ("shocking" fashion shows or gifts to the journalists). An interview can only work if it has contents, and where these are lacking, social gatherings become the only means for providing it.

Specialised press

There are two roles within the specialist press – the stylist and the journalist.

The stylists are responsible for selecting the articles from the various collections for the editorials. They are not involved in the preparation of texts. The journalists are usually mainly involved with customs and lifestyles. This has undoubtedly influenced the designers who have transformed collection presentations into shows, in order to be talked about. The competence of fashion stylists and journalists is almost always restricted to the aesthetics.

It is very hard for fashion journalists to have a technical or business background. This is because the fashion pages in magazines do not offer information about the quality, composition, comfort or other functional values of the articles. They are above all concerned with trends and image. The format of the magazines would not encourage a technical approach since the pages devoted to fashion match the editorials. They are thus advertising rather than information.

The stylist selects the items for a show, an advertising campaign or for an editorial, giving shape to sensations and atmosphere. The stylist needs two fundamental talents – aesthetic sensitivity and the ability to sense the mood of the moment. As they are the people with the ultimate responsibility for the image of one designer's offer (in the case of a show) or several designers (where the articles are chosen for editorials), the stylist sometimes plays a very important role in creating fashions and styles. Some people regard them as the 'opinion makers' behind the success of many designers because they put the designer's creations in touch with the real world. They not only decide which articles are the most important ones in a collection, but they also introduce changes right before the show (further evidence that many shows are still exclusively the result of aesthetic sensitivity alone). Most of them limit themselves to finding a location for fashion services.

10.2.3 The communication tools

There are many communication tools, as a firm's every action and public event is a form of communication (from the letter to shareholders to the choice of headquarters location).

One way of classifying communication tools is:

- *Seasonal* communication tools (for example fashion shows, media, catalogues and fairs)
- *Institutional* communication tools (for example the brand, the headquarters, shops, sponsorship and business magazines)
- *Relational* communication tools (for example website, direct marketing, relational marketing, mailing and events).

A further distinction applies between 'hot' and 'cold' media. Telephone and radio are examples of hot media, and television is the best example of cold media because those who watch it are very passive.

Seasonal communication tools
Catalogues
This is the most traditional tool in fashion. It was first used in the relationship between manufacturers and distributors to show collections.

Nowadays the increased contacts among subjects in the pipeline, the costs of printing and, above all, the advent of the Internet, have meant that catalogues have lost some of their importance. The classic distribution of catalogues in the sales point is not very useful because it is given to a customer who is already looking at the collection, and to a retailer that has already bought it. Firms are increasingly replacing this kind of catalogue with direct marketing. Direct marketing combines sending an advance catalogue to clients with personal invitations to specific events such as sales or displays of new collections (some firms are thinking of directing shows at small customer groups with similar attitudes and tastes), and sales point presentations. One-to-one direct marketing includes personal contacts (a birthday card, or an invitation for seasonal sales for example).

Fashion shows
Shows are the most important communication tool. This is because fashion communication has been identified for a long time with product communication. The fact that shows have become the most important communication event has resulted in a great change in their role. The show has become an exhibition where fashion is the simplest way to generate interest and shock. This is why the clothes on the catwalk are often different to those that will be put on sale. Not everything that is shown will be manufactured (the buyers make their own choices at a later date, when the collections are shown in *ad hoc* displays in the showrooms),

It has to be remembered that seasonal events in Milan, Paris, London and New York are the occasions when the fashion world is most visible.

Fairs
These are occasions for meetings among the operators from different parts of the textile pipeline. The sales function is less important, and fairs are a tool for pure business to business communication. The most important fairs, however, are also promotional tools aimed at the final consumer, thanks to the press and the series of events connected to them (shows, presentation of new lines or brands, round tables, and so on).

The media
The press
The press is the outstanding medium in the fashion system. It attracts most of the advertising investment, and it works through daily newspapers, periodicals and specialist magazines. Daily newspapers perform a social function because of their superior information value. From the point of view of advertisements, their advantages are in terms of timeliness, greater coverage, target (loyal readers), and the authority of their articles. These ele-

ments should have an effect on the credibility of the advertising message. The disadvantages are the lack of selectivity (generalised targets) and the reduced visual impact.

Periodicals, which are very widespread in Italy, offer greater specialisation than newspapers. Every magazine has an audience (the number of people reached in a given period of time by a message through the press, the radio or television). The audience is selected by the contents of the magazine itself (a predominantly male public versus female targets, a highly educated and high-income public versus a more popular one). The selectivity of magazines explains the wide use that the fashion system makes of them. The cosmetics industry has a monopoly on women's magazines in terms of advertising. As well as reliable targets, magazines offer the advantage of colour and better image reproduction. Their disadvantage is due to overcrowding, and the ratio between advertising and editorials makes many magazines look like interminable advertising catalogues. Further, many people in the field believe that over time most magazines are pretty much the same as regards target and contents. Finally, and with particular reference to men, there is currently no channel for non-specialised fashion communication.

Specialist magazines are an important tool for *business to business* communication. These provide more technical information.

The problem in Italy is that there are no communication methods that are unique to the industry. There is no difference between the images that are used for sell-ins (sales to the trade) and those that are used for sell-outs (sales to the end customer). The result is that even when addressing a public that works in the industry (such as distribution, for example), who would be interested in technical and qualitative details about the product, the language is exclusively emotional.

Television

Television has some programmes about fashion, but these are principally concerned with clothing. Television is not used as an advertising medium by designers' griffes because the audience is too wide. This is not the case for mass-market products like perfumes and sportswear.

Hoardings

This medium has a great impact, and in some cases it even becomes a form of urban decoration. Hoardings are much cheaper than newspaper advertisements, and they have a greater impact. This is why their use is increasing, above all for accessories (bags, shoes, perfumes and spectacles).

Multi-media channels: videos and CDs

Although the fashion industry is theoretically an ideal one for multimedia representation, only a few firms have gone beyond the classic promotional video (where parts of shows are generally shown and some production and back-stage images and the press campaign). These videos are used in the showrooms and flagship stores. Their objective is to renew communication when the collection arrives in the shop. They also supply information about ideal product matches for maintaining the collection's philosophy, and are an effective way of delivering this information to the consumer. The video is also a form of display in itself, a structural part of the shop that substitutes the traditional window-display. Video can also be used in fairs, at conventions, or within the firm itself as a work tool for people in the commercial area. Video can also be updated and put on the Internet and CDs, or for talking directly to the consumer. Video is also widely used in the *company tale* (where the firm tells its own story and describes its own roots). The company tale is a resource that firms, unfortunately, make little use of. The greatest advantages of CDs are interactivity and multimediality. A CD makes it possible to access the most interesting information, to zoom in on specific features, and to reach the information immediately. This is why some firms have replaced the traditional catalogue with a CD presentation.

Institutional communication tools

The brand

Communication about brand identity can be seen at two levels – the institutional and the business level.

Firms whose brand and corporate names are the same have always found brand communication valuable. The brand communicates the firm's vision and mission regarding its desired positioning. It does this through permanent visual codes that are recognisable because they are specified consistently and precisely. Toscani's famous campaigns for Benetton aim at communicating the concept of the union of differences, colours and races. This is something the group has always represented, irrespective of its seasonal product offerings.

Where the name of the brand is different to that of the firm, or where the firm has a brand portfolio, brand and institutional communication are not the same thing. This kind of firm has the problem of communicating at different levels. The corporate name will be used at the institutional level as a fame or guarantee factor of the whole offer system. Individual brands will communicate the area of taste relative to their specific business. Brand portfolios are more common in consumer goods industries than in fashion (Nestlé or Procter & Gamble).

The sales point

The increased importance of the sales point as a meeting point is the result of a change in the relationship between firms and consumers. The sales point has moved from being essentially a place for economic transactions towards being a multi-dimensional media delivering emotions. Sociologists speak about 'societing' rather than 'marketing', and of friendship in consumer dealings. The consumer's involvement with the firm is no longer seen as purely rational, but as the clash-confrontation-meeting between two worlds.

This is how the strategic importance of the sales point comes about. It is the theatre in which brand strategies are acted out, it is the perfect environment (just because it is a physical space) for creating and transferring an atmosphere, and it is the ideal place for a multiple relationship with the consumer where the consumption experience is 'in the round'. Distribution has a significance that it did not have in the past, because it is through distribution that consumer dialogue is established (forcing the firm to compare product and brand strategy). The shop is thus an integrated marketing tool; it is the first mass media of the firm's strategy. Many brands lack a consistent approach to brand

identity management and this can be seen very clearly by looking at their stores. Recently leading fashion houses began restructuring their shops with ambitious architecture making alliances with well known architects (Prada-Rem Koolhaas; Issey
Miyake-Frank Gehry and Hermes-Renzo Piano). The aim of the
new stores is to combine shopping with public space for more
cultural events.

Arts sponsorship
Fashion is coming ever closer to the arts, and to everything cultural. Designers are involved in artistic events (both as simple
sponsors and display curators). Some fashion houses have even
created special places such as the Prada Foundation or the
Trussardi's Marino alla Scala in Milan, where they hold exhibitions of avant-garde artists' work.

The marriage of art and fashion is controversial. They are undoubtedly close because of their common codes of aesthetic sensitivity[6], but they are separated by time (collections have to be
ready every season, while art is timeless). Art can certainly offer
fashion aesthetics and cultural legitimacy. Designers perform a
social role, organising exhibitions and restoring important works
in the Italian heritage, and they do this to restore credibility to a
world that is often perceived as trivial and unjustifiably expensive.

Arts sponsorship also brings fashion and music together.

Gianni Versace was a friend, partner and adviser to contemporary pop music stars, and he commented that in the last ten
years it has been rock stars that have given the strongest and
most modern image. They have completely replaced actors who
had been in the lead since Hollywood times. Increasing numbers of firms are supporting world tours and concerts, above all
in jeanswear and sportswear.

---

6. References to the world of pictures and the figurative arts do not occur by chance
   in fashion collections and advertisements. One thinks of Théodore Gericault's *La
   zattera della medusa* which was used in an advertising campaign by Vivienne West-
   wood.

Business magazines
Business magazines are more focused than catalogues, and they can be an important tool for building consumer loyalty.

> Elena Mirò, a Vestebene-Miroglio Group brand, is aimed at women with a size of 46 and above. The brand filled an editorial blank with the magazine *Le taglie del sorriso* (Smiling sizes). It was a huge success. In 1999 150,000 copies of the magazine were sent directly to customers, and a further 150,000 were distributed to boutiques and Elena Mirò corners. The transformation of the business catalogue into a real women's magazine came about because of a series of initiatives that were originally oriented towards participation. Women readers were involved in the management of the magazine. They wrote articles, letters (a book of ironic stories written by readers was planned around the subject of 'a little fatter'), they suggested topics to be discussed and even posed for photographs as 'fat models'. In the autumn of 1998 Mirò launched the first oversized modelling agency in Italy. It was called "*ciao magre*" (Bye-bye skinnies)'.

The relational tools
The Internet: from communication tool to a new business metaphor
The Internet is still not widely used by the fashion system. This is despite the fact that it could have many applications, both in the *business to consumer* area, and for *business to business* activities.

The objective in business to consumer should be to increase the amount of communication through 'widespread' access (as in the case of the show). It should also allow the firm to be in greater touch with its consumers (if the relation between *intention to buy* and net contact is a valid one). *Business to business* communication should, however, focus on making relationships within the productive and distributive pipeline more efficient.

The Internet can be used in the following ways by firms when dealing with consumers:

- As a *communication tool* for exhibiting collections, giving indications about where they can be found, telling those who log on about the firm's own history and the initiatives it is undertaking

> On Wednesday 29 September 1999 an Italian fashion show was broadcast for the first time on the Internet, at the same time as the show for the

Milan collections. It was possible to see the whole spring-summer collection for 2000 from anywhere in the world, by connecting to the Krizia site. This was preceded by an interview with the designer. All the Krizia shops had maxi-screens installed, to let customers follow the show, or to see it over the next two days. This gave buyers the advantage of not having to come to Italy. Compared to the nine hundred people who would normally have had access to the show, total estimates for the Internet attendance – taking account of time differences and the capacity of the Internet, were about 15,000 people per minute or 150,000 to 200,000 people.

When the American underwear brand Victoria's Secrets put Laetitia Casta on the internet for a fashion show, the rush was enough to blow out the Internet. Even models will be virtual soon. The joint work of Diesel and an Italian multimedia firm specialising in home entertainment, gave birth to Shadow Man, a killer zombie from the video game of the same name. He wears Diesel jeans as a virtual testimonial.

- For the *direct sale* of products
- For *gathering information* about the firm's own customers
- For *developing collections* thanks to the opinions, advice and contributions of net surfers
- As a means of entertainment, for example with articles from international magazines, close ups on facts and celebrities, pages devoted to entertainment, windows on the world of fashion and musical trends, the places and main events in night life, games, tests and interactive surveys.

Deciding to talk directly to consumers is not simple. There are many problems in terms of financial returns and lack of accuracy. *Most of this is related to the difficulty of communicating in an Internet-oriented way*, avoiding the simple reproduction of brochures or business catalogues. Different media require different contents and presentations, and there is an additional difficulty – it is not enough that the material is well prepared for the Internet, it also has to be constantly updated (otherwise the reason for logging on a second time is reduced). Too many brands still use the Internet as a window for the reproduction of images from the catalogue with a copy of the printed page. They lose the huge information and interactive potential of the tool by doing this. The television public was brought up on advertising bombardment. Internet navigators, however, can use the interactive tool to avoid mass messages. The capacity to offer interesting, useful and updated information is therefore fundamental.

The Internet is changing the relationships between the media and the firm in favour of the latter. The firm can now transfer information directly to the consumer without the need for intermediation. It is not by chance that in times of business crisis the Internet is used by 80% of firms, as it allows them to give customers all the information they need. This is something that could never happen with the traditional press. As far as using the Internet as a sales tool for clothing products is concerned, there are two absolute conditions:

- That the trust of the consumer in his dealings with the firm is established
- That the product is basic and has already been tested by the consumer (it is much easier to sell basic products online, like Levi's 501 jeans, Nike shoes or Gap T-shirts, than made to measure articles).

Italian ready-to-wear thus seems to have a disadvantage compared to the American casualwear product. On-line sales lead to some technical problems related to the transfer of warehousing from distribution to the firm, and thus to the width and assortment of the offer, sizes and drops. There is also the possibility of the cannibalisation of the traditional distributive structures. The time for approaching this new tool is medium-long term, and the firms that will achieve success first will be those that can count on the following:

- High sales volumes
- Global market
- Prevalence of current articles (not necessarily sportswear) or accessories in their offer structure.

In the short-term more opportunities are available for *business to business* networks with protected access through the Intranet and the Extranet. These allow for performing a series of operational functions on-line such as information, image and sound exchange, all of which can result in improved and more effective co-ordination.

Intranet networks (within the same organisation) are used to make the communication process more rapid and pervasive, and to spread knowledge among organisation members. This works both through the transmission of real-time reports, circulars, and initiatives, and the establishment of discussion groups and information exchange groups.

Extranet applications, however, are of particular interest. From the *business to business* viewpoint, communication has to increase the diffusion of information within the pipeline, in order to satisfy the increasingly well-informed and sophisticated consumer. Only firms that establish continuous learning processes and collect, elaborate and manage information can build long-term competitive advantages. The Internet can accumulate knowledge and make it available to the actors in pipeline. It does this in a context where production and sales points both benefit from synergies.

There are still few web sites moving in this direction. One of the most cited is wgsn.com (Worth Global Style Network). In return for the payment of an annual subscription it offers more than 180,000 pages that are updated on a daily basis, including the most complete on-line guide to news, information and studies in the fashion, style and design industry. The services offered by the site include:

- Review of the daily press and economic data about leading and emerging firms
- Calendars and reviews of fairs with photographs
- Specialist articles on trends and street styles supported by images and photographs of the trendiest places and streets in all the cities of the world
- Photographic archives of shows and virtual catalogues for fibres, textiles and finished articles
- Retail monitoring with more than 1,000 photographs a month of the 'hottest' windows in the 15 leading cities of the world in terms of style, and real time information about new openings
- Intelligence about the youth world and everything that causes trends
- News and in-depth information about new regulations (in particular those that concern the complexities of import/export tariffs)
- Graphics and comments about joint progress in the industry.

Sites that offer a similar service are not just a source of inspiration for ready fashion and for all those who want 'inspiration' for ready-to-wear models. Their real and much more important function is to *shorten the distances in the pipeline* by connecting the creation, production and sales stages through shared information. The problem of information overload, however, does not seem to have been solved. The service sites usually make a considerable amount of information available to operators, but they supply very little critical analysis, and they do not select from the mass of information on the basis of effective needs.

The Internet has been compared to an enormous library, where a huge number of books can be found, but these are not in any order. Managing the Internet effectively does not mean accessing all the information possible – it means only accessing information that is useful to the decisional process.

Co-marketing

This is the future for many firms. There are many examples of co-marketing, from Absolut Gucci (the collection that Tom Ford, Gucci's creative director, made in collaboration with Absolut Vodka) to joint promotional programmes involving textile and clothing firms or underwear firms and firms in the cosmetics industry. It is a route to diversification in the retail industry. It brings together products from different merchandise categories that have similar emotional contents that make it possible to transfer a world of reference more easily. Co-marketing allows similar brands to share location expenses, even if there are limits in terms of space.

10.3 A critical overview of fashion communication

10.3.1 Communicating the product

The main criticism of fashion communication is that it is not differentiated. It is difficult to distinguish different brand images because of the homogeneity of the messages that are transmitted and because of the overcrowding of the media themselves.[7]

To understand the reasons for this homogeneity it is necessary to look briefly at the development of communication in the fashion system. Fashion communication is a recent event. Up to the 1960s, the only communication tool was the show, and these were predominantly sales events rather than communication ones as they are today. The democratisation of fashion in the 1970s posed the problem of no longer addressing fashion shows to those who worked in the industry. With the advent of griffes in the 1980s fashion brands emerged and invaded the collective imagination.

During these years communication was managed on a trial and error basis. There was a frequent lack of well defined company mission, and this was reflected in the difficulty of transmitting precise and consistent communication codes to the various specialists in the communication pipeline. It was paradoxical that fashion firms, that should have expressed a huge potential for creativity and differentiation, were unable to break out of the rules of the game in communication because of their emphasis on the product over all the other variables in the marketing mix.

Fashion communication in the 1980s moved downwards from the designers. They often made decisions not only about the product/collection, but also about communication. This explains the particular structure of the marketing function in fashion firms. When the function existed at all, it was usually denied any strategic role and was essentially limited to marketing data analysis. The central role of the product in communication strategy led to a huge limitation in the tools that could be used. Communication was often left only to the show and to the catalogue, limiting the creative contribution to photographs of celebrities and top models. These are not distinctive skills, however, as they are available to anyone who can pay for them. The strong relationship between communication and the product has a series of implications:

---

7. This issue was discussed in an eloquently titled piece of research in 1988 commissioned by the Associazione Italiana Industriale dell'Abbigliamento at GPF&Associati on advertising in the fashion industry: 'Supernulla' (Super-Nothing).

- *The lack of a communication concept*: one effect of the centrality of the product has been that there is no clear creative brief to advertising, public relations and photographic agencies. These agencies have made their own decisions about objectives and strategies. The inadequate delegation of this role to outsiders has produced paradoxical effects, particularly in the past. One example is that of the item that was photographed. This was often not the best seller or the best representative of the creative concept behind the collection. It was often photographed because the stylist liked it, even though it was not available in the shops and had not been presented on the catwalk.

Taking the shortcut of *image communication* seems natural, and this has replaced the lack of a strong concept for many firms. Communication campaigns that were begun in the booming years of "Made in Italy" deliberately chose not to have consistent promises, specific objectives and distinctive positioning for products and brands and pursued a blurred, unclear image

- *Repetitiveness*: fashion that does not communicate becomes *conventional*, both in terms of the message transmitted and the medium used to transmit it. This is particularly the case of the designer. Regarding the medium, this takes the form of the same tools and the same media – the same photographers, the same top models, the choice of headed paper, the show as the high-point of communication that repeats the same scene with the same actors (journalists, Japanese buyers, celebrities, the so-called fashion community). All this leads to a split between the communication occasion and the consumer's real purchase occasion.

According to the manager in charge of external communications for a large fair in the industry, the repetitiveness of fashion advertising does not affect other industries such as cars because car images are found in magazines along with other products, while fashion is in specialist magazines which always show the same thing.

Regarding the message that is transmitted, the crowded images of unfriendly, inaccessible, sulky and aggressive models is in a certain sense anti-fashion because the distance between such scenes and ordinary people is always the same. The image that is transmitted is of a world for the very few, and it is typical of *haute couture* and the luxury that it represents. It does not vary with respect to the mission of individual brands. Everything is inexorably the same, and it conforms to the same aesthetic. Thus, to know which designer is talking, it is necessary to look for the name at the bottom. The result is that fashion advertising campaigns are less effective in terms of recognition of a specific brand

- *Self-referentiality*. The general impression is that communication in fashion is *self-referential*, that it is directed at those who already work in the industry. Fashion communication is almost never aimed at consumers but at opinion leaders. This confuses the instrument (which opinion leaders should be – for example the rock singer who becomes a testimonial for a label by wearing the clothes during a concert) with the recipient (the one who buys the clothes). There is a risk that the added value that is not declared will be clear only within a small group that understands it

- *Communication as cost*. From the economic perspective, the match between communication and product has meant that fashion firms consider communication expenses as *costs* and not as an investment. They thus eliminate any possibility of evaluating the effects of communication.

10.3.2 The new communication scenarios

Communication inefficiency and ineffectiveness could be excused during the 1980s. This was the golden period, for fashion in general and for "Made in Italy" in particular, when the market was so receptive that everything seemed simple and relatively cheap to communicate. The situation today is very different. Shrinking consumption, the higher number of competitors, the greater specialisation and fragmentation of the communication industry, and new channels like the Internet, all make fashion communication more difficult and expensive, and increasingly necessary to establish a brand identity.

The 1990s were also characterised by some changes within the fashion system that led to the emergence of new actors and new competitive thinking:

- Ready-to-wear fashion has to reach the consumer more quickly and directly
- Direct distribution has already become the key point for fashion communication, and is imposing consistent brand strategies
- New segments have burst onto the fashion scene and these communicate as *activewear* – the specialist product has become a product for all occasions thanks to communication (Nike's *swoosh* is both the brand logo and an immediate reference to sport) and *underwear* – from the *wonderbra* to products featuring as external clothing
- Even in the raw materials and intermediate products a communication revolution has begun. Communication is no longer business to business oriented, but is aimed at creating interest directly from the end consumer
- New critical areas have also emerged, such as licences. Additional complexity has led to the need for the licensee partners to maintain a strong image at the expense of the licensor's freedom of managing communication. It has also led to the licensee's need not to be forgotten or to be sufficiently involved in the communication strategy. This is an area where managing integrated communication is difficult, given that the reference is often to an inconsistent brand extension resulting from a speculative licensing policy
- The minimum level of investment required to be heard on the market is increasing. Compared with large firms operating in sportswear that spend tens millions of Euro on communication in one season, the real world of fashion is made of medium sized firms with small budgets devoted to communication. Few brands are able to overcome the

so-called 'sound barrier'. Being below it means getting no attention, or risking wasting the money that has been invested.

It is difficult to estimate exactly how much the fashion world invests in communication. The amount is always underestimated (it should be remembered that communication is not just advertising, but also the show, the flagship store, and investment in retail – these are all in the *below-the-line* area). The most important fact is the need for differentiation, given that the market is increasingly difficult, with the continuous birth and death of brands, and where the future of the griffe is itself under discussion. There is a need to be creative, to be capable of evolving rapidly and in harmony with new tastes in communication as well as in product strategy.

Those who have successfully changed the rules of the game have been rewarded, as the cases of Diesel and Calvin Klein show. They offered completely different worlds – irony and sexual ambiguity respectively – and they have been studied in marketing manuals, just because of the strength and connotation of the messages in their advertising campaigns. The actors have always been tempted to explore new directions through sports and arts sponsorship, co-marketing, and some hesitant movements in the direction of corporate communication.

10.3.3 From communicating by images to communicating by imaginaries

There was less emphasis on the product at the end of the 1990s, to such an extent that there were complaints about the opposite tendency - the disappearance of the clothes in magazines in favour of the overall context. Two different trends were noteworthy. On the one hand the physical product was shown in a barely descriptive way, particularly as regards accessories. On the other hand, only evocative images were used and their vagueness often did not justify their use. Earlier the photographic shooting was of details and the product characteristics, whereas now suggestion prevails. The focus is no longer on the model's clothes but on the environment in which they have to be worn. The predominant communication code seems to be suggesting rather than showing, evoking a sensation or emotion in which the clothes, the shoes are hidden if not entirely absent. In the shop windows of many of the leading brands, clothes and accessories are no longer seen at all – instead, there are some photographs of them as evidence of the already close link between the object and the image.

The problem is that there is a risk in this case as well, of remaining within image communication in the sense that if the atmosphere is the same for all, the message does not get through, exactly as in the past.

Fashion communication in the 1990s undoubtedly made an effort to move from product communication to *brand identity* communication. The conclusion of this process, which still has to start for many firms, is that firms move to more complex terrain, that of *imaginative communication*. The new terrain is fertile but potentially slippery. This implies that the firm communicates through its own world of reference, on the basis of its own identity and therefore of its recognition and self-justification for the final consumer.

The imagination is a larger and more pervasive concept than image. It goes beyond traditional segmentations based on lifestyles by suggesting brand identity as the key for a transversal interpretation of fashion where people live out the different experiences of their existence. Working on the imagination means starting from desire rather than need. This is a more difficult challenge. It can only be won if the consumer identifies himself as a character in a story. For this to happen, the brand has to be able to tell relevant, credible and consistent stories. This credibility can only be won if the *communication codes* are *permanent*. The object of the communication therefore has to be the brand. *Visual identity* has to match *stylistic identity*, and it has to be based on recognisable codes of communication that are distinct for each brand (Sicily for Dolce & Gabbana, irony for Diesel, the echo of classical Greece for Versace, the anti-fashion cry of Moschino, and so on).

No imagination can be credible if it does not find some correspondence in the product. Communication thus has to become, at least in part, information. The stylistic, functional and qualitative values, and the product's distinctive value for money, have to be communicated because they create differentiation and help the consumer to evolve.

Some examples of imaginative communication
Hermès
Hermès has a history (it came into existence in a Parisian workshop in 1843, and there is now the sixth generation in the firm). One of the business assets is thus the time factor. Time is written into its mission - making a product of outstanding quality with no concessions to the marketing (making a good product requires time). Hermès tries to innovate without ever turning away from the values of tradition. These values are also the subjects of its communication. For example, the mercantile spirit that has always characterised the history of Hermès has led to the development of an ethnic theme related to travel in its communication (under the headline 'Hermès, the only elegant luggage'). Hermès uses institutional communication that is intended to arouse emotion. Its objective is to communicate the world rather than the product (the house magazine is called 'The world of Hermès'). The imagination of Hermès is for the very few, almost aristocratic. It avoids the obvious use of the logo as a communication tool, and uses it only as a signature (like a painter's initials on a painting). The result is that the products do not have a label on the outside and the visuals of the brand campaign leave out the trademark. The communication codes are the colour orange (a random choice due to the wartime exhaustion of the traditional brown wrapping paper), the 'balduc' (the reel that is wrapped around packages), and the theme that the group offers each year. The whole communication system and some of the production system revolve around the theme. The tree theme is important as well as the travel theme. This is a symbol of growth. Its roots represent the past and the leaves the future. The image is a leaf with a drop of water, underneath which the 'balduc' could be seen (nature knows how to be essential, Hermes is essential for nature). In 1999 the dream was chosen as a theme. It began with a strong use of the colour code with loose fitting products in an orange background. It then became 'Hermes, messenger of dreams', with a foot that evoked Hermes, the messenger of the gods whose duty was to liase with the world of human beings.

Gucci
Gucci is an important name that was impoverished because of uncontrolled licensing and a dramatic family saga. It was both an unwieldy in-

heritance and at the same time a very valuable asset that it would have been neither correct nor possible to ignore when attempting to reposition the brand. There was one other variant. Guggio Gucci was gone, but there was an art director, Tom Ford. Like all designers who take on a brand, Ford could not start from his own ideas, but had to revitalise the label and make it fashionable once again. He had to get to the depths of the stylistic codes (which he had studied for months). At this level there was a precise imagination as a reference. In the past, all over the world, the Gucci moccasin had had a stirrup. One example of the modernisation of the codes was the re-editing of the famous Jackie bag (named in honour of Jackie Kennedy) in the original shape but in the latest colour. The reason for Tom Ford's success is his ability to speak to everyone – to those who work in fashion, to those who know the Jackie bag, and to a younger and fashion conscious public. The clothing itself becomes a communication tool in Gucci. The result is that it has to be very fashionable as an attractor in itself. It has to continuously renew the *raison d'etre* of objects from the past. It has to appear every season because Gucci is talked about every season.

10.4 Organisational implications

In conclusion, a very important subject in fashion firms is the *internal accreditation* of the communication function and its *placing within the organisation.*

One considerable limit to fashion communication is its placing. This has typically been a staff function that was basically related to public relations and press offices. Positioning communication at the strategic level where it should be would require strong support from senior management. The problem differs according to the size of the firm. Within small firms the owner makes the most significant decisions including those concerning communication. Here strong relationships with external professionals in advertising and communication agencies are favoured. These professionals are usually responsible for the whole process of image building, from making catalogues to advertising materials in support of the sales points. In medium and large firms the situation is different. There is usually a communication manager who acts as a bridge between the more disparate functions such as media and advertising, commercial, marketing, product design, human resources, purchasing, general services, information systems, and senior management. There is sometimes an advertising manager, but in other cases the managing director or communication manager are in charge of this. There is potential tension between these functions, and this is related to the assignment of responsibilities. This is specially the case with the commercial director because of the marginality of the marketing function in fashion firms. Marketing often occupies related areas such as communication, without however having the specific responsibilities. A role problem can also occur in the data elaboration centre, where the game of Internet control is played out. The information systems that are called in to set up the website at the beginning would like to control the design area as well. This is a communication tool with a strong strategic value. Internal communication is another possible area of conflict, in this case with 'human resources' that finds it hard to involve the *communication manager*. This produces negative effects for integrated communication (the classic example is that of the impersonal letter that is signed by the department).

The de-structuring of fashion firms is the main obstacle to communication, which has to have the objective of becoming an integrated process. This is only possible through measuring the attainment of fixed objectives (to the same standard that external agencies use when dealing with marketing directors). Continuous reporting is necessary, and the external sources have to be used for this purpose as well.

The accreditation of the communication function progresses through the delivering of concrete results. It should extend its influence to the Internet, to brochures, to the house organ (from the point of view of integrated communication it is important to take charge of internal communication as well). Tools and objectives must be shared with external actors, with account always being taken that the final aim is not to reach the media but consumers.

The Internet is a tool that can help the accreditation of the communication function because it makes it possible to quantify results directly (in terms of the number of connections). The ability to have a dialogue with different subjects, both within and without the firm, has to be the main talent of the communication manager. Creating a link between the designer and the shop architect or between the designer and the art director is as hard a task as developing a communication campaign that is consistent with brand identity.

Conclusions: the development of strategic archetypes in the fashion system

The development of fashion firms from the 1960s to the 1990s was characterised by a significant evolution in the key success factors of the competitive system, the features in the offer system, and the strategic models that were pursued. This development involved all countries to some extent, although at different times, and it led to an alignment of competitive thinking at the end of the 1990s. This evolution can be reduced to four stages, up to the current scenario of the fashion system that defines new actors and strategies.

First stage (1965-1975). The creation of a unique image
The concept of fashion during this first period was limited to the high end of the market (the haute couture and luxury ready-to-wear segments). Fashions came into existence and changed on the basis of prestige and exclusivity, and there was a strong social class connotation. The competitive system involved few firms, and these were mainly in Europe (France and Italy). The firms were craftsmanship/tailorshops, and they were centred on the figure of the tailor/*couturier* or a designer. The offer system had high quality products at high prices, and it was limited to cloth-

ing or leather items for a very select international clientele. The key success factors were based on product quality and originality of style. The entrepreneurial vision of the period was total product orientation. Markets were very segmented at national levels.

Second stage (1975-1985): the creation of brands

This stage of the international development of fashion closely followed the development of consumer society. New market segments came into existence (youth clothing, sportswear). Fashion began a process of 'democratisation' that would be completed in the periods that followed. The designers/*couturiers* became entrepreneurs managing firms that used licensing agreements to expand from clothing to accessories and perfumes. Thanks to the development of second and third lines (positioned in diffusion and bridge), they covered different market segments. The designer's name became a real 'umbrella' brand that guaranteed that all the products belonged to the same area of taste and identity. Along with product quality and style, commercial capacity emerged as a critical factor for successful competition. Thus began an orientation to the market and to sales. The traditional fashion houses became firms that invested in image and communication, and in wider distribution. They opened directly operated stores in the domestic and international markets. Global niches of affluent consumers began to form, and they stimulated the development of the internationalisation of fashion firms. New competitors appeared alongside the French and Italian designers, in particular American designers (Calvin Klein, Donna Karan, Ralph Lauren). These new competitors had a strong marketing and communication orientation, and they changed the rules of the game.

Third stage (1985-1995): industrial development

Consumer culture experienced its greatest development in these years. The interest in labels, which were already available to nearly everyone thanks to licensing, caused a rapid increase in business turnover. Fashion firms were by now industrial and commercial empires, a long way away from the original image of the designer/craftsman. Many fashion houses decided to take direct control of the productive and logistic stages of the value chain. This was done through partnerships or the acquisition of old licensees, and there was a progressive formation of integrated groups controlling the whole supply chain. The concept of the 'pipeline partnership' became increasingly important, because it meant the ability to connect the different production stages in order to ensure a greater service to the market. Management skills increased in most firms, and new professionals were acquired from other industries, as well as the creation of new organisational roles (marketing, integrated communication, licensing and information systems). Investment in global retailing and brand extension grew with the entry of new merchandise sectors through acquisitions or licenses. Product, commercial capacity and marketing were the new weapons in an increasingly global competition.

Fourth stage (from 1996): financial holding companies

The end of the 1990s was characterised by changes in the quality and structure of final demand, changes in the relationship between production and distribution, and changes in the international location of productive factors. Final demand sought alternatives to clothing consumption, and this resulted in a contraction of the industry's turnover. There was a polarisation between the high-end and mass market segments (the so-called hour glass effect). This caused a strong contraction of consumption in the traditional market of many industrial brands, the medium segment. Organised large distribution emerged as the new actor in the fashion scene at the international level. Its contractual power over the industry increased, and it brought together the lower stages of supply chain, giving rise to new, very successful entrepreneurial models. Finally, the growing cost differentials between the industrialised and developing countries, together with the growth of consumption in new areas of the world, brought about a shift of activity from the traditional markets to new countries, mainly East Asia. This contributed to the increasing international integration of the productive activities of fashion. All the firms in this complex scenario were pushed towards rationalisation in the search for greater value. Finance came into fashion. Acquisitions, mergers, stock market quotations, and the use of financial leverage to sustain development, were the hall-marks of the new era. Firms witnessed the creation of multi-brand companies, some of them acquiring brands after the death of the designer/founder. Wise management of the marketing mix was no longer enough. If the key success factors were the product and production in the past, they have now shifted towards more intangible elements such as strategic brand management, the control of retail, and human resources management.

Figure C.1 presents the entire development path of fashion firms.

FIGURA C.1   **DEVELOPMENT PATH OF FASHION FIRMS**

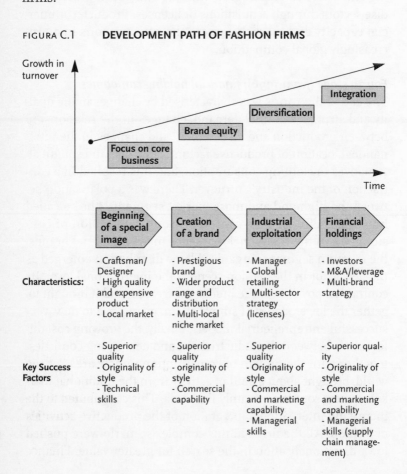

	Beginning of a special image	**Creation of a brand**	**Industrial exploitation**	**Financial holdings**
Characteristics:	- Craftsman/ Designer - High quality and expensive product - Local market	- Prestigious brand - Wider product range and distribution - Multi-local niche market	- Manager - Global retailing - Multi-sector strategy (licenses)	- Investors - M&A/leverage - Multi-brand strategy
Key Success Factors	- Superior quality - Originality of style - Technical skills	- Superior quality - originality of style - Commercial capability	- Superior quality - Originality of style - Commercial and marketing capability - Managerial skills	- Superior quality - Originality of style - Commercial and marketing capability - Managerial skills (supply chain management)

Organisational and entrepreneurial models in the fashion system have thus developed a lot in the last thirty years. The tailoring workshops of the *couturiers* have given way to integrated groups that use strategic management to control brand portfolios that are positioned in very different competitive environments. Although business size and professional management have both grown fairly uniformly, there has been no levelling of the strategic models for organising the business system and the supply chain. Two fundamental types of fashion firm can now be distinguished. Their characteristics and choices also have repercussions on the other actors in the supply chain that are connected to them:

- The vertically integrated firm
- The networked firm.

In the case of an integrated firm the business system is managed by one actor alone. This kind of firm is very common in Anglo-Saxon countries. It bases its success on economies of scale and the vertical integration of production and distribution (reduced transaction costs) and on product and process innovation. The key points of this entrepreneurial vision are as follows:

- Control of the whole process, possibly from yarn to finished product up to distribution
- The development of a high critical mass in all the stages, with the objective of maintaining high flexibility so as to be able to respond to a very changeable demand
- High investment in process technologies and information systems so as to introduce the most recent technological innovations and to bring together the needs of efficiency and flexibility
- International sourcing in countries that can optimise the quality/price ratio in the labour intensive productive stages
- A great emphasis on efficiency and service
- The development of a permanent learning process thanks to the control of information in the supply chain.

The model of the integrated firm has the following main limits:

- It is particularly suited to products that are not very subject to fashion (classic clothing, menswear, underwear, basic products and mass products)
- It requires high investment and implies significant managerial and organisational complexity.

The alternative to the vertically integrated firm model, above all in the Italian fashion system, is the 'network' model. In this case the business system is managed by a number of actors. The role of network leader (brand owner, producer or distributor) can be played by different actors and can change over time. The priorities of the networked firm are to achieve an efficient connection throughout the whole business system including product distribution, and to maintain a high level of flexibility with regard to variations in final demand.

The development of this model in medium-sized Italian firms, as well as those operating in certain special segments such as ready-to-wear, was favoured by the presence of small and very small firms in Italy, and their tradition of partnership relationships. The innovations and distinctive skills on which the network firm bases itself are mainly strategic and organisational rather than technological and productive. They are related to the capacity to develop a global entrepreneurial vision and to manage multiple relationships, all of which are part of the same general plan.

The most significant advantages of the network firm are:

- It guarantees the high flexibility of the productive system without requiring heavy investment in processes or information systems
- It offers considerable entrepreneurial space to those who want to take an active part in the network by establishing and developing their own firm (distribution, production or service)
- It reduces the financial burden connected to the management of inventories and guarantees an adequate service to the trade without high financial burdens

- It implies less financial investment when implementing development strategies (diversification and internationalisation).

Distinctly different roles can be identified within the network firm: the firm that is oriented to the market (this is the network 'director' in most cases), the producer firm, or the sub-contracting firm that focuses on technical and productive skills. The following activities in the value chain are carried out by the market oriented firm: product design and development, the purchase of raw materials and semi-finished goods (yarns and textiles), the logistics of semi-finished goods and finished articles, marketing and product distribution. In the producing firm the focus is on production. This can expand from manufacturing to include finishing, cutting and the purchase of some materials. Apart from the case of small sub-contractors, these firms are not manufacturers in the strict sense; they are often involved also in the product design, in research on new materials and so on. The fashion houses have been able to develop and grow through the support of this kind of firm. Sometimes the fashion houses have also invested into these firms.

The need for greater specialisation and co-ordination of the vertical pipeline encouraged many firms of different types (producers, fashion houses, distributors and textile suppliers) to look for ways of integrating in their organisational models, sometimes through direct intervention at different stages. Vertical integration strategies showed their worth above all in organisational solutions that allow a degree of flexibility within the pipeline.

Each firm can decide what role to play in the pipeline according to its own history, distinctive skills and strategic objectives. All the roles are equally worthwhile but they require the development of different skills. As has already been shown, each firm should find the correct integration of its managerial and creative skills. The history of Italian fashion shows that the network model has advantages in terms of innovation, management and creativity because of the greater stimuli that are offered by the number of actors in the network.

References

AAKER D.A., *Managing Brand Equity*, The Free Press, 1991.

AAKER D.A., JOACHIMSTHALER E., *Brand Leadership*, The Free Press, 2000.

ABELL D., *Defining the Business. The Starting Point of Strategic Planning*, Prentice Hall, 1980.

ABELL D., *Managing With Dual Strategies. Mastering the Present Preempting the Future*, The Free Press, 1993.

AMABILE T., "A Model of Creativity and Innovation in Organisations", in *Research in Organisational Behavior*, Vol. 10, 1988.

AMABILE T., "How to Kill Creativity", *Harvard Business Review*, Sept.-Oct. 1998.

AMABILE T., HENNESSE B.A., "The Condition of Creativity", in STERNBERG R.J. (ed.), *The Nature of Creativity*, Cambridge University Press, 1988.

ANDERSON BLACK J., GARLAND M., *A History of Fashion*, Orbis, 1978.

BARNARD M., *Fashion as Communication*, Routledge, 2001.

BARTHES R., *The Fashion System*, University of California Press, 1990.

BAUDRILLARD J., *Il sistema degli oggetti*, Bompiani, Milano, 1972.

BAUDRILLARD J., *Simulacra and Simulation (The Body, in Theory)*, University of Michigan Press, 1994.

BAUDRILLARD J., *The Consumer Society: Myths and Structures (Theory, Culture and Society)*, Sage Publications, 1998.

BERGADÀ M., FAURE C., PERRIEN J., "Enduring Involvement With Shopping", in *The Journal of Social Psychology*, 135 (1), 1995.

BERMAN B., EVANS J.R., *Retail Management: a Strategic Approach*, Prentice Hall, 1995.

BERTONE V., *Creatività Aziendale*, Franco Angeli, 1993.

BERTRAND D., *Lo sguardo semiotico*, Franco Angeli, Milano, 1997.

BLOCK F., POLANY K., STIGLITZ J., *The Great Transformation: The Political and Economic Origins of Our Time*, Beacon Press, 2001.

BLUMER H., "Fashion: From Class Differentiation to Collective Selection", in *Sociological Quarterly*, 10, 1969.

BONA M., ISNARDI F.A., STRANEO S.R., *Manuale di tecnologia tessile*, Zanichelli-Esac, 1981.

BRADLEY G.T., *Managing Customer Value*, Harper Collins, 1992.

BRAUDEL F., *La dinamica del capitalismo*, Il Mulino, Bologna, 1984.

CERIANI G., GRANDI R. (ed.), *Moda: regole e rappresentazioni*, Franco Angeli, 1995.

CHAN KIM W., MAUVBORGNE R., "Strategy, Value Innovation and the Knowledge Economy", in *Sloan Management Review*, Spring, 1999.

COPELAND M.T., "The Relation of Consumers' Buying Habits to Marketing Methods", in *Harvard Business Review*, April 1923.

D'AVENI R.A., *Hypercompetition*, New York Free Press, 1994.

DAVIS F., *Fashion, Culture, and Identity*, University of Chicago Press, 1992.

DEVOTO G., *Il dizionario della lingua italiano*, Le Monnier, 1995.

DOSSENA G., FROVA S., NOVA A., ORDANINI A., *L'industria meccanotessile in Italia. Comportamenti strategici, commerciali, finanziari*, Growing, 1996.

DRU J.M., *Disruption*, McGraw-Hill, 1996.

DRUCKER P.F., *Innovation and Entrepreneurship: Practice and Principles*, Harper Collins, 1985.

ECO U., *A Theory of Semiotics*, Indiana University Press, 1979.

FIOCCA R., *La comunicazione integrata nelle aziende*, Egea, 1994.

FISHER T., "The Designer's Self Identity - Myths of Creativity and the Management of Teams", in *Creativity and Innovation Management*, vol. 6, n. 1, March 1997.

FLUGEL J.C., *The Psychology of Clothes*, Hogarth Press, 1930.

FOMBRUN C.J., *Reputation*, Harvard Business School Press, 1996.

FORZA C., VINELLA A. (eds.), *Quick Response. La compressione dei tempi in progettazione, produzione e distribuzione*, CEDAM, 1996.

FRIEND S.C., WALKER P.H., "Welcome to the New World of Merchandising", *Harvard Business Review*, Nov. 2001.

GALLI F., *Moda e management. Il connubio*, Degree dissertation, Pavia University, 1993.

GARDNER H., *Frames of Mind. The Theory of Multiple Intelligences*, Basic Books, 1983.

GIANNELLI B., SAVIOLO S., *Il licensing nel Sistema Moda. Evoluzione, criticità, prospettive*, Etas, 2001.

GOBBI L., MORACE F., BAGNARA R., VALENTE F., *I Nuovi Boom*, Sperling & Kupfer Editori, 1993.

GOLEMAN D., *Emotional Intelligence*, Bantam Books, 1995.

HAMEL G., PRAHALAD C.K., "Competing for the Future", *Harvard Business School Press*, 1994.

HAMMER M., CHAMPY J., *Reengineering the corporation*, Harper Collins, 1993.

HANDY C., *The Age of Unreason*, Harvard Business School Press, 1990.

HART S., MURPHY J., *Brands. The new wealth creators*, Interbrand, Palgrave, 1998.

HENZEL P., "Imprese di moda e marketing: la semiotica come aiuto nelle decisioni" , in GRANDI R. (ed.), *Semiotica al marketing*, Franco Angeli, 1994.

HERBIG P., KOEHLER W., DAY K., "Marketing to the Baby Bust Generation", in *Journal of Consumer Marketing*, vol. 10, n. 1, 1993.

HINES T. BRUCE M. (ed.), *Fashion Marketing. Contemporary Issues*, Butterworth Heinemann, 2001.

HUNTER A., *Quick response in apparel manufacturing. A survey of the American scene*, The Textile Institute, 1990.

Il Grande Dizionario Garzanti della Lingua Italiana, 1993.

ISAKSEN S.G., *Frontiers of Creativity Research*, Bearly Press, 1987.

ITAMI H., ROEHL T.W., *Mobilizing Invisible Assets*, Harvard University Press, 1991.

JARNOW J., GUERREIRO M., *Inside the Fashion Business*, MacMillan Publishing Company, New York, 1991.

JOHNSON LAIRD P.N., *La comunicazione*, Edizioni Dedalo, Bari, 1992.

KAO J., *Jamming. The art and discipline of business creativity*, Harper Business, 1996.

KAPFERER J.N., *Strategic Brand Management*, New York Free Press, 1992.

KHANNA S.R., "Structural Changes in Asian Textile and Clothing Industries: The Second Migration of Production" *Textile Outlook International*, Economist Intelligence Unit, Sept. 1993.

KIM W.C., MAUBORGNE R., "Creating New Market Space", *Harvard Business Review*, vol. 77. Jan.-Feb. 1999.

KINCADE D.H., CASSILL N.L., WILLIAMSON N.L., "Quick Response management system: structure and components for the apparel industry", *Journal of the Textile Institute*, 84, 1993.

KING C.W., "Fashion Adoption: A Rebuttal to the Trickle Down Theory", in SPROLES G.B. (ed.), *Perspectives of Fashion*, Burgess, 1981.

KOHN A., *Punished by Rewards*, Houghton Mifflin, 1993.

KONIG R., *A La Mode; On the Social Psychology of Fashion*, Seabury, 1974.

LANE R., "You are what you wear", *Forbes* 400, October 14, 1996.

LEIBENSTEIN H., "Bandwagon, Snob and Vebelen Effects in the Theory of Consumer's Demand", *Quarterly Journal of Economics*, May 1950, 64(2).

LEVI PISETZKY R., *Il costume e la moda nella società italiana*, Einaudi, 1978.

LOWSON B., KING R., R. KING, HUNTER A., *Quick Response: Managing the Supply Chain to Meet Consumer Demand*, John Wiley & Sons, 1999.

MARIOTTI S., CAINARCA G., "The Evolution of Transaction Governance in the Textile-Clothing Industry", *Journal of Economic Behavior and Organization*, vol. 7, n. 4, 1986.

MARKIDES C., "Strategic Innovation", *Sloan Management Review*, Spring 1997.

MORACE F., *Metatendenze. Percorsi, prodotti e progetti per il terzo millennio*, Sperling & Kupfer, 1996.

MORRIS B., "In Paris, the Past Inspires Couture", *New York Times*, 24 Feb. 1987.

NAISBITT J., *Megatrends*, Sperling & Kupfer, 1984

PACKARD S., WINTERS A., AXELROD W., *Fashion Buying and Merchandising Management*, Fairchild Publications, 1983.

PARNES S., *The magic of your mind*, Bearly Press, 1981.

PASHIGIAN B.P., GOULD E., BOWEN B., "Fashion, Styling, and the Within-Season Decline in Automobile Prices", *The Journal of Law and Economics*, vol. XXXVIII, Oct. 1995.

PETERS T., *Thriving on Chaos: Handbook for a Management Revolution*, Harper & Row, 1987.

PESENDORFER W., "Design Innovation and Fashion Cycles", in *The American Economic Review*, vol. 5, Sept. 1995.

PINE J. II, GILMORE J.H., *The Experience Economy*, Harvard Business School Press, 1999.

POLHEMUS T., *Street Styles*, Thames and Hudson, 1994.

POLHEMUS T., PROCTER L., *Fashion and Anti-fashion and Anthropology of Clothing and Adornment*, Thames and Hudson, 1978.

PORTER M., *Competitive Advantage. Creating and Sustaining Superior Performance*, Free Press, 1985.

PORTER M., *The Competitive Advantage of Nations*, MacMillan Press, 1990.

RIDDLE E., BRADBARD D., THOMAS J., KINCADE D., "The role of electronic data interchange in Quick Response", *Journal of Fashion Marketing and Management*, 3, 1999.

RIES A., TROUT J., *Positioning: The battle for your Mind*, New York Warner Books, 1986.

ROBINSON A.G., STERN S., *Corporate Creativity* Berrett-Koehler Publisher Inc., 1997.

SABBADIN E., "La partnership verticale nel sistema moda", *Economia & Management*, n. 2, 1995.

SABBADIN E., *Marketing della distribuzione e marketing integrato. I casi Marks & Spencer e Benetton*, Egea, 1997.

SAPIR E., "Fashion", in *Encyclopedia of the Social Sciences*, 1931.

SAVIOLO S., "Gestire l'identità di marca nella moda. Il caso Artime – Sector No Limits", in *Economia & Management*, n. 5, 1997.

SCHANK R., *The Creative Attitude*, Mac Millan, 1988.

SCHMITT B., SIMONSON A., *Marketing Aesthetics*, New York Free Press, 1997.

SCHMITT B.H., *Experiential Marketing*, The Free Press, 1999.

SEMPRINI A. (ed.), *Lo sguardo semiotico*, Franco Angeli, 1997.

SIMMEL G., "Fashion", *American Journal of Sociology*, 62, 1957.

SIMON H.A., "Understanding Creativity and Creative Management", in KUHN R.L. (ed.), *Handbook for Creative and Innovative Managers*, McGraw-Hill, 1988.

STEELE V., *Paris Fashion, a Cultural History*, Oxford University Press, 1988.

STRAUSS W., HOWE N., *Generations : The History of America's Future, 1584 to 2069*, William Morrow & Co, 1992.

Street Trends. The Sputnik Minitrends Report, Harper Business, 1998.

SUN TZU, *The Art of War*, Delacorte Press, 1989.

TOFFLER A., *Powershift: Knowledge, Wealth, and Violence at the Edge of the 21st Century*, Mass Market Paperback, 1991.

TOFFLER A., *Third Wave*, Mass Market Paperback, 1991.

VARACCA P., "Lo sviluppo delle collezioni nel sistema moda: logiche e strumenti operativi", *Economia & Management*, n. 6, 1993.

VEBLEN T., *The Theory of the Leisure Class*, Macmillan, 1899.

Viewpoint, n. 6, September 1999.

WEISBERG R.W., *Creativity: Beyond the Myth of Genius*, Freeman, 1993.

www.thebesemer.com

www.clubdistretti.it

ZARA C. (ed.), *La marca e la creazione del valore di impresa*, Etas, 1997.

Afterword

The possibility for firms to remain competitive over time facing changes in demand, technology, and cost structures, depends on their capacity to produce and deliver on time, and where possible to anticipate developments in the above phenomena.

The greatest challenge facing western firms operating in labour-intensive industries, such as clothing, is the difference in the labour costs of developing countries. This difference was once unimportant because of physical distance and the backwardness of emerging markets. It is now increasingly significant given the growing liberalisation of international trade and reduced costs of transport and communication. Firms in industrialised countries thus suffer intense pressure to shift their labour-intensive manufacturing stages to cheaper regions. The migratory trend of labour-intensive activities is to some extent offset by repositioning strategies in the high end of the market and in global niches. These are the dominating strategies throughout the industrialised markets, or at least the main ones. This positioning requires, on the one hand, a continuous improvement in traditional skills to emphasise the difference between more price competitive but less sophisticated production. On the other hand, fashion industries have to enrich traditional manufacturing skills with innovative skills so as to give their products maximum excellence. This is done by the addition of intangible qualities that allow sufficient price premiums to compensate the greater costs compared with competing countries. It is very interesting to look at the successful cases where the distinctive skills of a firm have their roots in the historical, cultural economic, geographic and territorial environment in which it operates.

The relationships between the competitive advantages of firms and those of the national system (with reference, for example, to industrial districts) is a fascinating area of research that allows the macroeconomic dimension to be linked to the firm. Italian firms in the fashion system are one of the clearest examples of this type of beneficial osmosis. The economic system of fashion has not always had the features we recognise today. In the past there were two profoundly different situations with few points of contact, and Italian firms did not have a major role. High fashion was a highly skilled industry that served a very exclusive market dominated by the French. There was also an industrial sector that produced low price basic products for the mass market.

In the last thirty years Italian firms have been able to change the rules of the game. They have managed to find a synthesis between the creativity and stylistic innovation of high end products, and the quality/price ratio of organised manufacturing. Ready-to-wear came into existence and developed, but most importantly the ready-to-wear system (the marriage of style and industry, seasonally renewed collections, communicative strategy based on fashion shows, selective distributive strategy) was progressively transferred to other product categories (sportswear, underwear, leather items, accessories, perfumes and so on). This capacity to transform the industry's culture to its own advantage was made possible thanks to the ability of Italian firms to exploit the advantages of the national system. These circumstances included a very sophisticated demand with a widespread tradition of taste, the historical presence of an industrial pipeline in both textiles and leather, and a relatively small average firm size compared to foreign competitors that could respond very flexibly to fashion